CASEBOOK SERIES

GENERAL EDITOR: A. E. Dyson

PUBLISHED

T. S. Eliot

'Prufrock', 'Gerontion', *Ash Wednesday* and Other Shorter Poems

A CASEBOOK

EDITED BY

B. C. SOUTHAM

First published 1978 by
THE MACMILLAN PRESS LTD
London and Basingstoke
Associated companies in Delhi Dublin
Hong Kong Johannesburg Lagos Melbourne
New York Singapore and Tokyo

Printed in Great Britain by
REDWOOD BURN LIMITED
Trowbridge & Esher

British Library Cataloguing in Publication Data

T. S. Eliot, 'Prufrock', 'Gerontion', 'Ash Wednesday'
   and other shorter poems. – (Casebook series).
   1. Eliot, Thomas Stearns – Criticism and
   interpretation
   I. Southam, Brian Charles   II. Series
   821'.9'12   PR3509.L43

   ISBN 0-333-21232-0
   ISBN 0-333-21233-9   Pbk

CONTENTS

3. 'The Hollow Men', *Ash Wednesday* and
the Ariel Poems

ACKNOWLEDGEMENTS

The editor and publishers wish to thank the following who have kindly given permission for the use of copyright material: T. S. Eliot, extracts 'The Three Voices of Poetry', 'The Music of Poetry' plus other short quotations from *On Poetry and Poets*; 'Difficult Poetry' plus other short quotations from *The Use of Poetry and the Use of Criticism*; 'Shakespeare and the Stoicism of Seneca', 'Dante', 'Tradition and the Individual Talent' plus other short quotations from *Selected Essays*; 'What Dante Means to Me' and 'Reflections on *Vers Libre*' from *To Criticise The Critic*, reprinted by permission of Faber and Faber Ltd. Wallace Fowlie, extract from essay on 'Baudelaire and Eliot' in *T. S. Eliot: The Man and His Work*, ed. Allen Tate, reprinted by permission of Brandt and Brandt. Northrop Frye, extract from chapter 5, pp. 72–7, of *T. S. Eliot – Writers and Critics* (previously published by Oliver & Boyd, 1963), reprinted by permission of Longman Group Ltd. Helen Gardner, extracts from pp. 15–23 and 99–104 of *The Art of T. S. Eliot*, published by The Cresset Press (1949), reprinted by permission of Barrie & Jenkins Ltd. Robert Graves, extract from pp. 154–8 of the essay 'The Humorous Element' from *A Survey of Modernist Poetry* (1927), reprinted by permission of the author and A. P. Watt & Son. D. W. Harding, extract from *Experience Into Words*, reprinted by permission of the author and Chatto & Windus Ltd. Hugh Kenner, extract from essay on 'Eliot's Moral Dialectic', pp. 421–9 of *Hudson Review*, II (1949), reprinted by permission of the author. Hugh Kenner, extracts from pp. 3–11 and 76–9 of *The Invisible Poet: T. S. Eliot* (1960), reprinted by permission of W. H. Allen & Co. Ltd. F. R. Leavis, extract from 'The Dry Salvages' from *Scrutiny*, XI (1942) 61–3, reprinted by permission of the author and Cambridge University Press. F. R. Leavis, extract from pp. 75–87 and 114–32 of *New Bearings in English Poetry*, reprinted by permission of the author and Chatto & Windus Ltd. F. O. Matthiessen, extract from chapter 5 of *The Achievement of T. S. Eliot: An Essay on the Nature of Poetry, with a chapter on Eliot's later work by C. L. Barber*, Third Edition, © 1935, 1947, 1958 by Oxford University Press, Inc., reprinted by permission. Peter Mudford, essay on 'Sweeney among the Nightingales' from pp. 285–91 of *Essays in Criticism*, XIX (1969), reprinted by permission of the author and *Essays in Criticism*.

George Orwell, extract from review article on T. S. Eliot from *Poetry*, 2
July 1942, reprinted by permission of Mrs Sonia Brownell Orwell, the
publishers Martin Secker & Warburg, and A. M. Heath & Co.
Ltd on behalf of the Orwell Estate. D. D. Paige (ed.), short extract from *The
Selected Letters of Ezra Pound*, reprinted by permission of Faber & Faber
Ltd. Gertrude Patterson, extract from pp. 94–103 of *T. S. Eliot: Poems
in the Making* (1971), reprinted by permission of Manchester University
Press. Ezra Pound, essay on Eliot's 'Prufrock and other Observations'
from *Literary Essays of Ezra Pound*, ed. T. S. Eliot, reprinted by
permission of Faber and Faber Ltd. B. Rajan, extracts from essay on
'The Overwhelming Question' from *T. S. Eliot: The Man and His Work*,
ed. Allen Tate, reprinted by permission of Brandt and Brandt. John
Crowe Ransom, essay on 'Gerontion' from *T. S. Eliot: The Man and His
Work*, ed. Allen Tate, reprinted by permission of Brandt and Brandt.
Herbert Read, extract from 'T. S. E.: A Memoir' from *T. S. Eliot: The
Man and His Work*, ed. Allen Tate, reprinted by permission of Brandt
and Brandt. I. A. Richards, Appendix B of *The Principles of Literary
Criticism* (1926), reprinted by permission of Routledge & Kegan Paul
Ltd. Edgell Rickword, review article 'The Modern Poet' from *The
Calendar of Modern Letters*, © Edgell Rickword 1974, from *Essays &
Opinions 1921–31* (Manchester: Carcanet Press, 1974), reprinted by
permission of the author and publisher. Ernest Schanzer, essay on 'Mr.
Eliot's Sunday Morning Service' from *Essays in Criticism*, v (1955)
153–8, reprinted by permission of the author and *Essays in Criticism*. J.
Grover Smith, extracts from 'The Yellow Fog', pp. 21–3 and 24–5 of
T. S. Eliot's Poetry and Plays (1956), reprinted by permission of The
University of Chicago Press. C. K. Stead, extract from *The New Poetic*
(1964), reprinted by permission of Hutchinson Publishing Group Ltd.
Allen Tate, extracts from 'T. S. Eliot's *Ash Wednesday*' in *Essays of Four
Decades*, © 1959 by Allen Tate; and 'The Reading of Modern Poetry' in
Purpose, x, © 1938 by Allen Tate, reprinted by permission of the author
and The Swallow Press, Inc., Chicago. David Ward, extracts from
chapter 2, pp. 31–5, and chapter 5, pp. 164–71, of *Between Two Worlds:
A Reading of T. S. Eliot's Poetry and Plays* (1973), reprinted by permission
of Routledge & Kegan Paul Ltd. W. B. Yeats extract from Introduction
to *Oxford Book of Modern Verse*, reprinted by permission of M. B. Yeats
and Miss Ann Yeats. M. D. Zabel, review article, 'T. S. Eliot in Mid-
Career', from *Poetry*, xxxvi (1930), © 1930 by The Modern Poetry
Association, and reprinted by permission of the Editor of *Poetry*.

GENERAL EDITOR'S PREFACE

The Casebook series, launched in 1968, has become a well-regarded library of critical studies. The central concern of the series remains the 'single-author' volume, but suggestions from the academic community have led to an extension of the original plan, to include occasional volumes on such general themes as literary 'schools' and genres.

Each volume in the central category deals either with one well-known and influential work by an individual author, or with closely related works by one writer. The main section consists of critical readings, mostly modern, collected from books and journals. A selection of reviews and comments by the author's contemporaries is also included, and sometimes comment from the author himself. The Editor's introduction charts the reputation of the work or works from the first appearance to the present time.

Volumes in the 'general themes' category are variable in structure but follow the basic purpose of the series in presenting an integrated selection of readings, with an Introduction which explores the theme and discusses the literary and critical issues involved.

A single volume can represent no more than a small selection of critical opinions. Some critics are excluded for reasons of space, and it is hoped that readers will pursue the suggestions for further reading in the Select Bibliography. Other contributions are severed from their original context, to which some readers may wish to turn. Indeed, if they take a hint from the critics represented here, they certainly will.

A. E. DYSON

INTRODUCTION

The Waste Land and the *Four Quartets* have already been documented in separate volumes in the Casebook series; and this third Eliot volume is devoted to the rest of his poetry. The treatment is necessarily selective. Beyond the obvious choices, there have had to be many exclusions. For example, there are no separate critical items on 'Eyes that last I saw in tears', 'Sweeney Agonistes', 'Coriolan', 'La Figlia Che Piange', on any of the French poems or on *The Rock*, although these works are mentioned within the discussion of other poems. To have tried to cover a wide range of individual poems would have produced a thin and sketchy account. Instead, the critical documents focus on a smaller number of central and representative poems; and this narrowness of focus has been balanced by the section of 'Perspectives', which supplies wider-ranging views of Eliot's development and relates the 'minor' poems of this Casebook to his 'major' achievement in *The Waste Land* and the *Four Quartets*.

'Major' and 'minor' properly stand within inverted commas, for the nature of Eliot's achievement is still far from decided and agreed upon. The terms could be reversed. Some critics find the 'great' Eliot in the so-called 'minor' poetry, and a question-mark hangs over the *Four Quartets*. Is it the high-point of Eliot's career? Or a mannered and rhetorical decline? In the decade since his death, there has been a spate of critical and biographical studies. The discovery of *The Waste Land* manuscript (together with drafts of other poems) has stimulated research and rethinking. Valuation and revaluation go on and the discussion of Eliot's poetry is alive and continuing.

I

This Casebook illustrates some of the ways in which his work has been approached over the last sixty years and the force of its impact upon different critics (some of them considerable poets in their own right) across this period. It is not a steady and harmonious chorus of praise. There have been some notable dissenters, including Yvor Winters and W. B. Yeats. If a single truth emerges from this body of opinion, it is a

testimony to the necessary independence of critical judgement and the
obligation that rests on each individual reader to arrive at his own
understanding of what he reads. It was a moral that Eliot never tired of
repeating, indeed, was compelled to repeat in order to cope with the
long and persistent line of questioners, some simple-minded, some
scholarly, who came to enquire about the meaning of his poetry, the
significance of this or that line or image. Sometimes he would play
possum and keep quiet. Sometimes he would play willing, dropping
veiled hints, half opening doors. Sometimes he would brush them off
more flatly, as he did at the press conference in Edinburgh in 1953,
following the first performance of *The Cocktail Party*: 'As far as I am
concerned, it means what it says. If it had meant something else, I
would have said so.' 'But would you have said it so clearly?' 'No, I
would have said it just as obscurely.'

The 'meaning' of a poem is something notoriously difficult to define,
the subject of much critical debate. One theory is that a poem does not
mean, it *is*. Eliot's version was to say, for example, as he did of *The Waste
Land*, that at the time 'I wasn't even bothering whether I understood
what I was saying'; and that the 'meaning' of his poetry was only
something that arose afterwards, to satisfy those readers who wanted his
poetry to have meaning![1] But on one thing Eliot was clear. Confronted
with a collection of essays entitled *Interpretations*, which included an
analysis of 'Prufrock', he drew attention to the fallacy 'of assuming that
there must be just one interpretation of the poem as a whole, that must
be right'; 'as for the meaning of the poem as a whole, it is not exhausted
by any explanation, for the meaning is what the poem means to
different sensitive readers'.[2]

II

Part One of this collection presents quotations drawn from Eliot's own
prose. 'Never trust the teller, trust the tale' was D. H. Lawrence's neat
saying; Eliot's concession was that 'There may be much more in a poem
than the author was aware of.'[3] This, together with Eliot's jokiness, is a
warning to be attended to. None the less, embedded in Eliot's reviews
and critical essays is a body of commentary and explanation as
suggestive and illuminating as in all the formal criticism of Eliot's
poetry from other people. The connection between his poetry and prose
is deep and intimate. In 'The Frontiers of Criticism', he explained that

his critical writing was 'a by-product of my private poetry-workshop . . . a prolongation of the thinking that went into the formation of my own verse'.[4] He went on to say that 'I wrote best about poets whose works had influenced my own', a comment which he repeated, and significantly expanded upon, five years later, when in 1961 he added a historical gloss: 'in my earlier criticism, both in my general affirmations about poetry and in writing about authors who had influenced me, I was implicitly defending the sort of poetry that I and my friends wrote'.[5]

The particular friend (rather than 'friends') in question was Ezra Pound. From 1915, when Eliot's earliest reviews and essays began to appear, into the early 1920s, they were united in their efforts to create an informed public capable of responding to the sophistication, subtlety and European allusiveness of their poetry. Eliot's critical writings are valuable as criticism; some are classics of their kind; yet the pre-1920 pieces can also be read as the justifying, enabling, forerunning propaganda of a poet determined to shape the taste by which he could be appreciated. The principles of this criticism are practical rather than philosophical, as he said in a letter to Pound in February 1915: 'There can be no contemplative or easychair aesthetics, I think; only the aesthetics of the person who is about to do something.' And Eliot's early criticism is evidently the declaration of a writer 'about to do something'. Later, his Websterian and Jacobean verse is matched by essays on Webster and the other dramatists of that period; his metaphysical conceits and echoes by encomiums of metaphysical poetry; his Dantean images and themes by the celebration of Dante; his imitation of French symbolist poetic devices by praise for the symbolist poets. Even the essays written very much later can throw an informative light upon the earliest poetry.

We see this in, for example, the lecture 'What Dante Means to Me', given in 1950, where he looks back to the influence of Laforgue, whose work he was reading while still a student at Harvard and under whose impact he began to write imitations, culminating in the highly developed and creative Laforgueanism of 'Prufrock' and 'Portrait of a Lady'. In that lecture he also refers to the influence of Baudelaire, where 'I learned first, a precedent for the poetical possibilities, never developed by any poet writing in my own language, of the more sordid aspects of the modern metropolis, of the possibility of fusion between the sordidly realistic and the phantasmagoric, the possibility of the juxtaposition of the matter-of-fact and the fantastic' (see below, Part One, section 3. 1).

This statement makes an invaluable commentary on the subject-matter and vision of 'Preludes', 'Rhapsody' and the other poems that touch upon the experience of modern life in cities. It helps us to understand the insistence that both Pound and Eliot make in their early reviews and essays upon the *European* element in what they were then promoting as the best English and American school of modern poetry (meaning, of course, their own poetry!). It also helps us to understand, more precisely, the way in which Eliot can be described as a 'literary' poet and the complexity of his indebtedness to the past.

To take isolated sentences and passages from the close fabric of Eliot's prose is undeniably destructive. But the purpose of these extracts is not to display Eliot's qualities as a writer but to highlight specific ideas which are relevant to his poetry and which have played a part, directly or indirectly, in the criticism of his work. For example, there is the question of poetry and religious belief, an issue that has occupied many critics of *Ash Wednesday* and the Ariel poems. Another important idea, which Eliot returns to again and again, is the capacity of the creative imagination to bring together disparate, seemingly unconnected experiences – a feature of his own poetry, and widely discussed by the critics, sometimes to his advantage, sometimes to his disadvantage. Or there is his concept of the 'new art emotion' (see below, Part One, section 5. III) for which the structure of the poem provides the formula, a hint which some of Eliot's most recent critics have taken up.

I have also included some of Eliot's reflections on criticism itself: these are always illuminating and sometimes amusing too. In 'The Frontiers of Criticism' he talks about 'the lemon-squeezer school of criticism', whose practitioners seize a poem, 'analyse it stanza by stanza and line by line, and extract, tease, press every drop of meaning out of it that one can' (*On Poetry and Poets*, p. 113). The joke is double-edged. His quatrain poems are dense with remote allusion and obscure reference, baited with pedantry, a source-hunter's paradise, an explicator's dream, designedly grist to the lemon-squeezer's mill. So lemon-squeezing has not been wholly excluded from this collection.

Part One concludes with an extract from the very revealing *Paris Review* interview where Eliot explained the origins of his choice of *vers libre* (at first in imitation of Laforgue), and of his experimentation in a tight quatrain form, in imitation of Gautier. He also mentioned his campaigning relationship with Pound, and commented on the prevailing poetic fashions of that period, from about 1910 to 1920.

III

Fittingly, the section of 'Perspectives' (Part Two) opens with Pound's 1917 review of *Prufrock and Other Observations* and closes with an extract from Rajan's 1966 essay on 'the evolving logic of the *œuvre*'. These accounts of Eliot's poetic development provide a context for the criticism, in Part Three, of the individual poems and groups of poems. Pound's review carries a special authority, a special proximity to Eliot. When he first met Pound, in September 1914, Eliot was an unknown and rejected poet (Conrad Aiken having failed to get Harold Monro to take 'Prufrock' for *Poetry and Drama*) while Pound was already launched upon his career as a 'campaigner' (as Eliot called him)[6] for the modern movement. Pound at once wrote to Harriet Munroe, the editor of *Poetry* (Chicago), for whom he was scouting in Europe, exhilarated by his discovery of a poet who had 'actually trained himself *and* modernized himself *on his own*'.[7] 'Prufrock' he acclaimed as 'the best poem I have yet had or seen from an American'. But it took him six months' correspondence to beat down her reluctance to print a poem so strange and new, so unAmerican in its spirit and cultural ticket. In the years up to 1920, Pound was the driving force of the modern movement—championing artists of all kinds, musicians, painters and sculptors, as well as novelists and poets, raising money to support them, badgering the rich for their patronage, 'puffing', 'booming' (to use Pound's own language), taking up 'cudgels' on their behalf in the magazines he advised and wrote for. He was the pushing impresario of modernism, its *battistrada* ('outrider'), a 'hefty . . . battering ram' (as he described himself), breaking down resistance to the new movement and fighting for its recognition.[8]

Pound on 'Prufrock' is less a review than a declaration: a statement of the international standards by which this poet (and indeed all poets deserving the name) should then be judged; of the uninsularity of the new 'European' tradition in which he stands; of the completeness of his art, its 'intelligence' (a touchstone for both men, see below, Part One, section 5. II) and its remarkable, personal 'versification' (another touchstone shared with Eliot, see section 7. I). In the final paragraph, Pound hints that this is an intimate's review. He anticipates the charge of log-rolling – which, in truth, both men practised to their mutual benefit! But Pound had no qualms about its justification. At this time, Eliot and he were the only two critics capable of the level of informed and intelligent response that such poetry called for; and he regarded this as an opportunity to promote the cause, as he did so often, and on behalf of so many writers. In 1921, returning the typescript of *The Waste Land* to Eliot, with his comments and suggestions, he wrote with some pride, 'It is after all a grrrreat litttttttary period'.[9] Even down to the idiosyncrasy of his spelling, Pound had earned the right to claim a personal stake in its creation.

Rickword's 1925 review of *Poems 1909–1925* continues some of Pound's themes, including the supremacy of Eliot's art, the strength and refinement of his technique, and his contemporary historical significance. But with the advantage of a longer view, Rickword is able to comment more tellingly on Eliot's development. Dismissing the quatrain poems as 'mere *jeux d'esprit*', he identifies three main stages from 'Prufrock' to *The Waste Land*; and it is not, he ventures, a wholly progressive development.

A year later came the widely known Appendix B to the *Principles of Literary Criticism*. Richards tackles the issue of difficulty or obscurity when there is no followable thread of meaning to the poems. His solution is within the proposition that this poetry is not amenable to a mode of analysis that seeks an intellectual scheme but calls for the recognition of an emotional structure and unity. He identifies Eliot's technique as the 'music of ideas', a concept taken up by many later critics.

By 1930, Eliot's turning to religious faith, in *Ash Wednesday* and the Ariel Poems, was being remarked upon and a post-*Waste Land* period identified, if not always welcomed. Zabel finds this phase less convincing than the 'complete authority' of the earlier period, characterised by its 'profound conviction' and 'absolute creative certitude'. Matthiessen (1935) looks outside the poet and relates the changes in the poetry to the broad sweep of change in modern civilisation, to which the living poet cannot be immune. Yet, within this, he identifies a pattern of recurrent imagery linking the early and the later poetry. For Harding, in 1936, the poet's development looms as the main question, an uneasy question, posed by the change in taste which renders Eliot 'less *chic*' than in the previous decade. The 'protester' has become the poet of 'regret' and 'suffering', 'more personal and more mature'.

Yeats's Introduction to *The Oxford Book of Modern Verse* (1936) passes some very decisive judgements. Eliot is a 'satirist' rather than a 'poet', a writer whose verse has been contaminated by its subject: 'in describing this life that has lost heart his own art seems grey, cold, dry'. The Eliot selected by Yeats for posterity is a small, significant group: 'Preludes', 'The Hippopotamus', 'Whispers of Immortality', 'Sweeney among the Nightingales' (whose last two stanzas 'speak in the great manner'), 'The Hollow Men', *Journey of the Magi*, and 'The Eagle soars', from *The Rock*. Whatever the eccentricities and partialities of this choice, Yeats's views on Eliot have an inescapable weight as the judgement of one undeniably great poet upon another.

The extract from Tate's *The Reading of Modern Poetry* (1938) is valuable in its own right for its commentary upon 'Rhapsody on a Windy Night' and *Ash Wednesday*. But it has a historical interest, too, in registering the assaults which Eliot had suffered as a poet of obscurity. By this time, it was the stock denigration produced by those critics who still clung to older or more romantic notions of the 'poetic'. This reactionary anti-modernism ran to considerable length in Max Eastman's *The Literary Mind: Its Place in an Age of Science* (1931). According to its thesis, in the face of science modern writers were retreating, 'taking refuge in pure poetry and unintelligibility; the critics are conspiring with them'. This line of attack was followed up in 1934 in John Sparrow's *Sense and Poetry: Essays on the Place of Meaning in Contemporary Verse*. This ponderous title comes from Dryden, who claimed, rather circularly, to be writing for those 'who understand Sense and Poetry . . . when that Poetry and Sense is put into words they understand'. Sparrow's case was that modern poetry had departed 'from the paths of sense and intelligibility' and that its aim was to be 'as nearly as possible like a piece of life . . . reproducing as closely as possible a cultivated modern consciousness'. Tate confronts both these critics with the charge that they have misunderstood the nature of poetry, of modern poetry in particular.

A much more sustained and developed attack upon Eliot (and upon the modern movement) is made by Yvor Winters in *Primitivism and Decadence* (1937), *The Anatomy of Nonsense* (1943) and *On Modern Poets* (1957). His central objection is to Eliot's theory that the complexity of modern poetry is not individually peculiar to these poets, but a condition of writing in the contemporary world. As Eliot puts it, in a context of 'great variety and complexity' the modern poet can respond

only with 'various and complex results' (see below, Part One, section
1. 1). Winters dubs this 'the fallacy of expressive, or imitative form',
tracing it back to the aphorism of Henry Adams, 'that modern art must
be chaotic in order to express chaos'.

The publication of the separate parts of the *Four Quartets* between
1935 and 1942 provoked some sharp comparisons between the early
and the later poetry. Harding was reviewing the *Collected Poems
1909-1935* with 'Burnt Norton' as his point of reference; just as Orwell
was recollecting the earlier Eliot alongside 'Burnt Norton', 'East Coker'
and 'The Dry Salvages'. Orwell's verdict was sharp. There was a loss of
vitality, a 'current . . . switched off', leaving us with a poetry of
'gloomy despair' and 'melancholy faith'. This is an extreme account of
Eliot in decline. Against it, we can place three very different views.
Firstly, Helen Gardner's appraisal of the advance, after *The Waste Land*,
from the 'metrical virtuosity' achieved with the traditional heroic line,
to the discovery of freedom in a personal poetic voice. Next is Hugh
Kenner's contention that the division into an earlier and a later poetry
is more an idea in the minds of the critics than a feature of the texts
themselves. He suggests, instead, a more important unity: 'the principles of dramatic organisation that govern each poem govern also the
œuvre'. The concluding perspective is Rajan's claim for the organic
nature of the *œuvre*: that 'Prufrock' is 'a beginning which looks forward
to an end', just as 'Gerontion' looks forward to *The Waste Land* and as
'Prufrock' and *The Waste Land* are related 'in the symbolic continuum'.

IV

In Part Three, the first section runs from 'Prufrock' to 'Gerontion',
leaving the quatrain poems to the second section – an arrangement
which accords with the grouping usually followed by the critics. Section
I of Part Three opens with Pound's recommendation of 'Prufrock' to
Harriet Munroe, part of his attempt to get her to take the poem for
Poetry. These circumstances form an element of the historical background to which Leavis refers in *New Bearings in English Poetry*, as a
prelude to his account of 'Prufrock', 'Portrait of a Lady' and
'Gerontion' as the poetry of a 'modern sensibility . . . of one fully alive
in his own age'; and Kenner's chapter on 'Prufrock' can be read in part
as an extension of Leavis's point. Kenner also seems to be tracing a
perception very akin to Pound's comment on Eliot's 'mingling of a very

subtle observation with the unexpectedness of a backhanded cliché' (see below, Part Two, first piece). Kenner analyses the strategies that attend this 'small masterpiece', its remarkable detachment, its verbalism and its manipulation of nineteenth-century modes, especially the Tennysonian. The extract from Fowlie is in the same area, pointing to the literary traditions that attend the early poems – in particular, the influence of Baudelaire: his 'dandyism', the intensity of his poetic imagery and the poetry of memory. It is useful to compare this account with Eliot's own comment on Baudelaire (see below, Part One, section 8. III); and to refer to Eliot again (see section 5. III) alongside Patterson's discussion of the 'Preludes' and 'Rhapsody on a Windy Night'. Both these poems are explored for their Bergsonianism by Smith. The section ends with two pieces on 'Gerontion', a major essay by Ransom, who regards it as one of Eliot's greatest works, and an extract from Stead, who points to a sexual experience at the poem's centre and questions whether its 'coherence' and 'completeness' are fully achieved.

v

The quatrain poems, considered in section 2 of Part Three, constitute a very distinct group on their own: the form was one that Eliot practised for only two years, from the middle of 1917 to mid-1919, and its inspiration was literary-political, owing much to Pound's calculation of what their strategy should be in setting modern poetry, and, with it, contemporary taste, on what he felt to be the right course. Their decision was reached together, as Pound recorded the sequence of events, 'at a particular day, in a particular room', that Eliot should become an English Gautier, imitating the skilled and specialised technique of the Frenchman's hard, composed, sardonic verse in *Emaux et camées* , matching Gautier's 'L'Hippopotame' with his own Anglican 'Hippopotamus'. Eliot's Gautierism was designed to be purgative, to purify the state of English and American poetry, to drive out, with its supreme and displayed artistry, its virtuosity of form, its taut and structured quatrains, the loose, flabby inartistry of contemporary verse styles. According to Pound, the two men 'decided that the dilution of *vers libre*, Amygism, Lee Masterism, general floppiness had gone too far and that some counter-current must be set going. . . . Remedy prescribed "Émaux et Camées". . . . Rhyme and regular strophes.'[10] The composition of that 'Remedy' was explained by Eliot in the *Paris Review* interview: 'We studied Gautier's poems and then we thought, "Have I anything to say in which this form will be useful?" And we experimented. The form gave the impetus to the content.' (See below, Part One, section 9. II)

The quatrain poems provide a spectacular and sometimes explosive entertainment, fascinating, irritating, baffling, even offending their readers, as we see in the Graves and Riding account of 'Burbank'. Eliot is accused of indulging in a joky irresponsibility, of holding, for example, anti-Jewish and anti-American prejudices, for which, claiming the privileges of the comedian, 'he cannot be held morally accountable'. This view can usefully be compared with Bateson's, who regards the poem much more highly, as an exercise in 'semi-comic satire', and refers to the learnedness of Eliot's early poetry – evidence, he claims, 'of a certain gaiety of spirit' that disappears with *The Waste Land*. The most provocatively learned of these poems is 'Mr Eliot's Sunday Morning Service', which has excited some agitated lemon-squeezing. Schanzer's interpretation is not this; he admits, rather, to finding it a 'most bewildering and most fascinating' piece and raises the same question of 'coherence' that Stead puts to 'Gerontion'. Ward provides another account of this poem, whose tensions he relates to tensions in the poet, a line of analysis that effects a valuable distinction between the 'anxiety' of Eliot's metaphysical mode and the freedom and assurance achieved by the seventeenth-century metaphysical poets to whom he felt so compellingly drawn. Kenner calls 'Whispers of Immortality' 'the most celebrated of the quatrain poems', suggesting that in this group Eliot turns the traditional mock-heroic convention into 'a convention of mock-casualness'. 'Sweeney among the Nightingales' has puzzled or dissatisfied many critics and Mudford offers to set the record straight, not by skating over its local difficulties but by responding attentively to 'the different levels of intensity that the verse achieves'.

VI

Section 3 of Part Three covers the period following *The Waste Land*; and in bringing together 'The Hollow Men', *Ash Wednesday* and the Ariel poems, this collection again follows the grouping usually found in critical discussions.

Tate's view of *Ash Wednesday* makes an appropriate start chronologi-

cally and also because it takes up the important question of Eliot's
Anglicanism and the relationship between his declared religious
position and his poetry. As Tate comments, from the time of Eliot's
formal entry into the Church of England, in 1927, the poetry was
increasingly interpreted in an Anglo-Catholic light and increasingly
dismissed by those who admired *The Waste Land* for its pervasive irony
and its exposure of 'secular faith'. Tate urges a reading of *Ash Wednesday*
which is attentive to its tones and imagery as they really exist in the
poetry, not an interpretation keyed to the external fact of the poet's
religious declaration. This question continues into Leavis's account.
Although he accepts that the poetry of this phase 'may lack the charged
richness' and the range of 'Gerontion' and *The Waste Land*, he argues
(referring especially to *Ash Wednesday* and *Marina*) that 'it is, perhaps,
still more remarkable by reason of the strange and difficult regions of
experience that it explores'. His understanding of *Marina* is taken
further in a piece dated 1942, ten years later. Helen Gardner's
discussion of *Ash Wednesday* makes an interesting contrast, since she
addresses herself to the 'very complex' connection between the change
in Eliot's poetry and the 'momentousness' of his entry into the church.
The 'intensity of apprehension' of the earlier poetry becomes an
'intensity of meditation', with accompanying developments in the
rhythms and imagery.

Both Frye and Rajan relate the poems of this period to Eliot's earlier
and later work. Frye traces the significance of imagery and the
purgatorial vision in *Ash Wednesday* into the later poems and plays; while
Rajan regards it as 'a chapter' in the story of the quest', 'a dying into
life', where the earlier protagonists, Prufrock, Gerontion and Phlebas
endure something less fruitful. In these embracing interpretations, they
differ sharply from Read, who, in an account that can be placed
alongside Orwell's, takes 'The Hollow Men' to be the last example of
Eliot's *pure* poetry' and everything afterwards a decline into 'moralistic
poetry'. Finally, there is Ward's analysis of the Ariel poems, fixing on
the play of ideas and conveying a judgement on *Marina* very different
from that of Leavis.

VII

In 'Remembering Eliot' Stephen Spender compared that blissful time
in the late 1920s, when 'Eliot was a legend to the young poets', to our

present fallen state, 'Now, when his poems seem almost inseparable from the explanations of them. . . .'[11] A terrible fate, when the poems are lost in the criticism, the oak strangled by its parasitic ivy! But lest we end on too melodramatic a note, it is a relief to quote Eliot himself on the problem. He felt it too, but came to a positive and reassuring conclusion. After reading the collection of *Interpretations*, nearly all of which were of poems 'I had known and loved for many years', 'I found I was slow to recover my previous feeling about the poems. It was as if someone had taken a machine to pieces and left me with the task of reassembling the parts. I suspect, in fact, that a good deal of the value of an interpretation is – that it should be my own interpretation.'[12]

NOTES

1. *Paris Review*, XXI (1959) 53.
2. 'The Frontiers of Criticism' (1956); repr. in *On Poetry and Poets* (1957) p. 113.
3. 'The Music of Poetry' (1942); repr. in *On Poetry and Poets*, p. 31.
4. Repr. in *On Poetry and Poets*, p. 106.
5. *To Criticise the Critic* (1965) p. 16.
6. Introduction to *Literary Essays of Ezra Pound* (1954) p. xii. Elsewhere in this Introduction, Eliot describes Pound as 'more responsible for the xxth Century revolution in poetry than is any other individual' (p. xi).
7. *Letters of Ezra Pound*, ed. D. D. Paige (1951) p. 80: 30 Sep 1914.
8. Ibid., pp. 107, 191, 210, 213; Noel Stock, *Life of Ezra Pound* (1970) p. 206.
9. *Letters of Ezra Pound*, p. 235.
10. 'Harold Monro', *The Criterion*, July 1932, p. 590.
11. *Encounter*, Mar 1965.
12. 'The Frontiers of Criticism' (1956); repr. in *On Poetry and Poets*, p. 114.

Eliot on Poetry, Criticism and His Own Work

The extracts from Eliot's essays, lectures and reviews have been arranged, according to subject, in nine groups – as indicated in the Contents list and in the section-headings of Part One. It will be obvious that these divisions are arbitrary and that some extracts relate to a much larger field of discussion than the categories to which they are here assigned. None the less, these categories arise from Eliot's central preoccupations; and, as he confesses in extract 1 of section 8, whatever the poet-critic's 'ostensible purpose', he 'is always trying to defend the kind of poetry he is writing, or to formulate the kind that he wants to write'.

I. MODERN POETRY

ITS COMPLEXITY, THE DIVERSITY OF MATERIAL, AND THE PRINCIPLE OF POETIC UNITY

I

... We can only say that it appears likely that poets in our civilisation, as it exists at present, must be *difficult*. Our civilisation comprehends great variety and complexity, and this variety and complexity, playing upon a refined sensibility, must produce various and complex results. The poet must become more and more comprehensive, more allusive, more indirect, in order to force, to dislocate if necessary, language into his meaning. . . .

> SOURCE: extract from 'The Metaphysical Poets' (1921); reprinted in *Selected Essays* (1932; 2nd edition 1934) p. 289 (in 2nd edition). This collection is hereafter referred to as *S. E.*

II

The difficulty of poetry (and modern poetry is supposed to be difficult) may be due to one of several reasons. First, there may be personal causes which make it impossible for a poet to express himself in any way but an obscure way; while this may be regrettable, we should be glad, I think, that the man has been able to express himself at all. Or difficulty may be due just to novelty: we know the ridicule accorded in turn to Wordsworth, Shelley and Keats, Tennyson and Browning – but must remark that Browning was the first to be *called* difficult; hostile critics of the earlier poets found them difficult, but called them silly. Or difficulty may be caused by the reader's having been told, or having suggested to himself, that the poem is going to prove difficult. The ordinary reader, when warned against the obscurity of a poem, is apt to be thrown into a state of consternation very unfavourable to poetic receptivity. Instead of beginning, as he should, in a state of sensitivity he obfuscates his senses by the desire to be clever and to look very hard for something – he doesn't know what – or else by the desire not to be taken in. There is such a thing as stage fright, but what such readers have is pit or gallery fright. The more seasoned reader, he who has reached, in these matters, a state of greater *purity*, does not bother about understanding; not, at least, at first. I know that some of the poetry to which I am most devoted is poetry which I did not understand at first reading; some is poetry which I am not sure I understand yet: for instance, Shakespeare's. And finally, there is the difficulty caused by the author's having left out something which the reader is used to finding; so that the reader, bewildered, gropes about for what is absent, and puzzles his head for a kind of 'meaning' which is not there, and is not meant to be there.

The chief use of the 'meaning' of a poem, in the ordinary sense, may be (for here again I am speaking of some kinds of poetry and not all) to satisfy one habit of the reader, to keep his mind diverted and quiet, while the poem does its work upon him: much as the imaginary burglar is always provided with a bit of nice meat for the house-dog. This is a normal situation of which I approve. But the minds of all poets do not work that way; some of them, assuming that there are other minds like their own, become impatient of this 'meaning' which seems superfluous, and perceive possibilities of intensity through its elimination. I am not asserting that this situation is ideal; only that we must write our poetry as we can, and take it as we find it. It may be that for some periods of society a more relaxed form of writing is right, and for others a more concentrated. . . .

SOURCE: extract from *The Use of Poetry and the Use of Criticism* (1933); reprinted in *Selected Prose of T. S. Eliot*, ed. John Hayward (1953) pp. 92-3. (This material is under the heading '"Difficult" Poetry' in Hayward's selection. We can take it that this heading had Eliot's approval—it may even have been his choice—in view of his close friendship and literary collaboration with Hayward.)

III

. . . A thought to Donne was an experience; it modified his sensibility. When a poet's mind is perfectly equipped for its work, it is constantly amalgamating disparate experience; the ordinary man's experience is chaotic, irregular, fragmentary. The latter falls in love, or reads Spinoza, and these two experiences have nothing to do with each other, or with the noise of the typewriter or the smell of cooking; in the mind of the poet these experiences are always forming new wholes. . . .

SOURCE: extract from 'The Metaphysical Poets' (1921); in *S. E.*, 2nd edition, p. 287.

IV

. . . The poet's mind is in fact a receptacle for seizing and storing up
numberless feelings, phrases, images, which remain there until the
particles which can unite to form a new compound are present
together. . . .

> SOURCE: extract from 'Tradition and the Individual Talent'
> (1917); in *S. E.*, 2nd edition, p. 19.

V

. . . Whibley followed faithfully and easily the movement of his own
mind; he did not, as I and most people do, have to think up half a dozen
subjects to talk about and then shuffle them into the most suitable order;
the transition from one subject to the next suggested itself. Critics
sometimes comment upon the sudden transitions and juxtapositions of
modern poetry: that is, when right and successful, an application of
somewhat the same method without method. Whether the transition is
cogent or not, is merely a question of whether the mind is *serré* or *délié*,
whether the whole personality is involved; and certainly, the whole
personality of Whibley is present in whatever he wrote, and it is the
unity of a personality which gives an indissoluble unity to his variety of
subject. . . .

> SOURCE: extract from 'Charles Whibley' (1931); in *S. E.*, 2nd
> edition, p. 462.

VI

. . . One of the greatest distinctions of several of [Massinger's] elder
contemporaries – we name Middleton, Webster, Tourneur – is a gift
for combining, for fusing into a single phrase, two or more diverse
impressions.

. . . in her strong toil of grace

of Shakespeare is such a fusion; the metaphor identifies itself with what
suggests it; the resultant is one and is unique –

Does the silk worm *expend* her *yellow labours?* . . .
Why does yon fellow *falsify highways*
And lays his life between the judge's lips
To *refine* such a one? keeps horse and men
To *beat their valours* for her?

Let the common sewer take it from distinction. . . .
Lust and forgetfulness have been amongst us. . . .

These lines of Tourneur and of Middleton exhibit that perpetual slight alteration of language, words perpetually juxtaposed in new and sudden combinations, meanings perpetually *eingeschachtelt* into meanings, which evidences a very high development of the senses, a development of the English language which we have perhaps never equalled. And, indeed, with the end of Chapman, Middleton, Webster, Tourneur, Donne we end a period when the intellect was immediately at the tips of the senses. Sensation became word and word was sensation. . . .

SOURCE: extract from 'Philip Massinger' (1920); in *S. E.*, 2nd edition, pp. 209–10.

2. THE ENJOYMENT AND UNDERSTANDING OF POETRY

I

. . . it is better to be spurred to acquire scholarship because you enjoy the poetry, than to suppose that you enjoy the poetry because you have acquired the scholarship. I was passionately fond of certain French poetry long before I could have translated two verses of it correctly. With Dante the discrepancy between enjoyment and understanding was still wider. . . .

. . . If you get nothing out of [the *Divine Comedy*] at first, you probably never will; but if from your first deciphering of it there comes now and then some direct shock of poetic intensity, nothing but laziness can deaden the desire for fuller and fuller knowledge.

What is surprising about the poetry of Dante is that it is, in one sense, extremely easy to read. It is a test (a positive test, I do not assert that it is always valid negatively), that genuine poetry can communicate before it is understood. . . .

> SOURCE: extracts from 'Dante' (1929); in *S. E.*, 2nd edition, pp. 237, 238

II

. . . One can explain a poem by investigating what it is made of and the causes that brought it about; and explanation may be a necessary preparation for understanding. But to understand a poem it is also necessary, and I should say in most instances still more necessary, that we should endeavour to grasp what the poetry is aiming to be; one might say—though it is long since I have employed such terms with any assurance—endeavouring to grasp its entelechy. . . .

> SOURCE: extract from 'The Frontiers of Criticism' (1956); reprinted in *On Poetry and Poets* (1957) p. 110.

3. THE SOURCES AND RESOURCES OF POETRY

I

May I explain first why I have chosen, not to deliver a lecture about Dante, but to talk informally about his influence upon myself? What might appear egotism, in doing this, I present as modesty; and the modesty which it pretends to be is merely prudence. I am in no way a Dante scholar; and my general knowledge of Italian is such, that on this occasion, out of respect to the audience and to Dante himself, I shall refrain from quoting him in Italian. And I do not feel that I have anything more to contribute, on the subject of Dante's poetry, than I put, years ago, into a brief essay. As I explained in the original preface to that essay, I read Dante only with a prose translation beside the text. Forty years ago I began to puzzle out the Divine Comedy in this way; and when I thought I had grasped the meaning of a passage which especially delighted me, I committed it to memory; so that, for some years, I was able to recite a large part of one canto or another to myself, lying in bed or on a railway journey. Heaven knows what it would have sounded like, had I recited it aloud; but it was by this means that I steeped myself in Dante's poetry. And now it is twenty years since I set down all that my meagre attainments qualified me to say about Dante. But I thought it not uninteresting to myself, and possibly to others, to try to record in what my own debt to Dante consists. I do not think I can explain everything, even to myself; but as I still, after forty years, regard his poetry as the most persistent and deepest influence upon my own verse, I should like to establish at least some of the reasons for it. Perhaps confessions by poets, of what Dante has meant to them, may even contribute something to the appreciation of Dante himself. And finally, it is the only contribution that I can make.

The greatest debts are not always the most evident; at least, there are different kinds of debt. The kind of debt that I owe to Dante is the kind which goes on accumulating, the kind which is not the debt of one period or another of one's life. Of some poets I can say I learned a great deal from them at a particular stage. Of Jules Laforgue, for instance, I can say that he was the first to teach me how to speak, to teach me the poetic possibilities of my own idiom of speech. Such early influences, the influences which, so to speak, first introduce one to oneself, are, I think, due to an impression which is in one aspect, the recognition of a temperament akin to one's own, and in another aspect the discovery of a form of expression which gives a clue to the discovery of one's own form. These are not two things, but two aspects of the same thing. But the poet who can do this for a young writer, is unlikely to be one of the great masters. The latter are too exalted and too remote. They are like distant ancestors who have been almost deified; whereas the smaller poet, who has directed one's first steps, is more like an admired elder brother.

Then, among influences, there are the poets from whom one has learned some one thing, perhaps of capital importance to oneself, though not necessarily the greatest contribution these poets have made. I think that from Baudelaire I learned first, a precedent for the poetical possibilities, never developed by any poet writing in my own language, of the more sordid aspects of the modern metropolis, of the possibility of fusion between the sordidly realistic and the phantasmagoric, the possibility of the juxtaposition of the matter-of-fact and the fantastic. From him, as from Laforgue, I learned that the sort of material that I had, the sort of experience that an adolescent had had, in an industrial city in America, could be the material for poetry; and that the source of new poetry might be found in what had been regarded hitherto as the impossible, the sterile, the intractably unpoetic. That, in fact, the business of the poet was to make poetry out of the unexplored resources of the unpoetical; that the poet, in fact, was committed by his profession to turn the unpoetical into poetry. A great poet can give a younger poet everything that he has to give him, in a very few lines. It may be that I am indebted to Baudelaire chiefly for half a dozen lines out of the whole of *Fleurs du Mal*; and that his significance for me is summed up in the lines:

> Fourmillante Cité, cité pleine de rêves,
> Où le spectre en plein jour raccroche le passant . . .

I knew what *that* meant, because I had lived it before I knew that I wanted to turn it into verse on my own account.

I may seem to you to be very far from Dante. But I cannot give you any approximation of what Dante has done for me, without speaking of what other poets have done for me. When I have written about Baudelaire, or Dante, or any other poet who has had a capital importance in my own development, I have written *because* that poet has meant so much to me, but not about myself, but *about* that poet and his poetry. That is, the first impulse to write about a great poet is one of gratitude; but the reasons for which one is grateful may play a very small part in a critical appreciation of that poet.

One has other debts, innumerable debts, to poets, of another kind. There are poets who have been at the back of one's mind, or perhaps consciously there, when one has had some particular problem to settle, for which something they have written suggests the method. There are those from whom one has consciously borrowed, adapting a line of verse to a different language or period or context. There are those who remain in one's mind as having set the standard for a particular poetic virtue, as Villon for honesty, and Sappho for having fixed a particular emotion in the right and the minimum number of words, once and for all. There are also the great masters, to whom one slowly grows up. When I was young I felt much more at ease with the lesser Elizabethan dramatists than with Shakespeare: the former were, so to speak, playmates nearer my own size. One test of the great masters, of whom

Shakespeare is one, is that the appreciation of their poetry is a lifetime's task, because at every stage of maturing – and that should be one's whole life – you are able to understand them better. Among these are Shakespeare, Dante, Homer and Virgil.

SOURCE: 'What Dante Means to Me' (1950); reprinted in *To Criticise the Critic* (1966) pp. 125–7.

II

. . . One of the surest tests is the way in which a poet borrows. Immature poets imitate; mature poets steal; bad poets deface what they take, and good poets make it into something better, or at least something different. The good poet welds his theft into a whole of feeling which is unique, utterly different from that from which it was torn; the bad poet throws it into something which has no cohesion. A good poet will usually borrow from authors remote in time, or alien in language, or diverse in interest. . . .

SOURCE: extract from 'Philip Massinger' (1920); in *S. E.*, 2nd edition, p. 206.

III

. . . Only a part of an author's imagery comes from his reading. It comes from the whole of his sensitive life since early childhood. Why, for all of us, out of all that we have heard, seen, felt, in a lifetime, do certain images recur, charged with emotion, rather than others? The song of one bird, the leap of one fish, at a particular place and time, the scent of one flower, an old woman on a German mountain path, six ruffians seen through an open window playing cards at night at a small French railway junction where there was a water-mill:[1] such memories may have symbolic value, but of what we cannot tell, for they come to represent the depths of feeling into which we cannot peer. We might just as well ask why, when we try to recall visually some period in the past, we find in our memory just the few meagre arbitrarily chosen set of snapshots that we do find there, the faded poor souvenirs of passionate moments.

SOURCE: extract from *The Use of Poetry and the Use of Criticism*

(1933); reprinted in *Selected Prose*, ed. Hayward, p. 95, under the
heading 'Poetic Imagery'.

NOTE

1. Cf. *Journey of the Magi*, lines 21–8. [Hayward's note – Ed.]

IV

. . . It is an advantage to mankind in general to live in a beautiful
world; that no one can doubt. But for the poet is it so important? We
mean all sorts of things, I know, by Beauty. But the essential advantage
for a poet is not to have a beautiful world with which to deal: it is to be
able to see beneath both beauty and ugliness; to see the boredom, and
the horror, and the glory.

SOURCE: extract from *The Use of Poetry and the Use of Criticism*
(1933); in *Selected Prose*, ed. Hayward, p. 176, under the heading
'Arnold'.

4. POETRY AND RELIGIOUS BELIEF

I

. . . I doubt whether belief proper enters into the activity of a great
poet, *qua* poet. That is, Dante, *qua* poet, did not believe or disbelieve the
Thomist cosmology or theory of the soul: he merely made use of it, or a
fusion took place between his initial emotional impulses and a theory,
for the purpose of making poetry. The poet makes poetry, the
metaphysician makes metaphysics, the bee makes honey, the spider
secretes a filament; you can hardly say that any of these agents believes:
he merely does.

The problem of belief is very complicated and probably quite
insoluble. We must make allowance for differences in the emotional
quality of believing not only between persons of different occupation,
such as the philosopher and the poet, but between different periods of

time. The end of the sixteenth century is an epoch when it is particularly difficult to associate poetry with systems of thought or reasoned views of life. In making some very commonplace investigations of the 'thought' of Donne, I found it quite impossible to come to the conclusion that Donne believed anything. It seemed as if, at that time, the world was filled with broken fragments of systems, and that a man like Donne merely picked up, like a magpie, various shining fragments of ideas as they struck his eye, and stuck them about here and there in his verse. Miss Ramsay, in her learned and exhaustive study of Donne's sources, came to the conclusion that he was a 'mediaeval thinker'; I could not find either any 'mediaevalism' or any thinking, but only a vast jumble of incoherent erudition on which he drew for purely poetic effects. The recent work of Professor Schoell on the sources of Chapman seems to show Chapman engaged in the same task; and suggests that the 'profundity' and 'obscurity' of Chapman's dark thinking are largely due to his lifting long passages from the works of writers like Ficino and incorporating them in his poems completely out of their context.

I do not for a moment suggest that the method of Shakespeare was anything like this. Shakespeare was a much finer instrument for transformations than any of his contemporaries, finer perhaps even than Dante. He also needed less contact in order to be able to absorb all that he required. The element of Seneca is the most completely absorbed and transmogrified, because it was already the most diffused throughout Shakespeare's world. The element of Machiavelli is probably the most indirect, the element of Montaigne the most immediate. It has been said that Shakespeare lacks unity; it might, I think, be said equally well that it is Shakespeare chiefly that *is* the unity, that unifies so far as they could be unified all the tendencies of a time that certainly lacked unity. . . .

SOURCE: extract from 'Shakespeare and the Stoicism of Seneca' (1927); in *S. E.*, 2nd edition, pp. 138–9.

II

. . . My point is that you cannot afford to *ignore* Dante's philosophical and theological beliefs, or to skip the passages which express them most clearly; but that on the other hand you are not called upon to believe them yourself. It is wrong to think that there are parts of the *Divine*

Comedy which are of interest only to Catholics or to mediaevalists. For there is a difference (which here I hardly do more than assert) between philosophical *belief* and poetic *assent*. . . .

. . . You are not called upon to believe what Dante believed, for your belief will not give you a groat's worth more of understanding and appreciation; but you are called upon more and more to understand it. If you can read poetry as poetry, you will 'believe' in Dante's theology exactly as you believe in the physical reality of his journey; that is, you suspend both belief and disbelief. I will not deny that it may be in practice easier for a Catholic to grasp the meaning, in many places, than for the ordinary agnostic; but that is not because the Catholic believes, but because he has been instructed. It is a matter of knowledge and ignorance, not of belief or scepticism. The vital matter is that Dante's poem is a whole; that you must in the end come to understand every part in order to understand any part.

Furthermore, we can make a distinction between what Dante believes as a poet and what he believed as a man. Practically, it is hardly likely that even so great a poet as Dante could have composed the *Comedy* merely with understanding and without belief; but his private belief becomes a different thing in becoming poetry. It is interesting to hazard the suggestion that this is truer of Dante than of any other philosophical poet. With Goethe, for instance, I often feel too acutely 'this is what Goethe the man believed', instead of merely entering into a world which Goethe has created; with Lucretius also; less with the *Bhagavad-Gita*, which is the next greatest philosophical poem to the *Divine Comedy* within my experience. That is the advantage of a coherent traditional system of dogma and morals like the Catholic: it stands apart, for understanding and assent even without belief, from the single individual who propounds it. Goethe always arouses in me a strong sentiment of disbelief in what he believes: Dante does not. I believe that this is because Dante is the purer poet, not because I have more sympathy with Dante the man than Goethe the man.

We are not to take Dante for Aquinas or Aquinas for Dante. It would be a grievous error in psychology. The *belief attitude* of a man reading the *Summa* must be different from that of a man reading Dante, even when it is the same man, and that man a Catholic.

It is not necessary to have read the *Summa* (which usually means, in practice, reading some handbook) in order to understand Dante. But it is necessary to read the philosophical passages of Dante with the humility of a person visiting a new world, who admits that every part is essential to the whole. What is necessary to appreciate the poetry of the *Purgatorio* is not belief, but suspension of belief. Just as much effort is required of any modern person to accept Dante's allegorical method, as is required of the agnostic to accept his theology.

When I speak of understanding, I do not mean merely knowledge of books or words, any more than I mean belief: I mean a state of mind in which one sees certain beliefs, as the order of the deadly sins, in which treachery and pride are greater than lust, and despair the greatest, as *possible*, so that we suspend our judgement altogether. . . .

SOURCE: extracts from 'Dante' (1929); in *S. E.*, 2nd edition,
pp. 257, 258-9.

5. EMOTION AND THOUGHT IN POETRY

I

. . . The only way of expressing emotion in the form of art is by finding an 'objective correlative'; in other words, a set of objects, a situation, a chain of events which shall be the formula of that *particular* emotion; such that when the external facts, which must terminate in sensory experience, are given, the emotion is immediately invoked. . . .

SOURCE: extract from 'Hamlet' (1919); in *S. E.*, 2nd edition,
p. 145.

II

. . . The poet who 'thinks' is merely the poet who can express the emotional equivalent of thought. But he is not necessarily interested in the thought itself. We talk as if thought was precise and emotion was vague. In reality there is precise emotion and there is vague emotion. To express precise emotion requires as great intellectual power as to express precise thought. . . . When we enter into the world of Homer, or Sophocles, or Virgil, or Dante, or Shakespeare, we incline to believe that we are apprehending something that can be expressed intellectually; for every precise emotion tends towards intellectual formulation. . . . When Dante says

> la sua voluntade è nostra pace

it is great poetry, and there is a great philosophy behind it. When Shakespeare says

> As flies to wanton boys, are we to the gods;
> They kill us for their sport

it is equally great poetry, though the philosophy behind it is not great. But the essential is that each expresses, in perfect language, some permanent human impulse. Emotionally, the latter is just as strong, just as true, and just as informative – just as useful and benefical in the sense in which poetry is useful and beneficial, as the former.

What every poet starts from is his own emotions. And when we get down to these, there is not much to choose between Shakespeare and Dante. Dante's railings, his personal spleen – sometimes thinly disguised under Old Testamental prophetic denunciations – his nostalgia, his bitter regrets for past happiness – or for what seems happiness when it is past – and his brave attempts to fabricate something permanent and holy out of his personal animal feelings – as in the *Vita Nuova* – can all be matched out of Shakespeare. Shakespeare, too, was occupied with the struggle – which alone constitutes life for a poet – to transmute his personal and private agonies into something rich and strange, something universal and impersonal. The rage of Dante against Florence, or Pistoia, or what not, the deep surge of Shakespeare's general cynicism and disillusionment, are merely gigantic attempts to metamorphose private failures and disappointments. The great poet, in writing himself, writes his time.[1] Thus Dante, hardly knowing it, became the voice of the thirteenth century; Shakespeare, hardly knowing it, became the representative of the end of the sixteenth century, of a turning point in history. But you can hardly say that Dante believed, or did not believe, the Thomist philosophy; you can hardly say that Shakespeare believed, or did not believe, the mixed and muddled scepticism of the Renaissance. If Shakespeare had written according to a better philosophy, he would have written worse poetry; it was his business to express the greatest emotional intensity of his time, based on whatever his time happened to think. . . .

SOURCE: extracts from 'Shakespeare and the Stoicism of Seneca' (1927); in *S. E.*, 2nd edition, pp 135, 136–7.

NOTE

1. Remy de Gourmont said much the same thing, in speaking of Flaubert. [Eliot's note – Ed.]

III

. . . the poet has, not a 'personality' to express, but a particular medium, which is only a medium and not a personality, in which impressions and experiences combine in peculiar and unexpected ways. Impressions and experiences which are important for the man may take no place in the poetry, and those which become important in the poetry may play quite a negligible part in the man, the personality.

I will quote a passage which is unfamiliar enough to be regarded with fresh attention in the light – or darkness – of these observations:

> And now methinks I could e'en chide myself
> For doating on her beauty, though her death
> Shall be revenged after no common action.
> Does the silkworm expend her yellow labours
> For thee? For thee does she undo herself?
> Are lordships sold to maintain ladyships
> For the poor benefit of a bewildering minute?
> Why does yon fellow falsify highways,
> And put his life between the judge's lips,
> To refine such a thing – keeps horse and men
> To beat their valours for her? . . .

In this passage (as is evident if it is taken in its context) there is a combination of positive and negative emotions: an intensely strong attraction toward beauty and an equally intense fascination by the ugliness which is contrasted with it and which destroys it. This balance of contrasted emotion is in the dramatic situation to which the speech is pertinent, but that situation alone is inadequate to it. This is, so to speak, the structural emotion, provided by the drama. But the whole effect, the dominant tone, is due to the fact that a number of floating feelings, having an affinity to this emotion by no means superficially evident, have combined with it to give us a new art emotion.

It is not in his personal emotions, the emotions provoked by particular events in his life, that the poet is in any way remarkable or interesting. His particular emotions may be simple, or crude, or flat. The emotion in his poetry will be a very complex thing, but not with the complexity of the emotions of people who have very complex or unusual emotions in life. One error, in fact, of eccentricity in poetry is to seek for new human emotions to express; and in this search for novelty in the wrong place it discovers the perverse. The business of the poet is not to find new emotions, but to use the ordinary ones and, in working them up into poetry, to express feelings which are not in actual emotions at all. . . .

Source: extract from 'Tradition and the Individual Talent' (1917); in *S. E.*, 2nd edition, pp. 19–21.

6. MEANING AND INTERPRETATION

I

. . . [The poet] has something germinating in him for which he must find words; but he cannot know what words he wants until he has found the words; he cannot identify this embryo until it has been transformed into an arrangement of the right words in the right order. When you have the words for it, the 'thing' for which the words had to be found has disappeared, replaced by a poem. What you start from is nothing so definite as an emotion, in any ordinary sense; it is still more certainly not an idea; it is – to adapt two lines of Beddoes to a different meaning – a

> bodiless childful of life in the gloom
> Crying with frog voice, 'what shall I be?'

... In a poem which is neither didactic nor narrative, and not animated by any other social purpose, the poet may be concerned solely with expressing in verse – using all his resources of words, with their history, their connotations, their music – this obscure impulse. He does not know what he has to say until he has said it; and in the effort to say it he is not concerned with making other people understand anything. He is not concerned, at this stage, with other people at all: only with finding the right words or, anyhow, the least wrong words. He is not concerned whether anybody else will ever listen to them or not, or whether anybody else will ever understand them if he does. He is oppressed by a burden which he must bring to birth in order to obtain relief. Or, to change the figure of speech, he is haunted by a demon, a demon against which he feels powerless, because in its first manifestation it has no face, no name, nothing; and the words, the poem he makes, are a kind of form of exorcism of this demon. In other words again, he is going to all that trouble, not in order to communicate with anyone, but to gain relief from acute discomfort; and when the words are finally arranged in the right way – or in what he comes to accept as the best arrangement he can find – he may experience a moment of exhaustion, of appeasement, of absolution, and of something very near annihilation, which is in itself indescribable. And then he can say to the poem: 'Go away! Find a place for yourself in a book – and don't expect *me* to take any further interest in you.' ...

SOURCE: extracts from 'The Three Voices of Poetry' (1953); reprinted in Eliot's *On Poetry and Poets* (1957) pp. 97, 98. This collection is hereafter referred to as *On P. and P.*

II

... It is a commonplace to observe that the meaning of a poem may be something larger than its author's conscious purpose, and something remote from its origins. ... If we are moved by a poem, it has meant something, perhaps something important, to us; if we are not moved, then it is, as poetry, meaningless. We can be deeply stirred by hearing the recitation of a poem in a language of which we understand no word; but if we are then told that the poem is gibberish and has no meaning, we shall consider that we have been deluded – this was no poem, it was merely an imitation of instrumental music. If, as we are aware, only a part of the meaning can be conveyed by paraphrase, that is because the poet is occupied with frontiers of consciousness beyond which words fail, though meanings still exist. A poem may appear to mean very different things to different readers, and all of these meanings may be different from what the author thought he meant. For instance, the author may have been writing some peculiar personal experience, which he saw quite unrelated to anything outside; yet for the reader the poem may become the expression of a general situation, as well as of some private experience of his own. The reader's interpretation may differ from the author's and be equally valid – it may even be better. There may be much more in a poem than the author was aware of. The different interpretations may all be partial formulations of one thing; the ambiguities may be due to the fact that the poem means more, not less, than ordinary speech can communicate. . . .

> SOURCE: extracts from 'The Music of Poetry' (1942); in *On P. and*
> *P.*, pp. 30–1.

III

. . . The question of how far information about the poet helps us to understand the poetry is not so simple as one might think. Each reader must answer it for himself, and must answer it not generally but in particular instances, for it may be more important in the case of one poet and less important in the case of another. For the enjoyment of poetry can be a complex experience in which several forms of satisfaction are mingled; and they may be mingled in different proportions for different readers. . . .

> SOURCE: this and extracts IV, V and VI are from 'The Frontiers of
> Criticism' (1956); in *On P. and P.*, pp. 111, 112, 113.

IV

. . . there is in all great poetry, something which must remain unaccountable however complete might be our knowledge of the poet, and that is what matters most. When the poem has been made, something new has happened, something that cannot be wholly explained by *anything that went before*. That, I believe, is what we mean by 'creation'.

V

The explanation of poetry by examination of its sources is not the
method of all contemporary criticism by any means; but it is a method
which responds to the desire of a good many readers that poetry should
be explained to them in terms of something else: the chief part of the
letters I receive from persons unknown to me, concerning my own
poems, consists of requests for a kind of explanation that I cannot
possibly give. . . .

VI

. . . I imagine that some of the poets (they are all dead except myself)
would be surprised at learning what their poems mean: I had one or two
minor surprises myself, as on learning that the fog, mentioned early in
'Prufrock', had somehow got into the drawing-room. But the analysis of
'Prufrock' was not an attempt to find origins, either in literature or in
the darker recesses of my private life; it was an attempt to find out what
the poem really meant – whether that was what I had meant it to mean
or not. And for that I was grateful. . . . The first danger is that of
assuming that there must be just one interpretation of the poem as a
whole, that must be right. There will be details of explanation,
especially with poems written in another age than our own, matters of
fact, historical allusions, the meaning of certain words at a certain date,
which can be established, and the teacher can see that his pupils get
these right. But as for the meaning of the poem as a whole, it is not
exhausted by any explanation, for the meaning is what the poem means
to different sensitive readers. . . .

7. *VERS LIBRE*

I

... I do not minimize the services of modern poets in exploiting the possibilities of rhymeless verse. They prove the strength of a Movement, the utility of a Theory. What neither Blake nor Arnold could do alone is being done in our time. 'Blank verse' is the only accepted rhymeless verse in English – the inevitable iambic pentameter. The English ear is (or was) more sensitive to the music of the verse and less dependent upon the recurrence of identical sounds in this metre than in any other. There is no campaign against rhyme. But it is possible that excessive devotion to rhyme has thickened the modern ear. The rejection of rhyme is not a leap at facility; on the contrary, it imposes a much severer strain upon the language. When the comforting echo of rhyme is removed, success or failure in the choice of words, in the sentence structure, in the order, is at once more apparent. Rhyme removed, the poet is at once held up to the standards of prose. Rhyme removed, much ethereal music leaps up from the word, music which has hitherto chirped unnoticed in the expanse of prose. Any rhyme forbidden, many Shagpats were unwigged.

And this liberation from rhyme might be as well a liberation *of* rhyme. Freed from its exacting task of supporting lame verse, it could be applied with greater effect where it is most needed. There are often passages in an unrhymed poem where rhyme is wanted for some special effect, for a sudden tightening-up, for a cumulative insistence, or for an abrupt change of mood. But formal rhymed verse will certainly not lose its place. We only need the coming of a Satirist – no man of genius is rarer – to prove that the heroic couplet has lost none of its edge since Dryden and Pope laid it down. As for the sonnet I am not so sure. But the decay of intricate formal patterns has nothing to do with the advent of *vers libre*. It had set in long before. Only in a closely-knit and homogeneous society, where many men are at work on the same problems, such a society as those which produced the Greek chorus, the Elizabethan lyric, and the Troubadour canzone, will the development of such forms ever be carried to perfection. And as for *vers libre*, we conclude that it is not defined by absence of pattern or absence of rhyme, for other verse is without these; that it is not defined by non-existence of metre, since even the *worst* verse can be scanned; and we conclude that the division between Conservative Verse and *vers libre* does not exist, for there is only good verse, bad verse, and chaos.

SOURCE: extract from 'Reflections on *Vers Libre*' (1917); reprinted in *To Criticise the Critic*, pp. 188–9.

II

. . . As for 'free verse', I expressed my view twenty-five years ago by saying that no verse is free for the man who wants to do a good job. No one has better cause to know than I, that a great deal of bad prose has been written under the name of free verse; though whether its authors wrote bad verse, or bad verse in one style or in another, seems to me a matter of indifference. But only a bad poet could welcome free verse as a liberation from form. It was a revolt against dead form, and a preparation for new form or for the renewal of the old; it was an insistence upon the inner unity which is unique to every poem, against the outer unity which is typical. The poem comes before the form, in the sense that a form grows out of the attempt of somebody to say something; just as a system of prosody is only a formulation of the identities in the rhythms of a succession of poets influenced by each other.

SOURCE: extract from 'The Music of Poetry' (1942); in *On P. and P.*, p. 37.

8. CRITICISM

I

. . . I believe that the critical writings of poets, of which in the past there have been some very distinguished examples, owe a great deal of their interest to the fact that the poet, at the back of his mind, if not as his ostensible purpose, is always trying to defend the kind of poetry he is writing, or to formulate the kind that he wants to write. Especially when he is young, and actively engaged in battling for the kind of poetry which he practises, he sees the poetry of the past in relation to his own: and his gratitude to those dead poets from whom he has learned, as well

as his indifference to those whose aims have been alien to his own, may
be exaggerated. He is not so much a judge as an advocate.
His knowledge even is likely to be partial: for his studies will have led him to
concentrate on certain authors to the neglect of others. When he
theorizes about poetic creation, he is likely to be generalizing one type
of experience; when he ventures into aesthetics, he is likely to be less,
rather than more competent than the philosopher; and he may do best
merely to report, for the information of the philosopher, the data of his
own introspection. What he writes about poetry, in short, must be
assessed in relation to the poetry he writes. . . .

SOURCE: extract from 'The Music of Poetry' (1942); in *On P. and
P.*, p. 26.

II

. . . The best of my *literary* criticism – apart from a few notorious
phrases which have had a truly embarrassing success in the
world – consists of essays on poets and poetic dramatists who had
influenced me. It is a by-product of my private poetry-workshop; or a
prolongation of the thinking that went into the formation of my own
verse. In retrospect, I see that I wrote best about poets whose work had
influenced my own, and with whose poetry I had become thoroughly
familiar, long before I desired to write about them, or had found the
occasion to do so. My criticism has this in common with that of Ezra
Pound, that its merits and limitations can be fully appreciated only
when it is considered in relation to the poetry I have written myself. . . .

SOURCE: extract from 'The Frontiers of Criticism' (1956); in *On
P. and P.*, p. 106.

III

. . . It is not merely in the use of imagery of common life, not merely in
the use of imagery of the sordid life of a great metropolis, but in the
elevation of such imagery to the *first intensity* – presenting it as it is, and
yet making it represent something much more than itself – that
Baudelaire has created a mode of release and expression for other men.
This invention of language, at a moment when French poetry in
particular was famishing for such invention, is enough to make of

Baudelaire a great poet, a great landmark in poetry. Baudelaire is indeed the greatest examplar in *modern* poetry in any language, for his verse and language is the nearest thing to a complete renovation that we have experienced. But his renovation of an attitude towards life is no less radical and no less important. In his verse, he is now less a model to be imitated or a source to be drained than a reminder of the duty, the consecrated task, of sincerity. From a fundamental sincerity he could not deviate. The superficies of sincerity (as I think has not always been remarked) is not always there. As I have suggested, many of his poems are insufficiently removed from their romantic origins, from Byronic paternity and Satanic fraternity. The 'satanism' of the Black Mass was very much in the air; in exhibiting it Baudelaire is the voice of his time; but I would observe that in Baudelaire, as in no one else, it is redeemed by *meaning something else*. He uses the same paraphernalia, but cannot limit its symbolism even to all that of which he is conscious. . . .

SOURCE: extract from 'Baudelaire' (1930); in *S. E.*, 2nd edition, p. 388.

9. HIS OWN WORK

I

. . . When I was a young man at the university, in America, just beginning to write verse, Yeats was already a considerable figure in the world of poetry, and his early period was well defined. I cannot remember that his poetry at that stage made any deep impression upon me. A very young man, who is himself stirred to write, is not primarily critical or even widely appreciative. He is looking for masters who will elicit his consciousness of what he wants to say himself, of the kind of poetry that is in him to write. The taste of an adolescent writer is intense, but narrow: it is determined by personal needs. The kind of poetry that I needed, to teach me the use of my own voice, did not exist in English at all; it was only to be found in French. . . .

SOURCE: extract from 'Yeats' (1940); in *On P. and P.*, p. 252

II

. . . INTERVIEWER: I have another question about you and Pound and your earlier career. I have read somewhere that you and Pound decided to write quatrains, in the late teens, because *vers libre* had gone too far.

ELIOT: I think that's something Pound said. And the suggestion of writing quatrains was his. He put me onto *Émaux and Camées* [Gautier].

INTERVIEWER: I wonder about your ideas about the relation of form to subject. Would you have chosen the form before you knew quite what you were going to write in it?

ELIOT: Yes, in a way. One studied originals. We studied Gautier's poems and then we thought, 'Have I anything to say in which this form will be useful?' And we experimented. The form gave the impetus to the content.

INTERVIEWER: Why was *vers libre* the form you chose to use in your early poems?

ELIOT: My early *vers libre*, of course, was started under the endeavor to practise the same form as Laforgue. This meant merely rhyming lines of irregular length, with the rhymes coming in irregular places. It wasn't quite so *libre* as much *vers*, especially the sort which Ezra called 'Amygism'.[1] Then, of course, there were things in the next phase which were freer, like 'Rhapsody on a Windy Night'. I don't know whether I had any sort of model or practice in mind when I did that. It just came that way.

INTERVIEWER: Did you feel, possibly, that you were writing against something, more than from any model? Against the poet laureate perhaps?

ELIOT: No, no, no. I don't think one was constantly trying to reject things, but just trying to find out what was right for oneself. One really ignored poet laureates as such, the Robert Bridges. I don't think good poetry can be produced in a kind of political attempt to overthrow some existing form. I think it just supersedes. People find a way in which they can say something. 'I can't say it that way, what way can I find that will do?' One didn't really *bother* about the existing modes.

INTERVIEWER: I think it was after 'Prufrock' and before 'Geron-tion' that you wrote the poems in French which appear in your *Collected Poems*. I wonder how you happened to write them. Have you written any since?

ELIOT: No, and I never shall. That was a very curious thing which I can't altogether explain. At that period I thought I'd dried up completely. I hadn't written anything for some time and was rather desperate. I started writing a few things in French and found I *could*, at that period. I think it was that when I was writing in French I didn't take the poems so seriously, and that, not taking them seriously, I wasn't so worried about not being able to write. I did these things as a sort of *tour de force* to see what I could do. That went on for some months. The best of them have been printed. I must say that Ezra Pound went through them, and Edmond Dulac, a Frenchman we knew in London, helped with them a bit. We left out some, and I suppose they disappeared completely. Then I suddenly began writing in English again and lost all desire to go on with French. I think it was just something that helped me get started again.

INTERVIEWER: Did you think at all about becoming a French symbolist poet like the two Americans of the last century?

ELIOT: Stuart Merrill and Viele-Griffin. I only did that during the romantic year I spent in Paris after Harvard. I had at that time the idea of giving up English and trying to settle down and scrape along in Paris and gradually write French. But it would have been a foolish idea even if I'd been much more bilingual than I ever was, because, for one thing, I don't think that one can be a bilingual poet. I don't know of any case in which a man wrote great or even fine poems equally well in two languages. I think one language must be the one you express yourself in in poetry, and you've got to give up the other for that purpose. And I think that the English language really has more resources in some respects than the French. I think, in other words, I've probably done better in English than I ever would have in French even if I'd become as proficient in French as the poets you mentioned. . . .

INTERVIEWER: Are any of your minor poems actually sections cut out of longer works? There are two that sound like 'The Hollow Men'.

ELIOT: Oh, those were the preliminary sketches. Those things were earlier. Others I published in periodicals but not in my collected poems. You don't want to say the same thing twice in one book.

INTERVIEWER: You seem often to have written poems in sections. Did they begin as separate poems? I am thinking of *Ash Wednesday*, in particular.

ELIOT: Yes, like 'The Hollow Men' it originated out of separate poems. As I recall, one or two early drafts of parts of *Ash Wednesday* appeared in *Commerce* and elsewhere. Then gradually I came to see it as a sequence. That's one way in which my mind does seem to have worked throughout the years poetically – doing things separately and then seeing the possibility of fusing them together, altering them, and making a kind of whole of them. . . .

SOURCE: extracts from interview-article 'T. S. Eliot', in *Paris Review*, XXI (Spring/Summer 1959) 54–7, 58.

NOTE

1. A reference to Amy Lowell, who captured and transformed imagism. [Note in original – Ed.]

PART TWO

Perspectives, 1917–1966:
Eliot's Development
and the Unity of
His Achievement

Ezra Pound

CONFOUND IT, THE FELLOW CAN WRITE (1917)

Il n'y a de livres que ceux où un écrivain s'est raconté lui-même en racontant les mœurs de ses contemporains – leurs rêves, leurs vanités, leurs amours, et leurs folies. (Rémy de Gourmont.[1])

De Gourmont uses this sentence in writing of the incontestable superiority of *Madame Bovary*, *L'Éducation Sentimentale* and *Bouvard et Pécuchet* to *Salammbô* and *La Tentation de St Antoine*. A casual thought convinces one that it is true for all prose. Is it true also for poetry? One may give latitude to the interpretation of *rêves*; the gross public would have the poet write little else, but De Gourmont keeps a proportion. The vision should have its place in due setting if we are to believe its reality.

The few poems which Mr Eliot has given us maintain this proportion, as they maintain other proportions of art. After much contemporary work that is merely factitious, much that is good in intention but impotently unfinished and incomplete; much whose flaws are due to sheer ignorance which a year's study or thought might have remedied, it is a comfort to come upon complete art, naïve despite its intellectual subtlety, lacking all pretence.

It is quite safe to compare Mr Eliot's work with anything written in French, English or American since the death of Jules Laforgue. The reader will find nothing better, and he will be extremely fortunate if he finds much half as good.

The necessity, or at least the advisability of comparing English or American work with French work is not readily granted by the usual English or American writer. If you suggest it, the Englishman answers that he has not thought about it – he does not see why he should bother himself about what goes on south of the channel; the American replies by stating that you are 'no longer American'. This is the bitterest jibe in his vocabulary. The net result is that it is extremely difficult to read one's contemporaries. After a time one tires of 'promise'.

I should like the reader to note how complete is Mr Eliot's depiction of our contemporary condition. He has not confined himself to genre or to society portraiture. His 'lonely men in shirt-sleeves leaning out of windows' are as real as his ladies who 'come and go / Talking of Michelangelo'. His 'one night cheap hotels' are as much 'there' as are his

> four wax candles in the darkened room,
> Four rings of light upon the ceiling overhead,
> An atmosphere of Juliet's tomb.

And, above all, there is no rhetoric, although there is Elizabethan reading in the background. Were I a French critic, skilled in their elaborate art of writing books about books, I should probably go to some length discussing Mr Eliot's two sorts of metaphor: his wholly unrealizable, always apt, half ironic suggestion, and his precise realizable picture. It would be possible to point out his method of conveying a whole situation and half a character by three words of a quoted phrase; his constant aliveness, his mingling of a very subtle observation with the unexpectedness of a backhanded cliché. It is, however, extremely dangerous to point out such devices. The method is Mr Eliot's own, but as soon as one has reduced even a fragment of it to formula, some one else, not Mr Eliot, some one else wholly lacking in his aptitudes, will at once try to make poetry by mimicking his external procedure. And this indefinite 'some one' will, needless to say, make a botch of it.

For what the statement is worth, Mr Eliot's work interests me more than that of any other poet now writing in English. The most interesting poems in Victorian English are Browning's *Men and Women*, or, if that statement is too absolute, let me contend that the form of these poems is the most vital form of that period of English, and that the poems written in that form are the least like each other in content. Antiquity gave us Ovid's *Heroides* and Theocritus's woman using magic. The form of Browning's *Men and Women* is more alive than the epistolary form of the *Heroides*. Browning included a certain amount of ratiocination and of purely intellectual comment, and in just that proportion he lost intensity. Since Browning there have been very few good poems of this sort. Mr Eliot has made two notable additions to the list. And he has placed his people in contemporary settings, which is much more difficult than to render them with medieval romantic trappings. If it is permitted to make comparison with a different art, let me say that he has used contemporary detail very much as Velasquez used contemporary detail in *Las Meninas*; the cold gray-green tones of the Spanish painter have, it seems to me, an emotional value not unlike the emotional value of Mr Eliot's rhythms, and of his vocabulary.

James Joyce has written the best novel of my decade, and perhaps the best criticism of it has come from a Belgian who said, 'All this is as true of my country as of Ireland.' Eliot has a like ubiquity of application. Art does not avoid universals, it strikes at them all the harder in that it strikes through particulars. Eliot's work rests apart from that of the many new writers who have used the present freedoms to no advantage, who have gained no new precisions of language, and no variety in their cadence. His men in shirt-sleeves, and his society ladies, are not a local manifestation; they are the stuff of our modern world, and true of more countries than one. I would praise the work for its fine tone, its humanity, and its realism; for all good art is realism of one sort or another.

It is complained that Eliot is lacking in emotion. 'La Figlia Che Piange' is an adequate confutation.

If the reader wishes mastery of 'regular form' the 'Conversation Galante' is sufficient to show that symmetrical form is within Mr Eliot's grasp. You will hardly find such neatness save in France; such modern neatness, save in Laforgue.

De Gourmont's phrase to the contrary notwithstanding, the supreme test of a book is that we should feel some unusual intelligence working behind the words. By this test various other new books, that I have, or might have, beside me, go to pieces. The barrels of sham poetry that every decade and school and fashion produce, go to pieces. It is sometimes extremely difficult to find any other particular reason for their being so unsatisfactory. I have expressly written here not 'intellect' but 'intelligence'. There is no intelligence without emotion. The emotion may be anterior or concurrent. There may be emotion without much intelligence, but that does not concern us.

VERSIFICATION

A conviction as to the rightness or wrongness of *vers libre* is no guarantee of a poet. I doubt if there is much use trying to classify the various kinds of *vers libre*, but there is an anarchy which may be vastly overdone; and there is a monotony of bad usage as tiresome as any typical eighteenth or nineteenth century flatness.

In a recent article[2] Mr Eliot contended, or seemed to contend, that good *vers libre* was little more than a skilful evasion of the better known English metres. His article was defective in that he omitted all consideration of metres depending on quantity, alliteration, etc.; in fact, he wrote as if all metres were measured by accent. This may have been tactful on his part, it may have brought his article nearer to the comprehension of his readers (that is, those of the *New Statesman* people chiefly concerned with the sociology of the 'button' and 'unit' variety). But he came nearer the fact when he wrote elsewhere: 'No *vers* is *libre* for the man who wants to do a good job.'

Alexandrine and other grammarians have made cubby-holes for various groupings of syllables; they have put names upon them, and have given various labels to 'metres' consisting of combinations of these different groups.[3] Thus it would be hard to escape contact with some group or other; only an encyclopedist could ever be half sure he had done so. The known categories would allow a fair liberty to the most conscientious traditionalist. The most fanatical vers-librist will escape them with difficulty. However, I do not think there is any crying need for verse with absolutely no rhythmical basis.

On the other hand, I do not believe that Chopin wrote to a metronome. There is undoubtedly a sense of music that takes count of the 'shape' of the rhythm in a melody rather than of bar divisions, which came rather late in the history of written music and were certainly not the first or most important thing that musicians attempted to record. The creation of such shapes is part of thematic invention. Some musicians have the faculty of invention, rhythmic, melodic. Likewise some poets.

Treatises full of musical notes and of long and short marks have never been convincingly useful. Find a man with thematic invention and all he can say is that he gets what the Celts call a 'chune' in his head, and that the words 'go into it', or when they don't 'go into it' they 'stick out and worry him'.

You can not force a person to play a musical masterpiece correctly, even by having the notes 'correctly' printed on the paper before him; neither can you force a person to feel the movement of poetry, be the metre 'regular' or 'irregular'. I have heard Mr Yeats trying to read Burns, struggling in vain to fit 'The Birks o' Aberfeldy' and 'Bonnie Alexander' into the mournful keen of 'The Wind among the Reeds'. Even in regular metres there are incompatible systems of music.

I have heard the best orchestral conductor in England read poems in free verse, poems in which the rhythm was so faint as to be almost imperceptible. He[4] read them with the author's cadence, with flawless correctness. A distinguished statesman[5] read from the same book, with the intonations of a legal document, paying no attention to the movement inherent in the words before him. I have heard a celebrated Dante scholar and medieval enthusiast read the sonnets of the *Vita Nuova* as if they were not only prose, but the ignominious prose of a man devoid of emotions: an utter castration.

The leader of orchestra said to me, 'There is more for a musician in a few lines with something rough or uneven, such as Byron's

> There be none of Beauty's daughters
> With a magic like thee

than in whole pages of regular poetry.'

Unless a man can put some thematic invention into *vers libre*, he would perhaps do well to stick to 'regular' metres, which have certain chances of being musical from their form, and certain other chances of being musical through his failure in fitting the form. In *vers libre* his musical chances are but in sensitivity and invention.

Mr Eliot is one of the very few who have given a personal rhythm, an identifiable quality of sound as well as of style. And at any rate, his book is the best thing in poetry since . . . (for the sake of peace I will leave that date to the imagination). I have read most of the poems many times; I last read the whole book at breakfast time and from flimsy proof-sheets: I believe these are 'test conditions'. And, 'confound it, the fellow can write'.

SOURCE: review of Eliot's 'Prufrock and Other Observations', *Poetry*, x (1917); reprinted in *Literary Essays of Ezra Pound*, ed. T. S. Eliot (1954) pp. 418–22.

NOTES

1. [Trans.: 'The real books are those where a writer talks of himself in talking about the customs of his contemporaries – their dreams, their vanities, their loves and their follies' – Ed.]

2. ['Reflections on *Vers Libre*', *New Statesman*, 3 Mar 1917; an extract from this article appears above, as section 7. 1 of Part One – Ed.]

3. Prosody is the articulation of the total sound of a poem. [Note added by Pound in 1940 – Ed.]

4. Beecham.

5. Birrell.

Edgell Rickword

THE MODERN POET (1925)

If there were to be held a Congress of the Younger Poets, and it were
desired to make some kind of show of recognition to the poet who has
most effectively upheld the reality of the art in an age of preposterous
poeticising, it is impossible to think of any serious rival to the name of
T. S. Eliot. Yet, to secure the highest degree of unanimity, such a
resolution would have to be worded to the exclusion of certain
considerations, and it would concentrate attention on the significance of
this work to other poets, rather than on its possession of that quality of
'beauty' for which the ordinary reader looks, though we do not doubt
that on this count, too, perhaps the final one, it will slowly but certainly
gain the timid ears which only time can coax to an appreciation of the
unfamiliar.

'That Mr. T. S. Eliot is the poet who has approached most nearly the
solution of those problems which have stood in the way of our free poetic
expression', and 'that the contemporary sensibility, which otherwise
must have suffered dumbly, often becomes articulate in his verse', are
resolutions which express a sort of legal minimum to which individual
judgments must subscribe.

The impression we have always had of Mr. Eliot's work, reinforced
by this commodious collection in one volume [i.e. *Poems
1909 - 1925* – Ed.] may be analysed into two coincident but not quite
simultaneous impressions. The first is the urgency of the personality,
which seems sometimes oppressive, and comes near to breaking through
the so-finely-spun æsthetic fabric; the second is the technique which
spins this fabric and to which this slender volume owes its curious
ascendency over the bulky monsters of our time. For it is by his struggle
with technique that Mr. Eliot has been able to get closer than any other
poet to the physiology of our sensations (a poet does not speak merely for
himself) to explore and make palpable the more intimate distresses of a
generation for whom all the romantic escapes had been blocked. And,

though this may seem a heavy burden to lay on the back of technique, we can watch with the deepening of consciousness, a much finer realisation of language, reaching its height in passages in *The Waste Land* until it sinks under the strain and in 'The Hollow Men' becomes gnomically disarticulate.

The interval is filled with steady achievement, and though the seeds of dissolution are apparent rather early, there is a middle period in which certain things are done which make it impossible for the poet who has read them to regard his own particular problems of expression in the same way again; though he may refuse the path opened, a new field of force has come into being which exerts an influence, creates a tendency, even in despite of antipathy. Such a phenomenon is not in itself a measure of poetic achievement; Donne produced it in his generation; much smaller men, Denham and Waller, in theirs.

Let us take three main stages in this development of technique, the three poems which are, in essence, Mr. Eliot's poem, 'The Love Song of J. Alfred Prufrock', 'Gerontion' and *The Waste Land*. (The neo-satiric quatrains do not raise any fundamental queries, they are the most easily appreciated of Mr. Eliot's poems, after 'La Figlia Che Piange'. The French poems remind us of Dryden's prefaces (*vide* Swift), and there are half-a-dozen other mere *jeux d'esprit*.)

'Gerontion' is much nearer to *The Waste Land* than 'The Love Song' is to 'Gerontion'. The exquisite's witty drawing-room manner and the deliberate sentimental rhythms give way to more mysterious, further-reaching symbols, and simpler, not blatantly poetic rhythms. As an instance, we have in 'The Love Song':

> For I have known them all already, known them all:
> Have known the evenings, mornings, afternoons,
> I have measured out my life with coffee spoons.

But in *The Waste Land*:

> And I Tiresias have foresuffered all
> Enacted on this same divan or bed;
> I who have sat by Thebes below the wall
> And walked among the lowest of the dead.

The relation and the differences of these passages hardly need stressing, but, though I had not intended to enter into an examination of the psychological content of these poems, I find that this subject of fore-knowledge is cardinal to the matter. Fore-knowledge is fatal to the Active man, for whom impulse must not seem alien to the end, as it is to the vegetative life of the poets, whose ends are obscured in the means. The passage in 'Gerontion' beginning: 'After such knowledge, what forgiveness?' and the remainder of the poem are such profound commentary on the consequent annihilation of the will and desire that they must be left to more intimate consideration. The passage is a dramatic monologue, an adaptation one might hazard of the later Elizabethan soliloquy, down even to the Senecal:

> Think
> Neither fear nor courage saves us. Unnatural vices
> Are fathered by our heroism. Virtues
> Are forced upon us by our impudent crimes.

'Gerontion' is a poem which runs pretty close to *The Waste Land*, and it is free from the more mechanical devices of the later poem, but lacks its fine original verse-movements. In the Sweeney quatrains, especially in the last stanzas of 'Among the Nightingales', the noble and the base, the foul and fine, are brought together with a shock; the form has little elasticity, and tends to become, like the couplet, stereotyped antithesis. In the fluid medium of *The Waste Land* the contrast may be brought about just as violently, or it may be diffused. This contrast is not, of course, the whole content of the poem, but Mr. Eliot has most singularly solved by its means the problem of revoking that differentiation between poetic and real values which has so sterilised our recent poetry. His success is intermittent; after a short passage of exquisite verse he may bilk us with a foreign quotation, an anthropological ghost, or a mutilated quotation. We may appreciate his intention in these matters, the contrast, the parody, enriches the emotional aura surrounding an original passage, but each instance must be judged on its own merits; whether the parody, for instance is apposite. On this score Mr. Eliot cannot be acquitted of an occasional cheapness, nor of a somewhat complacent pedantry, and since we cannot believe that these deviations are intrinsic to the poetic mind, we must look for their explanation elsewhere. We find it in the intermittent working of Mr. Eliot's verbal imagination. He has the art of words, the skill which springs from sensitiveness, and an unmatched literary apprehension which enables him to create exquisite passages largely at second-hand (lines 60–77). It is when this faculty fails of imaginative support, as it must at times, that certain devices are called in; the intellect is asked to fill in gaps (possibly by reference to the notes, when they are, as they rarely are, helpful) which previous poets have filled in with rhetoric, perhaps, but at any rate by a verbal creation which stimulates the sensibility. The object of this verbal effort is not merely to stimulate the sensibility, since disjunctive syllables can do that, but to limit, control, and direct it towards a more intense apprehension of the whole poem. That is where a failure in verbal inventiveness is a definite poetic lapse. In a traditional poet it would result in a patch of dull verse, in Mr. Eliot's technique we get something like this:

> To Carthage then I came.
>
> Burning, burning, burning burning.
> O Lord thou pluckest me out
> O Lord thou pluckest
> burning.

Whether this is better or worse than dull verse I need not decide; that it is a failure, or the æsthetic scheme which would justify it is wrong, can I think be fairly upheld.

Though we may grasp the references to Buddah's Fire Sermon and Augustine's *Confessions*, and though Mr. Eliot may tell us that 'the collocation of these two representatives of eastern and western asceticism, as the culmination of this part of the poem, is not an accident', we find it difficult to be impressed. It is the danger of the æsthetic of *The Waste Land* that it tempts the poet to think the undeveloped theme a positive triumph and obscurity more precious than commonplace. The collocation of Buddah and Augustine is interesting enough, when known, but it is not poetically effective because the range of their association is only limited by widely dispersed elements in the poem, and the essential of poetry is the presence of concepts in mutual irritation.

This criticism might be extended to the general consideration of the technique of construction used in *The Waste Land*; it is still exploited as a method, rather than mastered. The apparently free, or subconsciously motivated, association of the elements of the poem allows that complexity of reaction which is essential to the poet now, when a stable emotional attitude seems a memory of historical grandeur. The freedom from metrical conformity, though not essential as *Don Juan* shows, is yet an added and important emancipation, when the regular metres languish with hardly an exception in the hands of mechanicians who are competent enough, but have no means of making their consciousness speak through and by the rhythm. Mr. Eliot's sense of rhythm will, perhaps, in the end, be found his most lasting innovation, as it is the quality which strikes from the reader the most immediate response.

SOURCE: review of Eliot's *Poems 1909–1925*, in *The Calendar of Modern Letters*, II (1925) 278–81.

I. A. Richards

A MUSIC OF IDEAS (1926)

We too readily forget that, unless something is very wrong with our civilisation, we should be producing three equal poets at least for every poet of high rank in our great-great-grandfathers' day. Something must indeed be wrong; and since Mr. Eliot is one of the very few poets that current conditions have not overcome, the difficulties which he has faced, and the cognate difficulties which his readers encounter, repay study.

Mr. Eliot's poetry has occasioned an unusual amount of irritated or enthusiastic bewilderment. The bewilderment has several sources. The most formidable is the unobtrusiveness, in some cases the absence, of any coherent intellectual thread upon which the items of the poem are strung. A reader of 'Gerontion', of 'Preludes', or of *The Waste Land*, may, if he will, after repeated readings, introduce such a thread. Another reader after much effort may fail to contrive one. But in either case energy will have been misapplied. For the items are united by the accord, contrast, and interaction of their emotional effects, not by an intellectual scheme that analysis must work out. The value lies in the unified response which this interaction creates in the right reader. The only intellectual activity required takes place in the realisation of the separate items. We can, of course, make a 'rationalisation' of the whole experience, as we can of any experience. If we do, we are adding something which does not belong to the poem. Such a logical scheme is, at best, a scaffolding that vanishes when the poem is constructed. But we have so built into our nervous systems a demand for intellectual coherence, even in poetry, that we find a difficulty in doing without it.

This point may be misunderstood, for the charge most usually brought against Mr. Eliot's poetry is that it is overintellectualised. One reason for this is his use of allusion. A reader who in one short poem picks up allusions to *The Aspern Papers*, *Othello*, 'A Toccata of Galuppi's', Marston, *The Phœnix and the Turtle*, *Antony and Cleopatra* (twice), 'The

Extasie', *Macbeth*, *The Merchant of Venice*, and Ruskin, feels that his wits are being unusually well exercised. He may easily leap to the conclusion that the basis of the poem is in wit also. But this would be a mistake. These things come in, not that the reader may be ingenious or admire the writer's erudition (this last accusation has tempted several critics to disgrace themselves), but for the sake of the emotional aura which they bring and the attitudes they incite. Allusion in Mr. Eliot's hands is a technical device for compression. *The Waste Land* is the equivalent in content to an epic. Without this device twelve books would have been needed. But these allusions and the notes in which some of them are elucidated have made many a petulant reader turn down his thumb at once. Such a reader has not begun to understand what it is all about.

This objection is connected with another, that of obscurity. To quote a recent pronouncement upon *The Waste Land* from Mr. Middleton Murry: 'The reader is compelled, in the mere effort to understand, to adopt an attitude of intellectual suspicion, which makes impossible the communication of feeling. The work offends against the most elementary canon of good writing: that the immediate effect should be unambiguous.' Consider first this 'canon'. What would happen, if we pressed it, to Shakespeare's greatest sonnets or to *Hamlet?* The truth is that very much of the best poetry is necessarily ambiguous in its immediate effect. Even the most careful and responsive reader must reread and do hard work before the poem forms itself clearly and unambiguously in his mind. An original poem, as much as a new branch of mathematics, compels the mind which receives it to grow, and this takes time. Anyone who upon reflection asserts the contrary for his own case must be either a demigod or dishonest; probably Mr. Murry was in haste. His remarks show that he has failed in his attempt to read the poem, and they reveal, in part, the reason for his failure – namely, his own overintellectual approach. To read it successfully he would have to discontinue his present self-mystifications.

The critical question in all cases is whether the poem is worth the trouble it entails. For *The Waste Land* this is considerable. There is Miss Weston's *From Ritual to Romance* to read, and its 'astral' trimmings to be discarded – they have nothing to do with Mr. Eliot's poem. There is Canto xxvi of the *Purgatorio* to be studied – the relevance of the close of that canto to the whole of Mr. Eliot's work must be insisted upon. It illuminates his persistent concern with sex, the problem of our generation, as religion was the problem of the last. There is the central position of Tiresias in the poem to be puzzled out – the cryptic form of the note which Mr. Eliot writes on this point is just a little tiresome. It is a way of underlining the fact that the poem is concerned with many aspects of the one fact of sex, a hint that is perhaps neither indispensable nor entirely successful.

When all this has been done by the reader, when the materials with which the words are to clothe themselves have been collected, the poem still remains to be read. And it is easy to fail in this undertaking. An 'attitude of intellectual suspicion' must certainly be abandoned. But this is not difficult to those who still know how to give their feelings precedence to their thoughts, who can accept and unify an experience without trying to catch it in an intellectual net or to squeeze out a doctrine. One form of this attempt must be mentioned. Some, misled no doubt by its origin in a Mystery, have endeavoured to give the poem a symbolical reading. But its symbols are not mystical, but emotional. They stand, that is, not for ineffable objects, but for normal human experience. The poem, in fact, is radically naturalistic; only its compression makes it appear otherwise. And in this it probably comes nearer to the original Mystery which it perpetuates than transcendentalism does.

If it were desired to label in three words the most characteristic feature of Mr. Eliot's technique, this might be done by calling his poetry a 'music of ideas'. The ideas are of all kinds, abstract and concrete, general and particular, and, like the musician's phrases, they are arranged, not that they may tell us something, but that their effects in us may combine into a coherent whole of feeling and attitude and produce a peculiar liberation of the will. They are there to be responded to, not to be pondered or worked out. This is, of course, a method used intermittently in very much poetry, and only an accentuation and isolation of one of its normal resources. The peculiarity of Mr. Eliot's later, more puzzling, work is his deliberate and almost exclusive employment of it. In the earlier poems this logical freedom appears only occasionally. In 'The Love Song of J. Alfred Prufrock', for example, there is a patch at the beginning and another at the end, but the rest of the poem is quite straightforward. In 'Gerontion', the first long poem in this manner, the air of monologue, of a stream of associations, is a kind of disguise, and the last two lines,

    Tenants of the house,
Thoughts of a dry brain in a dry season

are almost an excuse. The close of 'A Cooking Egg' is perhaps the passage in which the technique shows itself most clearly. The reader who appreciates the emotional relevance of the title has the key to the later poems in his hand. I take Pipit to be the retired nurse of the hero of the poem, and *Views of the Oxford Colleges* to be the, still treasured, present which he sent her when he went up to the University. The middle section of the poem I read as a specimen of the rather withered pleasantry in which contemporary culture has culminated and beyond which it finds much difficulty in passing. The final section gives the contrast which is pressed home by the title. Even the most mature egg was new laid once. The only other title of equal significance that I can recall is Mrs. Wharton's *The Age of Innocence*, which might well be studied in this connection. *The Waste Land* and 'The Hollow Men' (the most beautiful of Mr. Eliot's poems, and in the last section a new development) are purely a 'music of ideas', and the pretence of a continuous thread of associations is dropped.

How this technique lends itself to misunderstandings we have seen. But many readers who have failed in the end to escape bewilderment have begun by finding on almost every line that Mr. Eliot has written – if we except certain youthful poems on American topics – that personal stamp which is the hardest thing for the craftsman to imitate and perhaps the most certain sign that the experience, good or bad, rendered in the poem is authentic. Only those unfortunate persons who are incapable of reading poetry can resist Mr. Eliot's rhythms. The poem as a whole may elude us while every fragment, as a fragment, comes victoriously home. It is difficult to believe that this is Mr. Eliot's fault rather than his reader's, because a parallel case of a poet who so constantly achieves the hardest part of his task and yet fails in the easier is not to be found. It is much more likely that we have been trying to put the fragments together on a wrong principle.

Another doubt has been expressed. Mr. Eliot repeats himself in two ways. The nightingale, Cleopatra's barge, the rats, and the smoky candle-end, recur and recur. Is this a sign of a poverty of inspiration? A more plausible explanation is that this repetition is in part a conse-quence of the technique above described, and in part something which many writers who are not accused of poverty also show. Shelley, with his rivers, towers, and stars, Conrad, Hardy, Walt Whitman, and Dostoevski spring to mind. When a writer has found a theme or image which fixes a point of relative stability in the drift of experience, it is not to be expected that he will avoid it. Such themes are a means of orientation. And it is quite true that the central process in all Mr. Eliot's best poems is the same; the conjunction of feelings which, though superficially opposed, – as squalor, for example, is opposed to grandeur, – yet tend as they develop to change places and even to unite. If they do not develop far enough the intention of the poet is missed. Mr. Eliot is neither sighing after vanished glories nor holding contemporary experience up to scorn.

Both bitterness and desolation are superficial aspects of his poetry. There are those who think that he merely takes his readers into the Waste Land and leaves them there, that in his last poem he confesses his impotence to release the healing waters. The reply is that some readers find in his poetry not only a clearer, fuller realisation of their plight, the plight of a whole generation, than they find elsewhere, but also through the very energies set free in that realisation a return of the saving passion.

SOURCE: Appendix B in *The Principles of Literary Criticism* (1926)
pp. 289–95.

M. D. Zabel

T. S. ELIOT IN MID-CAREER
(1930)

If only because the history of Mr. Eliot's mind was for over a decade regarded as typical of the ordeal of the Twentieth Century intelligence progressing down the *via oscura* of the modern world, his latest encounters must command the attention of every contemporary. The hand that produced 'Sweeney', 'Prufrock', and *The Waste Land* unquestionably left its thumb-print on the thought and art of a generation. However little Eliot's former disciples may be able to follow the recent submissions of the poet from whom they learned the final accents of disillusionment, his experience remains one of the few authentic records of intellectual recovery in our time. For five years, that is, since his last appearance as a poet, he has perplexed his readers by a slow reversion (announced as fully achieved in the preface of *For Lancelot Andrewes*) to the moral absolutism of which the 'Hippopotamus' was an inverted parody, the 'Sunday Morning Service' a social indictment, 'Gerontion' a broken and pathetic echo, and the chorus of 'The Hollow Men' a derisive denial. What had long been implicit in his work was at length fully disclosed: Eliot had never succeeded in cutting the roots of native puritanism which bound him to the soil of Christianity. His nostalgia for the heroic and sanctified glories of the past, when man's rôle in the universe was less equivocal and his destiny mystically shrouded by the doctrine of redemption, had finally led him not to suicide but to the affirmations of faith. His explorations had never been conducted as far afield as those of a self-deluded des Esseintes or of Verlaine. His realism, though crossed with the subtle lineage of Donne, was in the more immediate line of Arnold, of the author of *The City of Dreadful Night*, of Housman and Hardy. Yet his return to faith might have been forecast by the courageous a dozen years ago. His early poems implicitly forecast a conversion as imminent

as the death-bed avowals of those *fin-de-siècle* apostates who ended by
espousing the creeds whereof they had made at worst a travesty, at best
a rich and sensuous symbolism for their emotional adventures. In their
luxuriating intoxications Eliot took no share. If anything made his
reaction surprising it was the clear-eyed confrontation of reality in *The
Waste Land*, or the withering and totally unflattering self-portraiture,
singularly unlike the elaborate conceit of the 'esthete', in 'Prufrock'. But
the element of self-pity was not lacking, and with it went an assumption
of premature senility, a Byronesque mockery of conventions, and the
extraordinary imaginative audacity which are unmistakeable vestiges
of a romanticism always mistrusted and finally rejected by Eliot in his
literary philosophy. The finality of his despairing self-scrutiny implied a
reserve of idealism to which, escaping suicide, he must some day fly for
recourse. 'The eagles and the trumpets' might be 'buried beneath some
snow-deep Alps,' but the posibility of digging them out remained. The
'old man in a dry month, / Being read to by a boy, waiting for rain' did
not release his last hope of a reviving shower, even where, across the
parched acres of the waste land, it failed to fall. The straw-stuffed men
in their idiotic dance around the prickly pear, waiting for the world to
end 'not with a bang but a whimper', could not forget the phrases of a
liturgy promising the resurrection and the life.

This poem, 'The Hollow Men' of 1925, serves as a link between the
earlier poems and *Ash Wednesday*. In its complete form it not only
provides an endpiece to the age of desolation and emptiness, but
contrives a plea for conciliation.

> This is the dead land
> This is the cactus land
> Here the stone images
> Are raised, here they receive
> The supplication of a dead man's hand
> Under the twinkle of a fading star.

Reality had claimed of its victim his last desire, but hope sent a
persistent echo through his brain.

> Sightless, unless
> The eyes reappear
> As the perpetual star
> Multifoliate rose

> Of death's twilight kingdom
> The hope only
> Of empty men.

And

> Between the desire
> And the spasm
> Between the potency
> And the existence
> Between the essence
> And the descent
> Falls the Shadow
> *For Thine is the Kingdom*

Here were probably the final lines of Mr. Eliot's *Inferno*. His present volume, along with the three pamphlet poems lately published, may be considered the opening cantos of his *Purgatorio*. These terms are not applied fortuitously. They are suggested both by Mr. Eliot's long and penetrating study of Dante, whereof his recent essay is a record, and by a symbolism which combines liturgical allusion with the properties of the *Commedia*: the 'multifoliate rose', the turning staircases, the 'blue of Mary's color' which suffuses the prospects of the future. From Dante Mr. Eliot has endeavored to derive the profound and salient simplicity which, in his own early poems, baffled so many readers by its resemblance to the ineluctable precision of Laforgue and Corbière; he has likewise seen in Dante the triumph of the visual imagination upon which the poet must rely for his direct, unequivocal, and *symbolical* approach to truth: a method natural to Mr. Eliot's creative temperament and wholly at variance with the discursive expositions of neo-classicism. 'Gerontion', 'Sweeney Among the Nightingales', and 'Burbank' employed that method on a miniature but precise scale, and the *The Waste Land* cut cleanest to the core of its inner meaning when it found symbolical instruments of unqualified accuracy (for instance, the first twenty lines; lines 77–110, 257–65; and the first half of part v). In Mr. Eliot's mind Dante's stylistic splendor is indissoluble from his mediaeval inheritance, the condition and certitude of his religious avowals, and the immediate veracity of his imagery. Dante has provided not only a tutelage for Mr. Eliot's literary concepts, but a guide toward the conversion which has now capped his career.

It was likely that Mr. Eliot should find this guide, not among the
exigencies of material life or through flaying his conscience with the rods
of logic and dialectic, but in a great poem. One is not debating his
sincerity when one recalls that his former despairs were tutored by
tragic and decadent poets, whose thoughts and feelings were imposed
on his mind as ineffaceably as their phrases were imposed on his poems.
From the desolation into which Webster, Donne, de Nerval, and
Baudelaire led him, Dante (not to mention the Bishops Bramhall and
Andrewes) stood ready to conduct him back to safety. The cure was
apparently as ready at hand as the torture. It remains to be seen if it was
adopted out of as extreme and inevitable a necessity, and if it has
yielded a poetry as distinguished by passion and clairvoyance, by
discipline in phrase and outline, by those qualities of 'equipoise, balance
and proportion of tones' which in the 'Homage to Dryden' won for
Marvell Mr. Eliot's incisive praise.

Mr. Eliot's approach to the doctrine of the Incarnation is presented
in *Journey of the Magi*; his persistent weariness in the face of the world's
burden – a weariness and a failure in moral courage hitherto counter-
balanced by the rigorous integrity of his craftmanship – reappears in *A
Song for Simeon*, where, with his 'eighty years and no tomorrow', the
tyranny of age and rationality still oppresses him. In *Ash Wednesday* the
torment of confusion and of exhausting intellectual scruples alike begin
to disappear.

> Because I do not hope to turn again
> Because I do not hope
> Because I do not hope to turn
> Desiring this man's gift and that man's scope
> I no longer strive to strive towards such things
> (Why should the aged eagle stretch its wings?)
> Why should I mourn
> The vanished power of the usual reign?
> . . .
> Consequently I rejoice . . .
> And pray to God to have mercy upon us
> And I pray that I may forget
> These matters that with myself I too much discuss
> Too much explain

> Because I do not hope to turn again
> Let these words answer. . . .

The poem, which is in six brief parts, is constructed around a paradoxical petition: 'Teach us to care and not to care'. Thus, by several allegorical devices the rejection of material concerns is described. The bones of mortal curiosity, 'scattered and shining', sing 'We are glad to be scattered, we did little good to each other.' The spirit, climbing three staircases to the cadence of 'Lord, I am not worthy, but speak the word only', leaves behind the deceitful demons of hope and despair. 'Mary's color' becomes the signal of promise as the poet reproaches himself with the memory of his gospel of desolation: 'O my people, what have I done unto thee.'

> Will the veiled sister between the slender
> Yew trees pray for those who offend her
> And are terrified and cannot surrender
> And affirm before the world and deny between the rocks
> In the last desert between the last blue rocks
> The desert in the garden the garden in the desert
> Of drouth, spitting from the mouth the withered apple-seed.

The final phrases, rejecting again the desperate realism of disillusionment, almost capture peace, the 'Shantih' of *The Waste Land*, in an evening of beatitude, charity, and exaltation, with 'Let my cry come unto Thee' on the poet's lips.

Mr. Eliot's religious experience has not thus far impressed one as conceived in intellectual necessity, or as imposed through other than esthetic forces on a crowded and exhausted mind. He will never be capable of forming a slovenly concept or judgement: his present essay and poems are distinguished by lucid statement and well-reasoned concision. They contain passages of subtle beauty. But of the impact of profound conviction and the absolute creative certitude of which the early poems partook and which still remains for Mr. Eliot's study in 'The Extasie', 'The Coy Mistress', in Baudelaire's 'La Mort', or even in the mathematical complexities of 'Charmes', one finds little here. The facility of design that made 'The Hollow Men' a flagging and dispirited declamation, devoid of organic fusion, has led to a desultory kind of allegory, subtle enough in itself, but unsharpened by wit or emotional

intensity, undistinguished by the complete formal synthesis which
Aquinas advocated as a moral property and Dante exemplified in his
slightest allusion. As a consequence, the contour of the design, as well as
the clean accuracy of reference and the pure aphoristic subtlety, which
alone would sustain the key of exaltation demanded by this quest for
illusion and transfiguration, is lacking. Eliot spoke with complete
authority in his first phase. In his second he displays a conciliatory
attitude which may persuade few of his contemporaries but which, as a
worse consequence, deprives his art of its once incomparable distinction
in style and tone. These brief poems, however, find their place in a
remarkable personal document which already contains some of the
finest poetry and some of the most significant entries in modern
literature.

SOURCE: review of *Ash Wednesday, Journey of the Magi, A Song for
Simeon* and 'Dante', in *Poetry*, XXXVI (1930) 330-7.

F. O. Matthiessen

THE SENSE OF HIS OWN AGE
(1935)

Even sympathetic readers of *Ash Wednesday* and 'Triumphal March' may feel that they show a decline from *The Waste Land* in that they do not give expression to so fully packed a range of experience. But, unfortunately for sociological critics, an artist's career cannot be regarded as a continual 'progress', nor plotted on a steadily rising curve. 'The Love Song of J. Alfred Prufrock' brought into union Eliot's ironic attitude with all the stimulus that he had received from his initial reading of Laforgue. As a result it possesses a finished mastery both of the material and of the form into which it is cast that puts it far beyond any of the other poems in his first volume of 1917 – with the exception of 'Portrait of a Lady' – though they were written during the following five years. In like manner, 'Gerontion', in 1919, marks a second crystallization and synthesis which lifts it entirely above the rank of the poems composed at about that time, such as 'The Hippopotamus' or 'Mr. Eliot's Sunday Morning Service', which read as though they were the work of a much younger, less mature man. Eliot himself, while commenting on Pound, has described the only way in which a poet's curve can be charted: his

work may proceed along two lines on an imaginary graph; one of the lines being his conscious and continuous effort in technical excellence, that is, in continually developing his medium for the moment when he really has something to say. The other line is just his normal human course of development, his accumulation and digestion of experience (experience is not sought for, it is merely accepted in consequence of doing what we really want to do), and by experience I mean the results of reading and reflection, varied interests of all sorts, contacts and acquaintances, as well as passion and adventure. Now and then the two lines may converge at a high peak, so that we get a masterpiece. That is to say, an accumulation of experience has crystallized to form material of art, and years of work in technique have prepared an adequate medium; and something results in which medium and material, form and content, are indistinguishable.

The very completeness of this union may cause confusion for the first readers of a new work: it may make them find difficulties that don't exist; mistake perfection for simpleness or slightness; or underestimate the force of what is being communicated. We tend too easily to pride ourselves on our superiority to the initial stupid reviewers of Wordsworth and Keats, and to forget that new art, a fresh way of interpreting life, has always to make its own audience. When Eliot's first poems appeared during the War, they were read, if at all, as an odd kind of *vers de société*; only gradually was it discovered that this slender volume was to have the effect, as Wyndham Lewis described it, of the little musk that scents a whole room.

In similar fashion, an impression of the comparative tenuousness of Eliot's later poems may prove illusory. It was probably impossible for him to strive towards a focused clarity of expression for his developing religious and political convictions without sacrificing part of his earlier complexity. But if there is loss in quickening surprise through the lessening of his sudden contrasts, there is in compensation a pervading, if less conspicuous quality: a sureness of accent and a quiet depth of tone. The one constant element through all the stages of his work has been his exact fitting of means to end, his rarely failing ability to perfect in each case the very kind of form he wanted for the particular content. The relative slimness of his production has tended to obscure his remarkable range in style. Indeed, as you read through his poems chronologically, he seems to have become expert in one mode of presentation only to move on to something else. After the 1917 volume the re-echoing manner of Laforgue diminishes, and such loosely flowing experiments as 'Rhapsody on a Windy Night' disappear altogether. Then, having carried his study of French versification to the point of writing some poems in that language, he mastered his handling of the quatrain of Gautier and thereafter has used it no more. Likewise his meeting of the late Elizabethan dramatists so completely on their own ground has never been repeated since 'Gerontion'. Both *The Waste Land* and *Ash Wednesday* are notable for the great variety of original verse forms that they employ within a short space; but the difference between these forms in the two poems is almost total.

Such versatility in style should in no degree be mistaken for mere technical virtuosity. Eliot is an example of the type of artist – and Joyce is another – whose motivating desire is to bring his expression to the greatest excellence he can, and then not to repeat it. Certain social implications can assuredly be drawn from the fact that not only Joyce and Eliot, but such other representative artists as Stravinsky and Picasso, have all felt within the past four decades a common urgency not to rest in the development of one manner, but to press on from each discovery to another. In the case of both the novelist and the poet their unwillingness to be confined long to any given method of presentation is obviously owing in part to their extraordinary historical consciousness, to their knowledge of so many possible techniques that they cannot remain satisfied with the limitations of any one. Probing beneath considerations of technique to the reasons for such a period of widespread experimentation in all the arts, one can undoubtedly link it with our contemporary sense of chaotic change and upheaval, of disequilibrium and insecurity. At the same time it is too easily forgotten in the current generalizations about the collapse of our culture that experiment, the trial of new possibilities, is a sign of life and not of death. And the ominous feeling that the fluctuation of the arts furnishes only one of many evidences that we are witnessing the final breakdown of all tradition often fails to take into consideration similar instability in other ages. Perhaps too much has been made of the fact that Donne's experiments, when seen against the background of his day, are even more radical than Eliot's; yet his restless invention of more than forty stanzaic forms is one unmistakable mark of his unsatisfied quest for certainty. But to take a seemingly far more traditional artist: it should not be obscured by time that Milton's whole career, his unending search for truth that rejected in turn the Anglican and Presbyterian creeds to pass to more and more independent definitions, is paralleled by the remarkably different stages in his development as a poet. Approached without preconceptions 'Arcades' and *Paradise Regained* would scarcely seem to be the work of the same man any more than *Chamber Music* and *Ulysses*. This juxtaposition may seem less incongruous the more one reflects on a remark that I heard Eliot make in conversation, that Joyce is the greatest master of the English language since Milton.

To return from this excursus: the value of any experiment in art lies in the length to which it is carried, whether it is merely the by-product of erratic or undisciplined fancy, or whether it has built up into a completed masterwork. Throughout Eliot's variety persists the enduring sameness that I have already noted, a result of the unusual degree to which he has composed all his work around certain focal centres that possess for him a special symbolical value. He has revealed other long preoccupations of a significance comparable to his persistent return to the twenty-sixth canto of the *Purgatorio*. A pattern could be made of his recurring images: of how often a sudden release of the spirit is expressed through sea-imagery which, with its exact notation of gulls and granite rocks and the details of sailing, seems always to spring from his own boyhood experience off the New England coast, just as his city-imagery belongs to Boston and London; of the equally numerous times when certain spring flowers, lilacs and hyacinths, appear in passages which express the stirring of desire warring against the memory of previous failure; of the widely varied occasions when he presents a moment of beauty and its loss by a glimpse of a girl, 'her hair over her arms and her arms full of flowers'; of how, in such different poems as 'Prufrock' and *Ash Wednesday*, a sudden ecstatic loveliness is caught in 'blown hair':

>   . . . brown hair over the mouth blown,
>   Lilac and brown hair;
>   Distraction. . . .

SOURCE: extract from chapter 5 of *The Achievement of T. S. Eliot* (1935) pp. 132–6.

D. W. Harding

THE SUBMISSION OF MATURITY
(1936)

This new volume is an opportunity, not for a review – for 'The Poetry of T. S. Eliot' begins to have the intimidating sound of a tripos question – but for asking whether anything in the development of the poetry accounts for the change in attitude that has made Mr. Eliot's work less *chic* now than it was ten years ago. Perhaps the ten years are a sufficient explanation – obvious changes in fashionable feeling have helped to make the sort-of-Communist poets popular. But, on the other hand, it may be that these poets gratify some taste that Mr. Eliot also gratified in his earlier work but not in his later. If so, it is surely a taste for evocations of the sense of protest that our circumstances set up in us; for it seems likely that at the present time it is expressions of protest in some form or other that most readily gain a poet popular sympathy. And up to *The Waste Land* and 'The Hollow Men' this protest – whether distressed, disgusted, or ironical – was still the dominant note of Mr. Eliot's work, through all the subtlety and sensitiveness of the forms it took. Yet already in these two poems the suggestion was creeping in that the sufferers were also failures. We are the hollow men, but there are, besides,

> Those who have crossed
> With direct eyes, to death's other Kingdom.

And in all the later work the stress tends to fall on the regret or suffering that arises from our own choice or our inherent limitations, or on the resignation that they make necessary. Without at the moment trying to define the change more closely, one can point out certain characteristics of the later work which are likely to displease those who create the fashions of taste in poetry today, and which also contrast with Mr. Eliot's earlier work. First, it is true that in some of the poems (most obviously in the choruses from *The Rock*) there are denunciations and preaching, both of which people like just now. But there is a vital difference between the denunciation here and that, say, in *The Dog Beneath the Skin*: Mr. Eliot doesn't invite you to step across a dividing line and join him in guaranteed rightness – he suggests at the most that you and he should both try, in familiar and difficult ways, not to live so badly. Failing to make it sound easy, and not putting much stress on the fellowship of the just, he offers no satisfaction to the craving for a life that is ethically and emotionally *simpler*.

And this characteristic goes with a deeper change of attitude that separates the later work from the earlier. Besides displaying little faith in a revolt against anything outside himself, Mr. Eliot in his recent work never invites you to believe that everything undesirable in you is due to outside influences that can be blamed for tampering with your original rightness. Not even in the perhaps over-simple *Animula* is there any suggestion that the 'simple soul' has suffered an avoidable wrong for which someone else can be given the blame. Mr. Eliot declines to sanction an implicit belief, almost universally held, which lies behind an immense amount of rationalization, self-pity, and childish protest – the belief that the very fact of being alive ought to ensure your being a satisfactory object in your own sight. He is nearer the more rational view that the process of living is at its best one of progressive dissatisfaction.

Throughout the earlier poems there are traces of what, if it were cruder and without irony and impersonality, would be felt at once as self-pity or futile protest: for example,

> Put your shoes at the door, sleep, prepare for life.
> The last twist of the knife.

or,

> Wipe your hand across your mouth, and laugh;
> The worlds revolve like ancient women
> Gathering fuel in vacant lots.

or again,

> The nightingales are singing near
> The Convent of the Sacred Heart,

> And sang within the bloody wood
> When Agamemnon cried aloud,
> And let their liquid siftings fall
> To stain the stiff dishonoured shroud.

Obviously this is only one aspect of the early poetry, and to lay much stress on it without qualification would be grotesquely unfair to 'Gerontion' especially and to other poems of that phase. But it is a prominent enough aspect of the work to have made critics, one might have thought, more liable to underrate the earlier poems than, with fashionable taste, the later ones. For there can be no doubt of the greater maturity of feeling in the later work:

> And I pray that I may forget
> These matters that with myself I too much discuss
> Too much explain
> Because I do not hope to turn again
> Let these words answer
> For what is done, not to be done again
> May the judgment not be too heavy upon us. . . .

This may be called religious submission, but essentially it is the submission of maturity.

What is peculiar to Mr. Eliot in the tone of his work, and not inherent in maturity or in religion, is that he does *submit* to what he knows rather than welcoming it. To say that his is a depressed poetry isn't true, because of the extraordinary toughness and resilience that always underlie it. They show, for instance, in the quality of the scorn he expresses for those who have tried to overlook what he sees:

> . . . the strained time-ridden faces
> Distracted from distraction by distraction
> Filled with fancies and empty of meaning
> Tumid apathy with no concentration
> Men and bits of paper. . . .

But to insist on the depression yields a half-truth. For though acceptance and understanding have taken the place of protest, the underlying experience remains one of suffering, and the renunciation is much more vividly communicated than the advance for the sake of which it was made. It is summed up in the ending of *Ash Wednesday*:

> Blessèd sister, holy mother, spirit of the fountain, spirit
>   of the garden,
> Suffer us not to mock ourselves with falsehood
> Teach us to care and not to care
> Teach us to sit still
> Even among these rocks,
> Our peace in His will
> And even among these rocks
> Sister, mother
> And spirit of the river, spirit of the sea,
> Suffer me not to be separated
> And let my cry come unto Thee.

This is the cry of the weaned child, I suppose the analyst might say; and without acquiescing in the genetic view that they would imply, one can agree that weaning stands as a type-experience of much that Mr. Eliot is interested in as a poet. It seems to be the clearer and more direct realization of this kind of experience that makes the later poems at the same time more personal and more mature. And in the presence of these poems many who liked saying they liked the earlier work feel both embarrassed and snubbed.

However, all of this might be said about a volume of collected sermons instead of poems. It ignores Mr. Eliot's amazing genius in the use of words and rhythms and his extraordinary fertility in styles of writing, each 'manner' apparently perfected from the first and often used only once (only once, that is, by Mr. Eliot, though most are like comets with a string of poetasters laboriously tailing after them). . . .

SOURCE: extract from review of Eliot's *Collected Poems, 1909–1935*, in *Scrutiny*, II (1936); reprinted in *The Importance of Scrutiny*, ed. Eric Bentley (1948) pp. 262–5.

W. B. Yeats

AN ALEXANDER POPE (1936)

Eliot has produced his great effect upon his generation because he has described men and women that get out of bed or into it from mere habit; in describing this life that has lost heart his own art seems grey, cold, dry. He is an Alexander Pope, working without apparent imagination, producing his effects by a rejection of all rhythms and metaphors used by the more popular romantics rather than by the discovery of his own, this rejection giving his work an unexaggerated plainness that has the effect of novelty. He has the rhythmical flatness of *The Essay on Man* – despite Miss Sitwell's advocacy I see Pope as Blake and Keats saw him – later, in *The Waste Land*, amid much that is moving in symbol and imagery there is much monotony of accent:

> When lovely woman stoops to folly and
> Paces about her room again, alone,
> She smooths her hair with automatic hand,
> And puts a record on the gramophone.

I was affected, as I am by these lines, when I saw for the first time a painting by Manet. I longed for the vivid colour and light of Rousseau and Courbet, I could not endure the grey middle-tint – and even to-day Manet gives me an incomplete pleasure; he had left the procession. Nor can I put the Eliot of these poems among those that descend from Shakespeare and the translators of the Bible. I think of him as satirist rather than poet. Once only does that early work speak in the great manner:

> The host with someone indistinct
> Converses at the door apart,
> The nightingales are singing near
> The Convent of the Sacred Heart,

And sang within the bloody wood
When Agamemnon cried aloud,
And let their liquid siftings fall
To stain the stiff dishonoured shroud.

Not until 'The Hollow Men' and *Ash Wednesday*, where he is helped by
the short lines, and in the dramatic poems where his remarkable sense of
actor, chanter, scene, sweeps him away, is there rhythmical animation.
Two or three of my friends attribute the change to an emotional
enrichment from religion, but his religion compared to that of John
Gray, Francis Thompson, Lionel Johnson in 'The Dark Angel', lacks all
strong emotion; a New England Protestant by descent, there is little self-
surrender in his personal relation to God and the soul. *Murder in the
Cathedral* is a powerful stage play because the actor, the monkish habit,
certain repeated words, symbolize what we know, not what the author
knows. Nowhere has the author explained how Becket and the King
differ in aim; Becket's people have been robbed and persecuted in his
absence; like the King he demands strong government. Speaking
through Becket's mouth Eliot confronts a world growing always more
terrible with a religion like that of some great statesman, a pity not less
poignant because it tempers the prayer book with the results of
mathematical philosophy.

Peace. And let them be, in their exaltation.
They speak better than they know, and beyond your
    understanding,
They know and do not know, that acting is suffering
And suffering is action. Neither does the actor suffer
Nor the patient act. But both are fixed
In an eternal action, an eternal patience
To which all must consent that it may be willed
And which all must suffer that they may will it,
That the pattern may subsist, for the pattern is the action
And the suffering, that the wheel may turn and still
Be forever still.

SOURCE: extract from Introduction to the *Oxford Book of Modern
Verse* (1936) pp. xxi–xxiii.

Allen Tate

LOGICAL VERSUS
PSYCHOLOGICAL UNITY (1938)

. . . most of the attacks on modern poetry involve [a] basic misconception as to the nature of poetry, a misconception which considers it a
bundle of items intrinsically poetic in themselves and neglects the
fundamental fact that the poetic effect is always dependent upon
relationships. Indeed, most statements that any given poem is unin-
telligible are simply confessions to the failure to find the intrinsically
poetic items existing in isolation.

But the general principle just laid down does not, or rather does not
seem to, take into account the charge that is most often made against
modern poetry – the charge of unintelligibility caused by an absence of
logical links. The critic may hold that he is quite willing to accept the
fact that a poem must be appreciated as a total organism but is unable to
do so without benefit of logical connection. In almost all cases this critic
will mean by logical connection the explicit general statement – he
does not mean that the connections between parts, or the general theme
of the poem, are not susceptible to a logical statement. He merely
refuses to attempt the leap himself. One critic, therefore, considers it a
deadly attack on some modern poems to say that the parts of a poem
'form a psychological, not a logical, unity'. The answer to this sort of
thing is simple: every successful poem creates a *psychological* unity, and
not even the simplest metaphor fails to violate a *logical* unity. The
distinction between the two kinds of unity is extremely important:
psychological unity is the aim of every poem; logical unity is a device to
achieve this aim, and may or may not be used.

A characteristic violation of this principle is committed in Mr.
Sparrow's attack on 'Rhapsody on a Windy Night', by T. S. Eliot. (The
critic, by the way, commits another violation of the principle of
psychological unity and indulges himself in a piece of forensic strategy,

by submitting to his readers only a part of the poem, the section from line 24 through line 47.)

Concerning his chosen passage the critic remarks in one place: 'clearly no canon of intelligibility has guided the selection, and no single structure of thought emerges'. Later, the same critic counsels us to 'suspect no meaning and ask for no interpretation'. Such comment by a serious critic, perhaps, justifies an exercise in interpretation that otherwise might appear superfluous. Here are the lines on which Mr. Sparrow comments:

> Half-past two,
> The street-lamp said,
> 'Remark the cat which flattens itself in the gutter,
> Slips out its tongue
> And devours a morsel of rancid butter.'
> So the hand of the child, automatic,
> Slipped out and pocketed a toy that was running along
> the quay.
> I could see nothing behind that child's eye.
> I have seen eyes in the street
> Trying to peer through lighted shutters,
> And a crab one afternoon in a pool,
> An old crab with barnacles on his back,
> Gripped the end of a stick which I held him.
>
> Half-past three,
> The lamp sputtered,
> The lamp muttered in the dark.
> The lamp hummed:
> 'Regard the moon,
> La lune ne garde aucune rancune,
> She winks a feeble eye,
> She smiles into corners.
> She smooths the hair of the grass.
> The moon has lost her memory. . . .'

The first two sections of the poem, which precede the passage in question, are primarily expository. This exposition may be summarised: the setting, a walk at night down deserted streets and an indication of the basic theme, the dissolving of the smug, easily-accepted organisation of life broken up here as seen under a different light, so that the memory of past life seems to have lost any vital pattern. (The theme somewhat resembles that in Section L of Tennyson's *In Memoriam* – 'Be near me when my light is low'.) The first image implies that memory is a sea. The items thrown up by memory are like the branch. The items of memory, when really experienced, were alive, growing, leafy, organic. Now, like the twisted branch, they are dead. The image of the world's skeleton is easily related. The content of memory is the world a person carries about with him, and he identifies himself in its terms. Under the influence of this occasion he discovers that the skeleton – the frame of the organisation for this world – is abstracted and dead like the branch. The image of the broken spring reënforces the meaning of the preceding lines by a parallel development of the idea. (Observe how the factors of stiffness, loss of resilience, hardness, et cetera, are used as the common denominator of meaning.)

The street lamp throwing its light on the cat seems to ask the man to regard it as it responds to brute appetite. So the child (the child of a particular memory as dramatised) responds to the toy, a thing worthless to an adult, with infantile curiosity and pleasure. And so the crab responded to the irritation of the stick. This image carries the further meaning that the difficulties and proddings of life had been planless, motiveless, and wanton. 'As flies to wanton boys. . . .' The child and the crab, then, are particular memories, memories aroused by association with the mechanical character of the cat's action, which in this case serves as the denominator of meaning.

The rest of the poem follows the same principle of composition.

The 'Rhapsody on a Windy Night', as has been said, illustrates a type of difficulty resulting from a lack of logical connection (or, to be exact, a lack of statement). The following passage from *Ash Wednesday*, which has been singled by Mr Eastman for special attack, illustrates a type of difficulty resulting, not from a lack of logical connection, but from what might be thought to be an excess of logic:

> If the lost word is lost, if the spent word is spent,
> If the unheard, unspoken
> Word is unspoken, unheard;
> Still is the unspoken word, the Word unheard,

> The Word without a word, the Word within
> The world and for the world;
> And the light shone in darkness and
> Against the Word the unstilled world still whirled
> About the centre of the silent Word.

Had Mr. Eastman, who calls the passage 'an oily puddle of emotional noises', read it with more care, he might have discovered that what baffled him was the presence of logic, rather than its absence. Even out of its context (and Mr. Eastman makes no effort to indicate the nature of its context) the passage can be paraphrased if one assumes even a rudimentary acquaintance with the Christian religion.

The passage is built about a set of oppositions, the most important of which is the opposition between the word and the Word, between the word as a common noun and the Word as the Christian Logos. To paraphrase: if the word of the gospel is lost, seems to be spent, is not heard, is not spoken, nevertheless, this unspoken gospel is the informing principle of the world, the Logos, which is the principle without temporal presentation, the Logos within the world, and for the world (*for* in the sense of providing a *basis for*); and the light (the Logos as Christ, the Light of the World) shone in the darkness just as the informing principle first shone over chaos, and against the Logos the unstilled world revolved. Obviously this statement does not take into account other levels of meaning in the term *word* and elsewhere in the passage. There is one further important statement clearly indicated, which turns upon the opposition between the two senses of the word *still*. In the foregoing statement we have taken it only in its sense of nevertheless, but the sense of fixity is also brought into sharp focus by the use of the word *unstilled*. The reader's sensitivity to such a play upon words has been sharpened by the fundamental opposition of meanings in the term *word*. It should not be forgotten, moreover, that the passage here is a fragment of a rather long poem, and that the meaning of this passage is substantially reënforced by the context provided by the poem and, as a matter of fact, by the total context provided by the poet's work.

These extracts have been used here because they were selected as test cases by two of the most vigorous and systematic antagonists of modern poetry. In both instances, the attack was on the ground of unintelligibility. Therefore the present argument does not attempt to evaluate the passages as poetry, but merely to demonstrate that a specific meaning is communicated. But such an evaluation would have to be undertaken, not on the grounds proposed by the critics, but by a consideration of the organic nature of any poem. Such an evaluation could scarcely begin by a ripping of the passages from a context. As a matter of fact, Eastman and Sparrow are not really objecting because the poetry does not communicate; they are objecting because it does not flatter certain preconceptions about the poetic effect. . . .

SOURCE: extract from 'The Reading of Modern Poetry', *Purpose*, x (1938) 36–40.

George Orwell

ESCAPE FROM THE CONSCIOUS-NESS OF FUTILITY (1942)

There is very little in Eliot's later work that makes any deep impression on me. That is a confession of something lacking in myself, but it is not, as it may appear at first sight, a reason for simply shutting up and saying no more, since the change in my own reaction probably points to some external change which is worth investigating.

I know a respectable quantity of Eliot's earlier work by heart. I did not sit down and learn it, it simply stuck in my mind as any passage of verse is liable to do when it has really rung the bell. Sometimes after only one reading it is possible to remember the whole of a poem of, say, twenty or thirty lines, the act of memory being partly an act of reconstruction. But as for these three latest poems, I suppose I have read each of them two or three times since they were published, and how much do I verbally remember? 'Time and the bell have buried the day', 'At the still point of the turning world', 'The vast waters of the petrel and the porpoise', and bits of the passage beginning 'O dark dark dark. They all go into the dark'. (I don't count 'In my end is my beginning', which is a quotation.) That is about all that sticks in my head of its own accord. Now one cannot take this as proving that 'Burnt Norton' and the rest are 'worse' than the more memorable early poems, and one might even take it as proving the contrary, since it is arguable that that which lodges itself most easily in the mind is the obvious and even the vulgar. But it is clear that something has departed, some kind of current has been switched off, the later verse does not *contain* the earlier, even if it is claimed as an improvement upon it. I think one is justified in explaining this by a deterioration in Mr Eliot's subject-matter. Before going any further, here are a couple of extracts, just near enough to one another in meaning to be comparable. The first is the concluding passage of 'The Dry Salvages':

> And right action is freedom
> From past and future also.
> For most of us, this is the aim
> Never here to be realised;
> Who are only undefeated
> Because we have gone on trying;
> We, content at the last
> If our temporal reversion nourish
> (Not too far from the yew-tree)
> The life of significant soil.

Here is an extract from a much earlier poem:

> Daffodil bulbs instead of balls
> Stared from the sockets of his eyes!
> He knew how thought clings round dead
>   limbs
> Tightening its lusts and luxuries.
>
> He knew the anguish of the marrow,
> The ague of the skeleton;
> No contact possible to flesh
> Allayed the fever of the bone.

The two passages will bear comparison since they both deal with the same subject, namely death. The first of them follows upon a longer passage in which it is explained, first of all, that scientific research is all nonsense, a childish superstition on the same level as fortune-telling, and then that the only people ever likely to reach an understanding of the universe are saints, the rest of us being reduced to 'hints and guesses'. The keynote of the closing passage is 'resignation'. There is a 'meaning' in life and also in death; unfortunately we don't know what it is, but the fact that it exists should be a comfort to us as we push up the crocuses, or whatever it is that grows under the yew-trees in country churchyards. But now look at the other two stanzas I have quoted. Though fathered onto somebody else, they probably express what Mr Eliot himself felt about death at that time, at least in certain moods. They are not voicing resignation. On the contrary, they are voicing the pagan attitude towards death, the belief in the next world as a shadowy place full of thin, squeaking ghosts, envious of the living, the belief that however bad life may be, death is worse. This conception of death seems to have been general in antiquity, and in a sense it is general now. 'The anguish of the marrow, the ague of the skeleton', Horace's famous ode 'Eheu fugaces', and Bloom's unuttered thoughts during Paddy Dignam's funeral, are all very much of a muchness. So long as man regards himself as an individual, his attitude towards death must be one of simple resentment. And however unsatisfactory this may be, if it is intensely felt it is more likely to produce good literature than a religious faith which is not really *felt* at all, but merely accepted against the emotional grain. So far as they can be compared, the two passages I have quoted seem to me to bear this out. I do not think it is questionable that the second of them is superior as verse, and also more intense in feeling, in spite of a tinge of burlesque.

What are these three poems, 'Burnt Norton', 'East Coker' and 'The Dry Salvages', 'about'? It is not so easy to say what they are about, but what they appear on the surface to be about is certain localities in England and America with which Mr Eliot has ancestral connections. Mixed up with this is a rather gloomy musing upon the nature and purpose of life, with the rather indefinite conclusion I have mentioned above. Life has a 'meaning', but it is not a meaning one feels inclined to grow lyrical about; there is faith, but not much hope, and certainly no enthusiasm. Now the subject-matter of Mr Eliot's early poems was very different from this. They were not hopeful, but neither were they depressed or depressing. If one wants to deal in antitheses, one might say that the later poems express a melancholy faith and the earlier ones a glowing despair. They were based on the dilemma of modern man, who despairs of life and does not want to be dead, and on top of this they expressed the horror of an over-civilised intellectual confronted with the ugliness and spiritual emptiness of the machine age. Instead of 'not too far from the yew-tree' the keynote was 'weeping, weeping multitudes', or perhaps 'the broken fingernails of dirty hands'. Naturally these poems were denounced as 'decadent' when they first appeared, the attacks only being called off when it was perceived that Eliot's political and social tendencies were reactionary. There was, however, a sense in which the charge of 'decadence' could be justified. Clearly these poems were an end-product, the last gasp of a cultural tradition, poems which spoke only for the cultivated third-generation rentier, for people able to feel and criticise but no longer able to act. E. M. Forster praised

'Prufrock', on its first appearance because 'it sang of people who were ineffectual and weak' and because it was 'innocent of public spirit' (this was during the other war, when public spirit was a good deal more rampant than it is now). The qualities by which any society which is to last longer than a generation actually has to be sustained – industry, courage, patriotism, frugality, philoprogenitiveness – obviously could not find any place in Eliot's early poems. There was only room for rentier values, the values of people too civilised to work, fight or even reproduce themselves. But that was the price that had to be paid, at any rate at that time, for writing a poem worth reading. The mood of lassitude, irony, disbelief, disgust, and not the sort of beefy enthusiasm demanded by the Squires and Herberts, was what sensitive people actually felt. It is fashionable to say that in verse only the words count and the 'meaning' is irrelevant, but in fact every poem contains a prose-meaning, and when the poem is any good it is a meaning which the poet urgently wishes to express. All art is to some extent propaganda. 'Prufrock' is an expression of futility, but it is also a poem of wonderful vitality and power, culminating in a sort of rocket-burst in the closing stanzas:

> I have seen them riding seaward on the waves
> Combing the white hair of the waves blown back
> When the wind blows the water white and black.
>
> We have lingered in the chambers of the sea
> By sea-girls wreathed with seaweed red and brown,
> Till human voices wake us, and we drown.

There is nothing like that in the later poems, although the rentier despair on which these lines are founded has been consciously dropped.

But the trouble is that conscious futility is something only for the young. One cannot go on 'despairing of life' into a ripe old age. One cannot go on and on being 'decadent', since decadence means falling and one can only be said to be falling if one is going to reach the bottom reasonably soon. Sooner or later one is obliged to adopt a positive attitude towards life and a society. It would be putting it too crudely to say that every poet in our time must either die young, enter the Catholic Church, or join the Communist Party, but in fact the escape from the consciousness of futility is along those general lines. There are other deaths besides physical death, and there are other sects and creeds besides the Catholic Church and the Communist Party, but it remains true that after a certain age one must either stop writing or dedicate oneself to some purpose not wholly aesthetic. . . .

SOURCE: extract from review of 'Burnt Norton', 'East Coker' and 'The Dry Salvages', in *Poetry*, 2 July 1942, 81–5.

Helen Gardner

AUDITORY IMAGINATION (1949)

. . . Mr Eliot was from the first a poet with a remarkable range of diction, and with a natural gift for the vividly memorable phrase. He was always consciously aware of the varied resources of English poetic diction and delighted to place an exotic word exactly, or to give us the sudden shock which the unexpected introduction of a commonplace word or phrase can provide. The development in his mature poetry is a development in naturalness: a more 'easy commerce of the old and the new'; a mastery of transitions on the large and the small scale, so that change and variety now 'give delight and hurt not'; and a capacity to employ without embarrassment the obviously poetic word and image. In his earliest poetry he showed a certain distaste for words with poetic associations, which suggested a limitation in his temperament and a certain lack of confidence in his art. Avoidance of the obvious is not the mark of the highest originality or of the genuinely bold artist. The change in Mr Eliot's poetic style which begins with 'The Hollow Men' in 1925 is accompanied by a change in his metric. The change in the metre is possibly the fundamental change, for it is the new metre that has made possible his new freedom with the language of poetry.

If we put this change as briefly as possible we might say that on the whole up to *The Waste Land* Mr Eliot's verse could be 'scanned' with as much or as little propriety as most English post-Spenserian verse can be. After 'The Hollow Men' this is not so. In this matter of metre the poets go before and the prosodists follow after, often a very long time after. What 'rules' prosodists of the future will discover that Mr Eliot has in practice obeyed I do not know. If I were to try to formulate any now I should almost certainly be proved wrong by whatever verse he writes next. All that someone who is neither a poet nor a prosodist can say at present is that there is a new beginning after *The Waste Land*, which is immediately recognizable, and which is best displayed by the juxtaposition of passages from the earlier and the later poetry. This new beginning is a break with the tradition of English non-lyrical verse, which has been dominant since Spenser displayed in *The Shepheardes Calender* the potentialities of the heroic line.

The characteristic metre of *Prufrock and Other Observations* (1917) is an irregularly rhyming verse paragraph in duple rising rhythm, with more or less variation in the length of the lines. Rhyme is used as a rhetorical ornament, not as part of a regular pattern; it is decorative and makes for emphasis, but it is not structural. There is, beside the variety in the number of stresses in the line, considerable variety in the amount of coincidence between speech stress and metrical stress; but all this we are accustomed to in verse from the seventeenth century onwards. The underlying rhythm is unmistakable; it remains a duple rising rhythm, the staple rhythm of English verse, the basis of our heroic line, whether the line is as short as 'Remark the cat', or as long as 'But as if a magic lantern threw the nerves in patterns on a screen'. The use of this metre, which is common to 'Prufrock', 'Portrait of a Lady', and, though it is naturally differently handled in the non-dramatic monologues, to 'Preludes' and 'Rhapsody on a Windy Night', is an attempt to get away from the dominant blank verse of the nineteenth-century masters of the poetic monologue. Mr Eliot develops instead the free treatment of the heroic line to create paragraphs adorned and pointed by rhyme which we find in poems such as Donne's 'The Apparition', or Herbert's 'The Collar', and in Milton's experiments before he created the blank verse of *Paradise Lost*: 'On Time', 'At a Solemn Music', and, of course, 'Lycidas'. What is original is the use to which the metre is put, not the metre itself. Two important poems in the 1917 volume are exceptional. In 'La Figlia Che Piange', though many of the lines if met separately would be identified as common variants of the heroic line, the incantatory repetitions of certain variants, such as the repeated strong stress on the first syllable, take the poem too far from that metrical norm for us to be aware of it as an underlying rhythm; though in the last paragraph we hear it again, in a singularly beautiful handling of this metre. In the other poem, 'Mr Apollinax', the ear discerns no hint of duple rhythm. We have a poem built upon a conversational phrase: a piece of free accentual verse. The speech stress is strong, the pause at the end of the line marked; as it must be for us to feel the pleasure this kind of verse can give, which is the pleasure of catching an emergent rhythm, not that of recognizing an underlying one.

The volume of *Poems* (1920) has abandoned the 'Prufrock' metre. In its place we have the blank verse of 'Gerontion'. The heroic line is handled here with the freedom of the later Elizabethan dramatists. If one can in any sense 'scan' the verse of Tourneur and Middleton, one can scan this. The characteristics of this verse are the extreme freedom in the disposition of the speech stresses, the absence of the strong beat which the co-incidence of speech and metrical stress gives, and the variety in the position of the pauses within the line. This, and other features such as the frequent omission of an initial unstressed syllable and the frequent addition of a final one, is all familiar to us from discussions of the development of Shakespearean and post-Shakespearean blank verse. But magnificent as 'Gerontion' is, there is a flavour in it of *pastiche*. One might call it Mr Eliot's *Hyperion*. We hear his voice through it, but we hear it rather in spite of a voice he is putting on. The majority of the poems in the 1920 volume are in quatrains. This common metre is handled with the greatest brilliance and confidence, reminding us again of the seventeenth century and the wonderful handling of the so-called octosyllabic by the lyric poets of that age. There are all the variations we are accustomed to find: the seven-syllabled and the nine-syllabled lines, the 'trisyllabic feet', but what delights us, as in Donne's 'The Fever', or Marvell's 'A Definition of Love' or Rochester's 'Absent from thee I languish still',[1] is the firmness of the duple rising rhythm, with its strongly marked beat, and the emphatic rhyme. The originality again is not in the metre or in the handling of it, but in the use to which it is put.

The Waste Land (1922) represents the culmination of this period of metrical virtuosity. Its basic measure is the heroic line, which it handles in almost every possible way. One could indeed give a demonstration of the varied music of which this line is capable from *The Waste Land* alone, giving parallels from the work of the most astonishingly diverse poets. We hear the voice of the Jacobean dramatists again in the voice of the thunder at the close. The Shakespearean echoes, apart from direct adaptation, are everywhere. The narrative sweetness of run-on rhyming verse is cruelly caught in

> But at my back from time to time I hear
> The sound of horns and motors, which shall bring
> Sweeney to Mrs Porter in the spring[2]

and the strength of the end-stopped line gives ironic dignity to the

carbuncular young man's encounter with the typist, with its regular
alternate rhymes. On the other hand, the beautiful and justly famous
opening lines, and the equally beautiful opening lines of the final section
have another rhythm, not the prevailing duple rising rhythm, but the
repeated falling cadences of 'La Figlia Che Piange'; and the speech of
Lou in the second section, like 'Mr Apollinax', has escaped entirely
from the characteristic rhythm of English dramatic or quasi-dramatic
verse. The voice of the 'poetry reciter' could make nothing of this.

It may be asked why, if Mr Eliot could do all these different things
with the heroic line, he felt it necessary to abandon it as the staple metre
of his verse. The answer may be partly given by quoting his adaptation
of a line from a Shakespearean sonnet at the opening of *Ash Wednesday*:

> Because I do not hope to turn again
> Because I do not hope
> Because I do not hope to turn
> Desiring this man's gift and that man's scope. . . .

One meaning of this, if not the principal one, is that from now on he will
try to speak in his own voice, which will express himself with all his
limitations, and not try to escape those limitations by imitating other
poets. The heroic line is a hindrance in this attempt, because it has so
long and glorious a history that when it is used as the metre of a long
poem it is almost impossible not to echo one or other of its great masters.
Mr Eliot's attack on the 'Chinese Wall' of Milton's verse has only
popularized what others have felt and said in the last seventy years or so:
the period after the work of Tennyson and Browning, the last poets to
show any originality in blank verse. Hopkins's 'sprung rhythm' and
Bridges's 'loose alexandrines' in *The Testament of Beauty* are different
reactions, the one fertile in influence, the other sterile, to the situation
described by Bridges in a review in *The Times Literary Supplement* in
1912:[3]

In all art when a great master appears he so exhausts the material at his disposal
as to make it impossible for any succeeding artist to be original, unless he can
either find new material or invent some new method of handling the old. In
painting and music this is almost demonstrable to the uninitiated; in poetry the
law may not be so strict, but it still holds; and any one may see that serious
rhyme is now exhausted in English verse, or that Milton's blank verse
practically ended as an original form with Milton. There are abundant signs

that English syllabic verse has long been in the stage of artistic exhaustion of form which follows great artistic effort. Now as far as regards the verse-form, Wordsworth was apparently unconscious of this predicament. It never occurred to him that he was working with blunted tools. His idea was to purify the diction and revivify English poetry by putting a new content into the old verse forms; and two reasons may be given for this conservatism. First, that in his time an artificial school of poetry had separated itself off from this older tradition, so that any return to the older style appeared to be a freshness; and secondly, he was part of that unaccountable flood of inspiration which in Keats and Shelley and in a few of Coleridge's lyrics transcended in some vital qualities whatever had been done before, and actually wrought miracles of original beauty within the old forms; but these bond-breaking efforts, we should say, more than completed the exhaustion, while the tedious quality of much of their work shows under what hampering conditions the genius of these poets attained excellence. Keats speaks very plainly; he says, for instance, that he relinquished *Hyperion* because he could not get away from Milton; and Mr Synge though he wrote but little verse, seems to have been fully conscious of the poetic situation; indeed he thought it so desperate as to question whether 'before verse can be human again it must not learn to be brutal'.

Up to *The Waste Land* Mr Eliot is on the whole doing what Bridges says the Romantics did: trying to put new content into old forms, and to revive the forms by returning to older handlings of them. Bridges's praise of Keats and Shelley as having 'wrought miracles of original beauty in the old forms' can be applied to him as well as to them. But *The Waste Land* revealed to him, whether consciously or unconsciously, where his own 'Chinese Wall' lay. At all its greatest moments we are conscious of the inescapable power over the poet's ear of the rhythms of the dramatic blank verse of Shakespeare and his followers. Milton, who was deeply read in the dramatists and echoes them again and again in his poetry, escaped from dependence on them by creating his own music. When he had done this, by restoring as the basis of his prosody syllabic regularity, the Shakespearean tone becomes one among the other beauties of *Paradise Lost*. Mr Eliot has not, I think, realized how similar his problem was to Milton's. Milton came at the end of the astonishing development of blank verse on the stage. By the time he reached maturity it had reached decadence. His problem, which one understands best, not by reading *Paradise Lost* in which he has solved it, but by reading *Comus* in which as Johnson says 'may very plainly be discerned the dawn or twilight of *Paradise Lost*', was to do something which Shakespeare had not already done better than he could hope to. In his British Academy lecture (1947) on Milton Mr Eliot does not quite see this because of the too rigid distinction he makes between dramatic and non-dramatic verse. But his coupling of Shakespeare and Milton together, as poets to be escaped from, gives us the truth which his long critical quarrel with Milton has disguised: that Shakespeare was the real obstacle to his discovery of his own voice:

Milton made a great epic impossible for succeeding generations; Shakespeare made a great poetic drama impossible; such a situation is inevitable, and it persists until the language has so altered that there is no danger, because no possibility, of imitation. Anyone who tries to write poetic drama, even today, should know that half his energy must be exhausted in the effort to escape from the constricting toils of Shakespeare: the moment his attention is relaxed, or his mind fatigued, he will lapse into bad Shakespearian verse. For a long time after an epic poet like Milton, or a dramatic poet like Shakespeare, nothing can be done. Yet the effort must be repeatedly made; for we can never know in advance when the moment is approaching at which a new epic, or a new drama, will be possible; and when the moment does draw near it may be that the genius of an individual poet will perform the last mutation of idiom and versification which will bring that new poetry into being. . . .

SOURCE: extract from chapter 5 of *The Art of T. S. Eliot* (1949) pp. 15–23.

NOTES

1. I refer to these particular poems because of their masculine vigour. Although they employ two rhymes to the quatrain, where Mr Eliot has only one, this seems less important than the similarity in the run of the verse and the finality of each stanza. The attempt in 'Burbank' to avoid stanzaic finality does not seem to me successful. I feel it to be a failure in metrical taste.

2. I find it difficult to forgive the outrage committed on Marvell's line, even though it does illustrate well that the 'heroic line' when used in this way often takes ten syllables to say what could be better said in eight. The fondness of the seventeenth century for the 'octosyllabic' is a reaction against the diffuseness of much earlier writing in the 'decasyllabic'.

3. See *Collected Essays and Papers*, vol. II, no. 13.

Hugh Kenner

ELIOT'S MORAL DIALECTIC
(1949)

Discussion of Eliot's poetry as a whole has always been bedevilled by its notorious separability into 'earlier' and 'later'. This distinction is less evident in the texts than in critical history; it would be easy to show that Eliot has had not so much a succession of manners as a succession of reputations, reputation in the world of reviewers and enlightened gossip being based on the most extrinsic factors in a poetic corpus. No sooner had Mr. Eliot rebuked the Noel Cowardish adherents who applauded his expressing, in *The Waste Land*, 'the disillusionment of a generation', than as author of *Ash Wednesday* he was being regarded as traitor to the banners of despair, and adopted as the congenial poet of a new intellectual milieu whose focus is less Bloomsbury than Canterbury. He has never concealed his intense concern with moral states; but when he turned his attention to moral states thought by professing Christians to be congenial, or at least desiderated, one group of admirers simply replaced another. The resulting earthquakes in the world of literary reputations grotesquely distort what actually happens in the book and on the page. It is not possible to show that 'The Hollow Men' is agnostic on the premises that render *Ash Wednesday* Christian, or that Mr. Eliot's omnivorous perspicacity or his dramatic skill are less evident in *Four Quartets* than in 'Sweeney Agonistes'. The verse of *Four Quartets* has a different *texture* from that of *The Waste Land*, but this technical distinction, indicated in Mr. Eliot's discussion, in his 'Dante' essay, of opaque and transparent diction, cannot be held to justify such rapid fluctuations in market quotations allegedly based on congeniality of preoccupation alone. For Mr. Eliot has never changed his pre-occupations. His poetic corpus constitutes a developing action, and the verse of *Four Quartets* differs from that of 'Sweeney Agonistes' only as (to take a notorious instance) the verse of the last act of *Antony and Cleopatra* differs from that of the first. In this perspective, the onset of the *stil nuovo* enacts not a recantation but a third-act climax. Poem is juxtaposed with poem, as line with line and word with word. The personae persist. Tiresias makes his initial appearance in 'Mélange Adultère de Tout', is metamorphosed in *Ash Wednesday* and continues to 'foresuffer all' in 'East Coker'. Prufrock fills his most significant role as an anti-self to be purged away by Becket, just as twenty years earlier St. John the Baptist and Lazarus had presented themselves as anti-selves for Prufrock. The principles of dramatic organization that govern each poem govern also the *œuvre*: without an understanding of this there can be no understanding of the poems. And those principles, which will be investigated in the next few pages, are not technical merely but moral; or technical only in the sense in which realized techniques are inseparable from the projection of a succession of moral worlds. They illuminate, for example, as we shall see, so baffling a poem – the reader may be surprised, but it has proved baffling – as *Ash Wednesday*.

The assumption that it is a beautiful elaboration of Christian commonplaces probably explains why none of Eliot's later admirers has given a helpful analysis of *Ash Wednesday*, just as embarrassment at its Christian content probably explains why even Dr. Leavis has not really succeeded. Contemporary criticism is dominated, the best like the worst, by a preoccupation with the moral worth of poetry: a theme acutely sensed but badly formulated. The critic who can elucidate a symbol-cluster with the aplomb of an Empson still fumbles at spiritual themes with the impeccable clumsiness of an Arnold. Of the latter Eliot writes,

Like many people the vanishing of whose religious faith has left behind only habits, he placed an exaggerated emphasis upon morals. Such people often confuse morals with their own good habits, the result of a sensible upbringing, prudence, and the absence of any very powerful temptation; but I do not speak of Arnold or of any particular person, for only God knows. Morals for the saint are only a preliminary matter; for the poet a secondary matter. How Arnold finds morals in poetry is not clear. . . .   (*The Use of Poetry and the Use of Criticism* (1933) p. 114.)

And what exactly is to be found admirable in *Ash Wednesday*, when it is read as a search for faith, is not clear.[1] But there is no doubt that Eliot's contemporary reputation rests largely upon the notion that since it is admirable to be searching resolutely for faith, one ought to admire the poet who casts a lovely sentiment over this search: especially when, guided by Dante, he has stumbled into the right camp. 'Mr. Eliot means what is meant by any Christian', writes a not unperceptive analyst, 'and it should be clear that the experience behind the second half of 'The Dry Salvages' is meant to suggest that of spiritual rebirth.' For 'any Christian' to imagine that he was in possession of the 'meaning' of 'The Dry Salvages' a priori would be at least overconfidence: so one might insist; with what chance, amid so much undiscriminating praise, of being understood? The later poetry of Eliot, that is, is thought to offer an ethical example: which is, after all, not very different from a 'message' except that it is vague enough to suit the most up-to-date notions of the poetical. Here again, with perhaps one eye on his own expositors, Eliot displays his customary acuteness:

. . . I am concerned further with criticism as evidence of the conception of the use of poetry in the critic's time, and assert that in order to compare the work of different critics we must investigate their assumptions as to what poetry does and ought to do. Examination of the criticism of our time leads me to believe that we are still in the Arnold period. (*The Use of Poetry*, p. 129.)

It is evident that the nature of Eliot's moral preoccupation has yet to be defined: perhaps 'isolated' would be a better word. We may expect it to be most isolable in the later poems, where he has isolated it himself: Eliot is one of those poets – Joyce is another – whose development has been such as continually to reduce and reduce the possibilities of misunderstanding. There are fewer ways of misreading *Four Quartets* with some comfort than of misreading 'Prufrock': which means that the inadequate reader is going to find the *Quartets* much more 'difficult' and uncongenial. The most spectacular instance of this policy of excluding the uncomprehending was the publication of the Ariel Poems: when a whole battalion of Eliot-worshippers suddenly realized that they had been bowing at the wrong shrine and made for the door. Yet Eliot's continuity remained unbroken; *Journey of the Magi* has obvious analogies with part v of *The Waste Land*, though it would embarrass most admirers of *The Waste Land* to notice what they were. Indeed, despite the importance Eliot obviously attaches to them (vide his recent Harvard recordings) very little has ever been said about the Ariel Poems; they are neither sufficiently skeptical for the skeptics nor sufficiently assured for the Christians. Yet to say, as is usually said, that in *A Song for Simeon* Eliot is searching for faith is to say that he has not written a poem. As a matter of fact, he is writing a careful counterpart to 'Gerontion'.

> My life is light, waiting for the death wind,
> Like a feather on the back of my hand.
> Dust in sunlight and memory in corners
> Wait for the wind that chills toward the land,

is meant to be closely connected with the

> old man driven by the Trades
> To a sleepy corner

who awaits the ultimate dissolution of the cleansing blast:

> Gull against the wind, in the windy straits
> Of Belle Isle, or running on the Horn,
> White feathers in the snow. . . .

Yet it is manifestly the *difference* between the two poems that counts.
Gerontion habitually clothes his dryness in sonorous rhetoric. What he
has never done:

> I was neither at the hot gates
> Nor fought in the warm rain
> Nor knee deep in the salt marsh, heaving a cutlass,
> Bitten by flies, fought

is more moving in its rocking rhythms and abrupt caesuras than
Simeon's lifelong resilient achievement:

> I have walked many years in this city,
> Kept faith and fast, provided for the poor,
> Have given and taken honour and ease.
> There went never any rejected from my door.

Though Gerontion's old age is of a piece with the evasions of his young
manhood, yet paradoxically, between 'Bitten by flies, fought' and 'My
house is a decayed house', what the changing pace of the verse insists on
is an illusion of contrast: after such glory, what a shabby finish! This is a
dramatic device for projecting a mode of glozing self-consciousness
inappropriate to Simeon; for the *conceptual* contrast between Simeon's
high deserts and the fate of his descendants is negated by a level
transition from one theme to the other without even a stanza break:

There went never any rejected from my door.
Who shall remember my house, where shall live my children's
  children
When the time of sorrow is come?
They will take to the goat's path and the fox's home,
Fleeing from the foreign faces and the foreign swords.

– the actual contrast between the man and his fortune hidden,
deprecated, not dramatized nor, as in 'Gerontion', trumped up. The
technique of 'Gerontion' involves a dramatization of the speaker's
plight that constantly returns to itself –

Here I am, an old man in a dry month . . .

I an old man,
A dull head among windy spaces. . . .

I have no ghosts,
An old man in a draughty house
Under a windy knob. . . .

We have not reached conclusion, when I
Stiffen in a rented house.

– in order to invest itself with new glamour from ostensibly contrasting
heroic vistas. Eliot has explained the technique in an essay written a few
months before 'Gerontion':

The really fine rhetoric of Shakespeare occurs in situations where a character in
the play *sees himself* in a dramatic light. . . . A speech in a play should never be
intended to move us as it might conceivably move other characters in the play,
for it is essential that we should preserve our position of spectators, and observe
always from the outside though with complete understanding. . . . And in the
rhetorical speeches from Shakespeare which have been cited, we have this
necessary advantage of a new clue to the character, in noting the angle from
which he views himself. But when a character *in* a play makes a direct appeal to
us, we are either the victim of our own sentiment, or we are in the presence of a
vicious rhetoric. ('Rhetoric and Poetic Drama'.)

One may conclude that many applauders of Gerontion's refined despair
have been victims of their own sentiment; that Gerontion is constantly

regarding himself in a dramatic light (like Othello); and that the point
to be grasped about Simeon is that he is not regarding himself at all. His

> Not for me the martyrdom, the ecstasy of thought and prayer,
> Not for me the ultimate vision

is instantly retrieved from self-pity by the calmly juxtaposed 'Grant me
thy peace'.

In the same way, one of the most stirring moments in 'Gerontion',

> Signs are taken for wonders. 'We would see a sign!'
> The word within a word, unable to speak a word,
> Swaddled with darkness. In the juvescence of the year
> Came Christ the tiger

is in *A Song for Simeon* emptied of its paradoxical intensity to be the
vehicle for poignancy of a wholly different kind:

> Now at this birth season of decease,
> Let the Infant, the still unspeaking and unspoken Word,
> Grant Israel's consolation
> To one who has eighty years and no tomorrow.

The lithe tiger in the darkness has no place in Simeon's glamourless
calm.

The elaborately-textured contrasts of 'Gerontion', then, are ma-
nipulated according to a rhetorical decorum which Eliot explicitly
connects with the moral state of the protagonist. In *A Song for Simeon*,
rhythm is used to enact the failure of rhythm, and dramatic devices to
convey the absence of drama. This is not to say that *Simeon* is a poem
that works by the absence of poetry, that it secures its effects merely by
having 'Gerontion' available for contrast. The two opening lines should
be enough to convince anyone of its power; though, as Eliot has
remarked of readers of Dante, 'It is apparently easier to accept
damnation as poetic material than purgation or beatitude; less is
involved that is strange to the modern mind.' Simeon inhabits a positive
spiritual state, whose tension, because not within himself but between
himself and an order outside himself, is purer and more taut than
Gerontion's stirring self-contemplation. Gerontion's hopeless attempt

to unite his will instant by instant with that of the tiger ('I would meet you upon this, honestly') dramatizes a conflict between the mind that suffers and the will that thinks; a conflict offered in the opening lines by the juxtaposition of the obedient, reading boy and the dry month. *Simeon* focuses a state: 'Gerontion' a parody of that state. It is consciously ironical that the epigraph to 'Gerontion' leads us to the Duke's speech in *Measure for Measure*, III i, which opens with words that might stand as epigraph for *Simeon*: 'Be absolute for death. . . .' *Simeon* the state: 'Gerontion' the parody. That is its mode. The sacramental Tiger is eaten, divided, drunk among whispers of social and financial intrigue that parody the hushed voices of Churchgoers. Mr. Silvero walks all night like one examining his conscience. Hakagawa 'bowing among the Titians' is a priest genuflecting at the profane altars of social decorum. The candles shifted in the dark room recall those of the altar; Fräulein von Kulp, 'who turned in the hall, one hand on the door', climaxes the series with an epiphany of guilty terror that throws over the preceding eight lines the lurid malaise of some cosmopolitan Black Mass. And the next words, 'Vacant shuttles weave the wind', allude to Stephen Dedalus' meditation, in the first chapter of *Ulysses*, on Mulligan the parody-priest: 'Words Mulligan had spoken a moment since in mockery to the stranger. Idle mockery. The void awaits surely all them that weave the wind: a menace, a disarming and a worsting from those embattled angels of the church' [Penguin edition, p. 27 – Ed.]. The void awaits them:

> De Bailhache, Fresca, Mrs. Cammel, whirled
> Beyond the circuit of the shuddering Bear
> In fractured atoms.

'Gerontion' and *A Song for Simeon* explore two modes of negative being: the first annihilation, the second self-surrender. And annihilation closely resembles self-surrender. Only an accession of self-consciousness is needed to turn the latter into the former. Annihilation is a parody of self-surrender.

'Parody' may be thought a strong term. It is justified, at any rate, in 'Prufrock', where, even so early, the theme is fundamental. Prufrock as a John the Baptist who has been executed without having denounced the adultery of his hostess; a Lazarus who fears to return from the dead lest he be misunderstood; a Falstaff who resembles the fat knight only in

being a butt and growing old; a Hamlet who is all soliloquies and no
heroism, fustily annihilated like Polonius – Prufrock is in every way a
caricature of his exemplars, who were 'absolute for death'.

> Should I, after tea and cakes and ices,
> Have the strength to force the moment to its crisis?
> But though I have wept and fasted, wept and prayed,
> Though I have seen my head (grown slightly bald)
>   brought in upon a platter,
> I am no prophet – and here's no great matter;
> I have seen the moment of my greatness flicker,
> And I have seen the eternal Footman hold my coat, and
>   snicker,
> And in short, I was afraid.

SOURCE: extract from essay in *Hudson Review*, II (1949) 421–9.

NOTE

1. I do not say that Dr. Leavis, in *New Bearings in English Poetry*, reads it as a
search for faith, though his approach to Eliot has other inadequacies. He is at
some points close to the weaker side of Arnold. But his refutation of Eliot's
inferior critics, favorable and unfavorable, is so telling that the reader
sympathetic to the present study, should regard him as an important ally, and
should comprehend *Ash Wednesday* in Dr. Leavis's way before trying to do any
more.

B. Rajan

THE UNITY OF THE *ŒUVRE* (1966)

. . . The shape of Mr Eliot's poetry is . . . composed by two forces: the spiral of process and the circle of design. Each necessitates the other and both stipulate the search for reality as a condition of man's being. It is not a search which can end in decisive findings: humankind cannot bear very much reality, and the enchainment of past and future protects mankind from heaven as well as from damnation. The sea of doubt is man's natural element, and the hints and guesses at the truth which illuminate that sea are designed not so much to end doubt as to save it from the whirlpool of despair. Eliot's poetry as an *œuvre* is thus given a unique and, as it were, double honesty, by its sense of a pattern won out of experience and by the manner in which the nature of the pattern entails a further commitment to experience through which the pattern is once again validated.

If these circumnavigations are not irrelevant, 'Prufrock' must take its place not simply as a beginning, but as a beginning which looks forward to an end, and which defines the terms of the unending inquiry. It has been remarked more than once that Prufrock's love song is never sung; what should be added is that his inability to sing it is not simply ironic, but part of the specifications of failure. To sing is to achieve a definition and Prufrock's fate is to fall short of definition, to bring momentous news only to thresholds. At the outset we are told that we will be taken through certain half-deserted streets

> that follow like a tedious argument
> Of insidious intent
> To lead you to an overwhelming question. . . .

The slumming tour is also a return to underground life, and it is plain even at this stage that the overwhelming question is more than the

proposal of marriage to a lady, that the love song must eventually be
sung to Beatrice. In these circumstances Prufrock's 'Oh, do not ask,
"What is it?"' is also more than a suggestion that the question will
reveal itself as one strolls along. Much is in character here: the
exaggeration that does not really exaggerate, the turning away from
definition, and the implication that further inquiry would not be in
good taste. We are in fact moving on two levels, and Prufrock's gestures,
volubly in excess of the occasion, correlate fully to another order of
reality which Prufrock unfortunately cannot confront and make
explicit. He is too much the child of his milieu to achieve the
outrageousness of proper definition; and since the ambience of 'Prufrock' is comic, the framing of the question must be an exercise in
outrage, not, as in 'Gerontion', a diagnosis of guilt. Eliot's favourite
life–death ambiguity is potent here as nearly everywhere else. What
seems to be life is death and to die into the true life one must die away
from the salon. The paradox is sharpened at the climax of the poem
when Prufrock drowns because he is awakened by human voices. But
submarine or underground existence is not the answer and Prufrock
does not undergo true death by drowning; the staircase he climbs is also,
for the same reason, not a purgatorial stair. The reader is aware,
through Prufrock, of the shocking nature of knowledge:

> Do I dare
> Disturb the universe?

But the scandal of recognition is beyond Prufrock himself. It is Lazarus
and John the Baptist who are the proper ambassadors of reality to the
salon, who can convey to it the angry, clawing truth. Prufrock still lives
(and fails to live) by a minor and less taxing scale of values. Visions and
decisions shade off into revisions. An eternal footman holds a coat, and
the confession 'in short, I was afraid' reduces the deeper terror to
everyday nervousness. 'Would it have been worth it, after all. . . .?'
Prufrock asks reassuringly, and the size of the exaggeration dismisses the
enterprise:

> To have squeezed the universe into a ball
> To roll it towards some overwhelming question. . . .

At a deeper level, however, the responsibility continues. The echo from
Marvell reminds us that Marvell's suitor was more daring. As the poem

develops, Prufrock's initial 'do not ask, "What is it?"' takes its proper place in the outline of failure. The overwhelming question has to be asked. It cannot be left to define or uncover itself. It must be forced into being in that passion for definition which can seize the moment and drive it to its crisis. The cost of definition will be more than ridicule. One is entitled to fear the cost. But not to meet it means the death of the man. The gesture of comic and yet of cosmic defiance – 'Do I dare / Disturb the universe?' – collapses now into mere sartorial rebellion:

> Shall I part my hair behind? Do I dare to eat a peach?
> I shall wear white flannel trousers, and walk upon the beach.

If the ambience of 'Prufrock' is comic, the Jacobean corridors of 'Gerontion' are slippery with images of evasion and betrayal. Gerontion, an old man arithmetically, has known neither natural youth nor natural age. He is in fact that typical Eliot character who cannot die because he has not lived. The thought is mentioned in the second line and does not recur until the last line links the dry brain to the dry season. Cut off from the organic world, Gerontion is cut off also from the living truth, the sustaining sense of relatedness. He knows that Christ the tiger is also the helpless child of Lancelot Andrewes's sermon; but his mind cannot keep the paradox in balance, and as guilt drives him mercilessly against the wall it is the tiger that stalks through his unnatural year. The confrontation of reality cannot be endured; the images twist away into rites of expiation and anxiety, surrogates for the truth that will not be faced. It is this falling short, this failure of metaphysical nerve, that makes the difference between dying and dying into life. So the tree of life becomes the tree of wrath, and neither fear nor courage can save us, because both fear and courage acquire their full nature only when they are morally rooted.

> The tiger springs in the new year. Us he devours.

This is the death of annihilation that looks forward to, yet is completely different from, another devouring in the desert by three white leopards. Gerontion's vehement declarations of design ('We have not reached conclusion. . . . I have not made this show purposelessly'), with the repeated 'Think now' and the final 'Think at last' forcing the moment to its intellectual crisis, do seem to result in a last-minute facing of reality:

> I would meet you upon this honestly.

But it is the honesty of the man against the wall, not that deeper confrontation which Eliot describes as 'that peculiar honesty, which, in a world too frightened to be honest, is peculiarly terrifying'. Gerontion's response is that of fear, not courage, in the metaphysical sense, and both its content and emptiness are pitilessly exposed in what is perhaps the most moving passage of the poem, as the imagery of the old age blends into the sense of withering away from God:

> I that was near your heart was removed therefrom
> To lose beauty in terror, terror in inquisition.
> I have lost my passion: why should I need to keep it
> Since what is kept must be adulterated?
> I have lost my sight, smell, hearing, taste and touch:
> How should I use them for your closer contact?

In terms which are closer to the nerves of pity and terror, Gerontion's predicament is that of Prufrock. He has moved forward in the act of definition, but he cannot cross the threshold, cannot make that surrender to reality which involves the death of the illusion which is his life. When the question is not asked the collapse into triviality must follow:

> These with a thousand small deliberations
> Protract the profit of their chilled delirium,
> Excite the membrane, when the sense has cooled,
> With pungent sauces, multiply variety
> In a wilderness of mirrors.

Gerontion's frivolity may be more opulent than that of Prufrock, but the terms of failure are not dissimilar; the darker colouring is the result of a more sombre ambience, with the sense of guilt blocking the tentative effort at definition, just as the fear of ridicule did in the earlier poem. The death of the self follows the failure to achieve relationship, notwithstanding the multiplying of the self in mirrors; the poem's threatening rhetoric here calls for a grimmer extinction than Prufrock's elegant drowning. Gerontion's identity is disintegrated and even pulverized. His mind may have its fragments, but it is permitted no ruins against which to shore them, and the vestigial white feathers in the snow of oblivion, drawn into a gulf that is more than geographical, express vividly the sense of sheer obliteration, even down to the collapsing cadence.

When Pound dissuaded Eliot from making 'Gerontion' a part of *The Waste Land*, he could not have been aware of the evolving logic of the *œuvre*. Nevertheless, his action contributed to that logic. 'Gerontion' looks forward to *The Waste Land* if only because there must be a world at the bottom of Dover cliff. Gerontion himself is unable to enter that world. His monologue, made up of the thoughts 'of a dry brain in a dry season', is carefully distanced from experience, and even the encounter to which he reaches imaginatively cannot be totally faced. To go forward from this point is to enter the abyss and to be prepared to prove nothingness on one's pulses. When one accepts the risk one also discovers that the risk is the only possibility of survival.

Seen in the symbolic continuum, the waste land is Prufrock's world more fully realized, a world where prophecy has fallen to fortune-telling, where love has hardened into the expertise of lust, where April is the cruellest month, and where the dead are no longer buried but planted in gardens. . . .

SOURCE: extract from 'The Overwhelming Question', in *T. S. Eliot: The Man and His Work*, ed. Allen Tate (1966) pp. 366–71.

PART THREE

Criticism of Individual Poems and Groups of Poems, 1915–1973

1. 'PRUFROCK' TO 'GERONTION'

Ezra Pound   'Prufrock' (1915)

... Now as to Eliot: 'Mr Prufrock' does not 'go off at the end'. It is a portrait of failure, or of a character which fails, and it would be false art to make it end on a note of triumph. I dislike the paragraph about Hamlet, but it is an early and cherished bit and T. E. won't give it up, and as it is the only portion of the poem that most readers will like at first reading, I don't see that it will do much harm.

For the rest: a portrait satire on futility can't end by turning that quintessence of futility, Mr P., into a reformed character breathing out fire and ozone. . . . I assure you it is better, 'more unique', than the other poems of Eliot which I have seen. . . .

> SOURCE: extracts from letter to Harriet Monroe, 31 January 1915; in *The Letters of Ezra Pound, 1907–1941*, ed. D. D. Paige (1951).

F. R. Leavis   'Prufrock', 'Portrait of a Lady', 'Gerontion' (1932)

The situation upon which Mr Eliot impinged has now been fairly described. The magnitude of the impact may be said to have been registered with the publication of *Poems 1909–1925*; but the contents of that volume had appeared at various times earlier. 'Prufrock', the earliest section, which is dated 1917, itself constitutes an important event in the history of English poetry. The title poem, 'The Love Song of J. Alfred Prufrock', which is printed at the beginning of *Poems 1909–1925*, represents a complete break with the nineteenth-century tradition, and a new start. It must indeed have been difficult to take seriously in 1917, for it defies the traditional canon of seriousness:

> I grow old . . . I grow old . . .
> I shall wear the bottoms of my trousers rolled.

Can this be poetry? And yet there are passages that, for all their oddness of imagery and tone, do not immediately condemn themselves as 'unpoetical' even by anthological standards:

> The yellow fog that rubs its back upon the window-panes,
> The yellow smoke that rubs its muzzle on the window-panes
> Licked its tongue into the corners of the evening,
> Lingered upon the pools that stand in drains,
> Let fall upon its back the soot that falls from chimneys,
> Slipped by the terrace, made a sudden leap,
> And seeing it was a soft October night,
> Curled once about the house, and fell asleep.

– Indeed, it is as necessary to revise the traditional idea of the distinction between seriousness and levity in approaching this poetry as in approaching the Metaphysical poetry of the seventeenth century. And as striking as this subtlety and flexibility of tone, this complexity of attitude, is the nature (exemplified in the passage just quoted) of the imagery. The canons of the poetical are forgotten; the poet assumes the right to make use of any materials that seem to him significant. We have here, in short, poetry that expresses freely a modern sensibility, the ways of feeling, the modes of experience, of one fully alive in his own age. Already the technical achievement is such as to be rich in promise of development and application.

Yet it must be admitted that if 'The Love Song of J. Alfred Prufrock' stood alone there would be some excuse for unreadiness to recognize in it this kind of significance. A certain heaviness about the gestures ('heavy' in the sense of caricature) –

> Do I dare
> Disturb the universe?

and

> Though I have seen my head (grown slightly bald) brought in upon a
>   platter

– emphasizes the touch of conscious elegance in the disillusion, and makes 'clever' seem a more adequate description than it ought:

> I have seen the moment of my greatness flicker,
> And I have seen the eternal Footman hold my coat,
>   and snicker,
> And in short, I was afraid.

But in 'Portrait of a Lady' the poise is more subtle, and it is maintained with sure and exquisite delicacy. The poet's command both of his experience and of his technique (if we can distinguish) is perfect. Without any limiting suggestion of caricature he can write:

> And I must borrow every changing shape
> To find expression . . . dance, dance
> Like a dancing bear,
> Cry like a parrot, chatter like an ape.
> Let us take the air, in a tobacco trance –
> Well! and what if she should die some afternoon,
> Afternoon grey and smoky, evening yellow and rose;
> Should die and leave me sitting pen in hand
> With the smoke coming down above the housetops . . . .

The flexibility and the control of this are maintained throughout the poem. The utterances of the lady are in the idiom and cadence of modern speech, and they go perfectly with the movement of the verse, which for all its freedom and variety, is nevertheless very strict and precise. The poet is as close to the contemporary world as any novelist could be, and his formal verse medium makes possible a concentration and a directness, audacities of transition and psychological notation, such as are forbidden to the novelist. Only a very strong originality could so have triumphed over traditional habits, and only very strong preconceptions could hinder the poem's being recognized as the work of a major poet.

'Portrait of a Lady' is the most remarkable thing in the 'Prufrock' section. 'Preludes' and 'Rhapsody on a Windy Night' develop that imagery of urban disillusion which has since done so much service in the verse of adolescent romantic pessimists. The use of this imagery relates him to Baudelaire, and the occasion now arises to note his debt to certain later French poets. To a young practitioner faced with Mr Eliot's problems Tristan Corbière and Jules Laforgue offered starting points such as were not to be found in English poetry of the nineteenth century. How closely he studied French verse may be gathered from the verse, retained in *Poems 1909–1925*, that he himself wrote in French. He learnt, by his own account, from Jules Laforgue in particular, and the evidence is apparent in his early work. The evidence lies not so much in a Laforguian exercise like 'Conversation Galante' as in 'The Love Song of J. Alfred Prufrock' and 'Portrait of a Lady'. It is difficult to distinguish between attitude and technique: he was able to derive means of expression from Laforgue because of a certain community with him in situation and sensibility. The self-ironical, self-distrustful attitudes of 'Prufrock' owe their definition largely to Laforgue, and there the technical debt shows itself; it shows itself in the ironical transitions, and also in the handling of the verse. But this last head has been made too much of by some critics: French moves so differently from English that to learn from French verse an English poet must be strongly original. And to learn as Mr Eliot learnt in general from Laforgue is to be original to the point of genius. Already in the collection of 1917 he is himself as only a major poet can be.

The other derivation he assigns to his verse – 'the form in which I began to write, in 1908 or 1909, was directly drawn from the study of Laforgue together with the later Elizabethan drama'[1] – manifests itself plainly in the first poem of the section following 'Prufrock', that dated 1920. It is not for nothing that in 'Gerontion' he alludes to one of the finest passages of Middleton:

> I that was near your heart was removed therefrom
> To lose beauty in terror, terror in inquisition.
> I have lost my passion: why should I need to keep it
> Since what is kept must be adulterated?
>
> ('Gerontion')

> I that am of your blood was taken from you
> For your better health; look no more upon it,
> But cast it to the ground regardlessly.
> Let the common sewer take it from distinction.
>
> (*The Changeling*, v iii)

The comparison would be worth making at greater length in order to bring out, not only the likeness in movement of Mr Eliot's verse to mature Elizabethan dramatic verse, but also Mr Eliot's astonishing power. Nowhere in Middleton, or, for that matter, Webster, Tourneur, or anywhere outside Shakespeare, can we find a passage so sustained in quality as 'Gerontion'. In his essay on Massinger[2] he says: 'with the end of Chapman, Middleton, Webster, Tourneur, Donne we end a period when the intellect was immediately at the tips of the senses. Sensation became word and word sensation.' 'Gerontion' answers to this description as well as anything by any of the authors enumerated: it expresses psychological subtleties and complexities in imagery of varied richness and marvellously sure realization. The whole body of the words seems to be used. Qualities that (if we ignore Hopkins as he was ignored) have been absent from English poetry since the period that Mr Eliot describes (his critical preoccupation with it is significant) reappear with him.

The effect of his few and brief critical references to Milton is notorious. The effect upon Miltonic influence of his practice is likely to be even more radical. If we look at the first *Hyperion* of Keats we see that it points forward to Tennyson and backward to Milton. This simple reminder (a safe generalization would call for more qualifying than is in place here) serves to bring home the prevalence of certain limitations in the way in which English has been used in poetry since Milton. Milton and Tennyson are very different, but when Tennyson, or any other poet of the nineteenth century (which saw a rough first draft in the revised *Hyperion*), wrote blank verse, even when he intended it to be dramatic, it followed Milton rather than Shakespeare – a Milton who could be associated with Spenser. Even when Shakespeare was consciously the model, it was a Shakespeare felt through Milton. Language was used in a generally Miltonic way even in unMiltonic verse. To justify the phrase, 'a generally Miltonic way', a difficult and varying analysis would be necessary; but I have in mind Milton's habit of exploiting language as a kind of musical medium outside himself, as it were. There is no pressure in his verse of any complex and varying current of feeling and sensation; the words have little substance or muscular quality: Milton is using only a small part of the resources of the English language. The remoteness of his poetic idiom from his own speech is to be considered here. ('English must be kept up', said Keats, explaining his abandonment of the Miltonic first *Hyperion*). A man's most vivid emotional and sensuous experience is inevitably bound up with the language that he actually speaks.

The brief account given above of the relation of 'Gerontion' to Middleton and his contemporaries must not be allowed to suggest that Mr Eliot's verse has anything in it of pastiche. For all its richness and variety and power of assimilating odds and ends from Lancelot Andrewes (for instance), its staple idiom and movement derive immediately from modern speech.

These considerations have been put too briefly to be critically impregnable: no simple formula will cover poetic practice in the nineteenth century. That they can be put so briefly and yet serve their purpose, that one can take so much for understood, is due to Mr Eliot. That young practitioners are now using words very differently from the poets of the last age is also due mainly to him.

The dramatic derivation of the verse is not all that there is dramatic about 'Gerontion': it has a really dramatic detachment. In this respect it represents a great advance upon anything printed earlier in *Poems 1909–1925*. 'Prufrock' and 'Portrait of a Lady' are concerned with the directly personal embarrassments, disillusions and distresses of a sophisticated young man. It is not a superficial difference that 'Gerontion' has for *persona* an old man, embodying a situation remote from that of the poet. From a position far above his immediate concerns as a particular individual, projecting himself, as it were, into a comprehensive and representative human consciousness, the poet contemplates human life and asks what it all comes to. The introductory quotation gives the hint:

> *Thou hast nor youth nor age*
> *But as it were an after dinner sleep*
> *Dreaming of both.*

– 'Gerontion' has the impersonality of great poetry.

In method, too, 'Gerontion' represents a development. Since the method is that, or a large part of that, of *The Waste Land*, it seems better to risk some elementary observations upon it, for *The Waste Land* has been found difficult. Instructions how to read the poem (should anything more than the title and the epigraph be necessary) are given in the last line:

> Tenants of the house,
> Thoughts of a dry brain in a dry season.

It has neither narrative nor logical continuity, and the only theatre in which the characters mentioned come together, or could, is the mind of the old man. The Jew who squats on the window-sill could not hear the old man even if he spoke his thoughts aloud, and the field overhead in which the goat coughs has no geographical relation to the house. All the persons, incidents and images are there to evoke the immediate consciousness of the old man as he broods over a life lived through and asks what is the outcome, what the meaning, what the residue. This seems simple enough, and the transitions and associations are not obscure.

The poem opens with what is to be a recurrent theme of Mr Eliot's: the mixing of 'memory and desire' in present barrenness. The old man in his 'dry month', waiting for the life-giving 'rain' that he knows will never come, is stirred to envy, then to poignant recollection, by the story of hot-blooded vitality, which contrasts with the squalor of his actual surroundings. Youthful desire mingles in memory with the most exalted emotions, those associated with the mysteries of religion:

> The word within a word, unable to speak a word,
> Swaddled with darkness. In the juvescence of the year
> Came Christ the tiger.
>
> In depraved May. . . .

Here, in the last two phrases, Mr Eliot does in concentration what he does by his notorious transitions from theme to theme: widely different emotions and feelings are contrasted and fused. It is the kind of effect that Shakespeare gets in such a line as 'Lilies that fester smell far worse than weeds',[3] where the associations that cluster round 'lilies' – fragrant flowers and emblems of purity – are contrasted and fused with those attaching to 'fester', which applies to rotting flesh.

In 'Gerontion' the contrast is developed: the emotional intensities evoked by the reference to the Sacrament are contrasted with the stale cosmopolitan depravity evoked by the names and by the suggested incidents and associations:

> To be eaten, to be divided, to be drunk
> Among whispers; by Mr Silvero
> With caressing hands, at Limoges
> Who walked all night in the next room;
> By Hakagawa, bowing among the Titians;
> By Madame de Tornquist, in the dark room
> Shifting the candles; Fraulein von Kulp
> Who turned in the hall, one hand on the door.

'Among whispers' may be pointed to as a characteristic transition. They are first the whispers of religious awe; then, in the new context, they become clandestine and sinister, the whispers of intrigue. The reference to 'the Titians' brings in art: art and religion, the two refuges from time and the sordid actuality, suffer the same staling depravation. Fraulein von Kulp is seen vividly, a precise particular figure in a precise particular posture, but far in the past; she serves only to emphasize the present vacancy:

> Vacant shuttles
> Weave the wind. I have no ghosts,
> An old man in a draughty house
> Under a windy knob.

But this kind of elucidation is perhaps insulting. At any rate, no more can be needed: more than enough has been done to illustrate the method. And only an analysis on Mr Empson's lines[4] could be anything like fair to the subtleties of the poem; for Mr Eliot's effects depend a great deal upon ambiguity. One of the most obvious instances occurs near the end:

> De Bailhache, Fresca, Mrs Cammel, whirled
> Beyond the circuit of the shuddering Bear
> In fractured atoms. Gull against the wind, in the windy straits
> Of Belle Isle, or running on the Horn,
> White feathers in the snow, the Gulf claims,
> And an old man driven by the Trades
> To a sleepy corner.

The gull following upon those names that evoke *The News of the World* enforces partly the inevitable end, the common reduction to 'fractured atoms.' A bunch of feathers blown in the gale, it brings home poignantly the puny helplessness of the individual life. But also, in its clean, swift vitality, it contrasts with the frowsy squalor of finance, crime and divorce. Similarly with respect to the old man: it stands to him for inevitable death and dissolution; but it also stands for the strength and ardour that he has lost. . . .

SOURCE: extract from chapter 3 of *New Bearings in English Poetry* (1932) pp. 75–87.

NOTES

1. *Selected Poems of Ezra Pound* (1928): Introduction, p. viii.
2. *The Sacred Wood* (1920) p. 117.
3. *Sonnet* XCIV.
4. See *Seven Types of Ambiguity* (1930).

Hugh Kenner 'Prufrock' (1960)

The name of Prufrock-Littau, furniture wholesalers, appeared in advertisements in St. Louis, Missouri, in the first decade of the present century; in 1911 a young Missourian's whimsical feline humour prefixed the name of Prufrock to what has become the best-known English poem since the *Rubaiyat*. The savour of that act had faded from the memory of the sexagenarian London man of letters who wrote to a mid-century inquirer that his appropriation of the now-famous German surname must have been 'quite unconscious'. There would be no point in denying that it probably was; but the unconscious mind of T. S. Eliot once glimmered with a rich mischief which for many years has been more cautiously disclosed than it was in 1911.

The query itself must have amused him, however; Mr. Eliot's dealings with people who wanted to know what he was concealing have for two decades afforded some of the richest comedy in the annals of literary anecdote. Letter after letter, visitor after visitor, he answers with

unfailing lambent courtesy. After *The Confidential Clerk* was produced, a journalist, teased by implications he couldn't pin down, or
perhaps simply assigned a turn of duty at poet-baiting, wanted to know
what it meant. It means what it says, said Mr. Eliot patiently. No more?
Certainly, no more. But supposing, the journalist pursued, supposing
you had meant *something else*, would you not have put some other
meaning more plainly? 'No,' Mr. Eliot replied, 'I should have put it just
as obscurely.'

No other writer's verse has inspired so tenacious a conviction that it
means more than it seems to. Certainly no other modern verses so
invade the mind, attracting to themselves in the months following their
ingestion reminiscence, desire, and speculation. Eliot deals in effects,
not ideas; and the effects are in an odd way wholly verbal, seemingly
endemic to the language, scrupulously concocted out of the expressive
gestures of what a reader whose taste has been educated in the
nineteenth-century classics takes poetry to be.

That is why they will not leave the mind, which grows bored with
ideas but will never leave off fondling phrases. How much of the
grotesque melancholy of 'Prufrock' radiates from the protagonist's
name would be difficult to estimate. It was surgical economy that used
the marvellous name once only, in the title, and compounded it with a
fatuous 'J. Alfred'. It was a talent already finely schooled that with nice
audacity weighed in a single phrase the implications of this name
against those of 'Love Song'. It was genius that separated the speaker of
the monologue from the writer of the poem by the solitary device of
affixing an unforgettable title. Having done that, Eliot didn't need to
keep fending off his protagonist with facile irony; the result was a poised
intimacy which could draw on every emotion the young author knew
without incurring the liabilities of 'self-expression'.

This complex deftness in the title of his first long poem epitomizes the
nature of Eliot's best early verse. Every phrase seems composed as
though the destiny of the author's soul depended on it, yet it is un-
profitable not to consider the phrases as arrangements of words before
considering them as anything else. Like the thousand little gestures that
constitute good manners, their meaning is contained in themselves
alone. Eliot is the most verbal of the eminent poets: more verbal than
Swinburne. If he has carried verbalism far beyond the mere extirpation
of jarring consonants, it is because of his intimate understanding of what
language can do: how its 'tentacular roots', as he once said, reach 'down

to the deepest terrors and desires'. Only a poet who came after the nineteenth century and grew up in its shadow could have acquired this understanding. Eliot acquired it early, and was able to coerce a small masterpiece into existence at a time when (according to his later standards) he understood very little else.

'Prufrock' exploits the nineteenth century's specialized plangencies at every turn.

> I grow old . . . I grow old . . .
> I shall wear the bottoms of my trousers rolled.

Everyone remembers these lines. They manage to be ridiculous without being funny (the speaker is not making a joke) or cruel (a joke is not being made about the speaker). Their mechanism is allied to the mock-heroic but it doesn't burlesque anything. Like a side-show mermaid, this non-sequitur of an aging Bostonian floats embalmed in dark sonorities whose cloudiness almost conceals the stitching between mammal and fish. We feel that the two halves won't conjoin at the very instant of being persuaded they do. The vowels sound very fine, the syllables are impeccably cadenced; but vaguely within one's pleasure at Tennysonian excellence there struggles an intimation of the absurd, with no more chance of winging clear into view than a wasp in a jar of molasses.

The phenomenon of sound obscuring deficiencies of sense from writer and reader is often to be observed in English poetry; the Romantics may be said to have elevated it into a method. Mr. Eliot's originality consisted in allowing the deficiency to be concealed only from the speaker. The writer is too cool not to have known what he was about, and as for the reader, his pleasure consists precisely in experiencing a disproportion difficult to isolate. The certainty that Prufrock himself understands it no better than we do checks any pursuit of 'metaphysical' analogies between senility and trouser-bottoms; and as for Prufrock's mind, where the collocation is supposed to be taking place, its workings are nowhere very profoundly explored. His *sensibility* is plumbed to the uttermost, but that is not what is usually meant when a poet is praised for revealing a human soul. To say that Prufrock is contemplating a young blade's gesture, or alternatively an old castoff's, rolling up his trousers because he either hasn't learnt to care for dignity or has outgrown its claims, is to substitute for the poetic effect a formula that

fails to exhaust it because incapable of touching it. For the purposes of
the effect, the pathos of the character of Prufrock is no more than a
donnée. And the effect is unique, and no reader has ever forgotten it.

'The Love Song of J. Alfred Prufrock' most clings to the memory
whenever it exploits, as a foil to undistinguished middle age, the
authorized sonorities of the best English verse, *circa* 1870:

> In the room the women come and go
> Talking of Michelangelo.

The closed and open o's, the assonances of 'room', 'women', and 'come',
the pointed caesura before the polysyllabic burst of 'Michelangelo',
weave a context of grandeur within which our feeling about these trivial
women determines itself. The heroic sound, and especially the carefully
dramatized sound of the painter's name, is what muffles these women.
The lines scale down severely in French:

> Dans la pièce les femmes vont et viennet
> En parlant des maîtres de Sienne.

That the translator has caught the sense and approximated the
movement is an achievement strangely insufficient for lines whose
poetic mechanism, one might have thought, depended on so simple a
contrast of conceptions: talking women, and a heroic visionary. But
Eliot's effects traffic only marginally with conceptions. Hence –
again – the elusive disproportion from which his humour arises, a
delicate vapour in whose aura the lights twinkle.

Tennyson, to whom Eliot owes so much, does not smile; 'He really
did hold', as G. K. Chesterton said, 'many of the same ideas as Queen
Victoria, though gifted with a more fortunate literary style.' It was in
the nature of things impossible for him to realize that the peculiar
medium he had perfected from Coleridgean beginnings was a totally
unsuitable climate for the conducting of human thought. This perception was reserved for his friend Edward Lear, another of Eliot's
mentors, whose wistful incantations –

> Where the purple river rolls fast and dim
> And the Ivory Ibis starlike skim,
> Wing to wing we dance around,
> Stamping our feet with a flumpy sound,

– provide a sort of middle term between Coleridge's incantation on the running of Alph the Sacred River and

> I grow old . . . I grow old . . .
> I shall wear the bottoms of my trousers rolled.

This embryology isn't adduced in belittlement; whatever Coleridge and Lear may have been up to, Eliot has so disciplined the procedures for securing 'an *air of meaning* rather than meaning itself'[1] that – in his later work at least – the spectacle of their operation can itself imply meaning of a still more austere kind.

Lear, however, wasn't a technical innovator; he discovered his comic method by contemplating not the state of the poetic tradition but (Prufrock-like) his own artistic futility. Tennyson remains the Victorian norm. 'His feelings', Eliot has noted, 'were more honest than his mind', and his feeling found continually exact expression –

> but far away
> The noise of life begins again,
> And ghastly thro' the drizzling rain
> On the bald street breaks the blank day.

But he made, notoriously, attempts to *think* in this kind of verse – 'Are God and Nature then at strife?' – which are really mistaken attempts to exploit the apparent inclusiveness of his poetic world (it contains so much that it ought to contain everything) and which emphasize by their fatuity the sacrifices through which that air of inclusiveness has been achieved. A sphere is self-bounded because its surface is turning away at every instant from possible tangents.

What was bequeathed to the young poets of 1910 by their predecessors in England was a world made out of words; much of Tennyson and most of Swinburne has no more bite on the realities outside the dictionary than have the verses of 'Jabberwocky'. Coherence was obtained by exploiting the sounds of the words and the implications concealed in their sounds; 'A cry that shivered to the tingling stars' would be a strikingly impoverished line if the English language could be suddenly purged of the words 'twinkling' and 'tinkling'. T. S. Eliot from the first has leaned on words in that way; it was the *name* of Prufrock that attracted him; no information about the

St. Louis bearers of that name can throw the smallest light on his poem.
In the few juvenilia that have been preserved we find him manipulating
sounds in Jonson's way –

> The flowers I sent thee when the dew
> Was trembling on the vine
> Were withered ere the wild bee flew
> To pluck the eglantine   (1905)

or Swinburne's –

> Their petals are fanged and red
> With hideous streak and stain   (1908)

or Tennyson's –

> The moonflower opens to the moth,
> The mist crawls in from the sea;
> A great white bird, a snowy owl,
> Slips from the alder tree.   (1909)

Two years later he wrote 'Prufrock'. It was the Tennysonian medium
that he learned to use; characteristically, he took what it seemed proper
to take at the time, the manner of his immediate elders. He learned to
use it; he never made the mistake of trying to think in it. Aware both of
its limitations and of its extraordinary emotional inclusiveness, he
contrives instead to give the impression that thought is going on
alongside the poetic process, that sardonic eyes are being frequently
bent on the pretensions toward which rhythmic speech incorrigibly
reaches, and that whole areas of human life which the sentiments of
romantic verbalism have appropriated are patently, to a rational
vision, entoiled in richly muffled absurdity – 'They will say: "But how
his arms and legs are thin!"'

Such is the situation that 'Prufrock' dramatizes: a muffling of rational
behaviour by rhetoric. To the aggrandizement of that situation the
poet brings every conceivable wile. The epigraph is a piece of calculated
opportunism:

> *S'io credesse che mia risposta fosse . . .*

'If I thought that my response would be addressed to one who might go back
alive, this flame would shake no more; but since no one ever goes back alive out
of these deeps (if what I hear be true), without fear of infamy I answer you.'

Senza tema d'infamia ti rispondo.

From these Italian words the English speech moves forward without a
break – 'Let us go then, you and I . . .' – effecting a liaison between
this situation and Dante's which is all the smoother for the reflective,
lingering rhythm of the opening phrase. For the next twenty lines Eliot
brings all his melodic resources to the incantation of a quiet *fin-de-siècle*
inferno, equipped with nightmare streets that 'follow' and are omin-
ously 'half-deserted', and inimical clouds of yellow fog. It is a hell
neither sustained by a theology nor gradated by degrees of crime; a
genteel accumulation of stage effects, nothing quite in excess. It isn't a
punishment so much as a state. Somewhere beyond or around it lies the
world where questions have answers, but the moment an 'overwhelming question' is mentioned we are cautioned, 'Oh, do not ask, "What is
it?"'

    Above this monotonous emotional pedal-point runs a coruscating
texture of effects. For twelve lines the word 'time' reverberates, struck
again and again, while (punctuated once by the startling precision of
'To prepare a face to meet the faces that you meet') portentousness
overlays mere sonority:

> And indeed there will be time
> For the yellow smoke that slides along the street,
> Rubbing its back upon the window-panes;
> There will be time, there will be time
> To prepare a face to meet the faces that you meet;
> There will be time to murder and create,
> And time for all the works and days of hands
> That lift and drop a question on your plate;
> Time for you and time for me,
> And time yet for a hundred indecisions,
> And for a hundred visions and revisions,
> Before the taking of a toast and tea.

What 'murder and create' may mean we cannot tell, though it is plain
what the phrase can *do*; the words have lost their connexion with the
active world, lost in fact everything but their potential for neurasthenic

shock. 'Time for you and time for me' is as hypnotic and as meaningless
as a phrase on the 'cellos. The yellow smoke rubbing its back upon
window-panes is a half-realizable picture; the detail about the hands
and the plate has the air of being a picture but in fact isn't, the thing that
is dropped on the plate being 'a question', and the hands – blurred by
the phrase 'works and days' which is a fusion of Hesiod and Ecclesiastes
(3 : 1 – 8) – being not quite those of God and not quite those of a butler.

> And time for all the works and days of hands
> That lift and drop a question on your plate;

these gravely irrational words evoke a nervous system snubbed by the
Absolute without committing themselves as to whether that Absolute is
the moral rigour of an implacable Creator or the systemized social
discomfort of a Boston tea-party.

The first half of 'Prufrock', in fact, is devoted to a systematic
confusion of temporal and eternal disciplines; this man's doom is an
endless party-going –

> For I have known them all already, known them all: –
> Have known the evenings, mornings, afternoons,

– which he is no more at liberty to modify than one of Dante's subjects
can desert his circle of Hell. As he moves wearily through the fog toward
yet another entrance-hall he can toy with images of rebellion –

> And indeed there will be time
> To wonder, 'Do I dare?' and, 'Do I dare?'
> Time to turn back and descend the stair,
> With a bald spot in the middle of my hair –
> (They will say: 'How his hair is growing thin!')

But one doesn't – the switch from social to cosmic is typical – 'disturb
the universe'. In Hell you do what you are doing.

SOURCE: extract from *The Invisible Poet: T. S. Eliot* (1960)
pp. 3–11.

NOTE

1. Miss Elizabeth Schneider's description of *Kubla Khan*.

Wallace Fowlie   'Prufrock',
'Gerontion' and Baudelaire (1966)

. . . In 1910 Eliot lived in France and in Paris, where he took courses at
the Sorbonne, and private French lessons from Alain-Fournier, who
was to publish *Le Grand Meaulnes* in 1913. The Paris which Eliot
observed in 1910 was the past and the future of the city: the *Cahiers de la
Quinzaine* were appearing at that time in Péguy's shop, enthusiasm for
Henri Bergson filled to capacity every week an auditorium in the
Collège de France, *La Nouvelle Revue Française* was really new. Many
years later, in speaking of the year 1910, in an article of homage to
Jacques Rivière, Eliot said that 'France represented poetry' for him at
that time. There he was attracted to the work of Laforgue, Corbière,
Verlaine, Baudelaire, Rimbaud, and Gautier. He was also reading at
that time certain French prose writers: Stendhal, Flaubert, the
Goncourt brothers, Benda, and Maritain.

Of all these French writers, Baudelaire had the deepest influence on
Eliot. With Baudelaire he felt the closest affinities. Affinities even in
temperament and reserve of character, in the liking for self-discipline
and for the challenge of a difficult art, in the desire to create a different
art. Baudelairian dandyism, visible in Eliot's personality, was first an
isolation, but it was especially the heroism of concentration, the
spiritual struggle for inner perfection.

Almost at the same time in their careers, when they were still quite
young, Baudelaire and Eliot realized that the poet and the critic are
one. At its highest degree of lucidity, the critical mind is transformed
into poetic inspiration. Both poets felt the reciprocal dependence of
their critical and creative faculties.

Baudelaire's example and influence are especially apparent in the
early poems of Eliot and in those that preceded *The Waste Land* of 1922.
The first poems are fragmentary pictures of a civilization in a state of
disintegration. The poet's vision is intense in these first exercises in
which he is learning how to fashion an instrument suitable to reveal
what he has seen.

Baudelaire taught him ways by which to renew the poetic art by
drawing from the daily life of a large metropolis. He taught the
American poet especially the way to translate ideas into sensations.

'Prufrock', as a 'love song', is reminiscent of the *Complaintes* of Laforgue, or even of *La Chanson du malaimé* of Apollinaire. But Prufrock has also a Baudelairian temperament: he sees around him concupiscence, turpitude, evil. He is sickened by the vulgarity of a large city. Eliot's word tends to fill the void between poetry, or what was traditionally understood by poetry, and the modern world. And this is exactly what Apollinaire and Max Jacob have done in France in the twentieth century. . . .

Alone among the French poets – romantics, symbolists, decadents – Baudelaire revealed an understanding of Christianity which Eliot was to continue. The French poet of the nineteenth century, like Villon in the century of Jeanne d'Arc, had a very personal sense of religious values. He was also obsessed by vice and sin, an obsession which Eliot will not have. But Eliot studied in the writings of Baudelaire the Christian meaning of the real which is concealed beneath the appearances of the real. Baudelaire speaks of that very imprecise restlessness of men which comes with evening: 'Aux uns portant la paix, aux autres le souc'. And Eliot recasts the image:

> When evening quickens faintly in the street,
> Wakening the appetites of life in some. . . .

There is an even more striking example in the same sonnet of 'Recueillement', where the clouds, coloured by the setting sun, appear as balconies in the sky, and the poet's past appears in the form of women in old-fashioned dresses on the balconies:

> Vois se pencher les défuntes Années,
> Sur les balcons du ciel, en robes surannées. . . .

And the opening of the 'Love Song', where evening is compared to a sick person on an operating table, is reminiscent of 'Recueillement':

> When the evening is spread out against the sky
> Like a patient etherised upon a table. . . .

The affinity is not only in the images designating the tranquillity of evening. It is especially in the feelings and thoughts of the two poets. Eliot saw in Baudelaire the example of a writer for whom criticism and poetry are converging aspects of the same literary process. The books of each one represent the search for a form of analysis capable of translating the consciousness of an age, when it is a question of poetic creation, or a form of analysis capable of translating the consciousness of an objective work, when it is a question of criticism. Whether it is a poem or a critical essay, the definitive result recapitulates a personal reaction in which the intelligence of the writer and his sensibility are similarly engaged.

'Le Voyage' of Baudelaire and 'Gerontion' of Eliot are two poems which can be explained in terms of a cultural context. For Baudelaire, the world has become so small that it is reduced to what a single man sees, to the image of the inner life of a man:

> Amer savoir, celui qu'on tire voyage!
> Le monde, monotone et petit, aujourd'hui,
> Hier, demain, toujours, nous fait voir notre image. . . .

The same motifs of time, of consciousness of evil, and of spatial and chronological ambiguities are to be found in 'Gerontion':

> After such knowledge, what forgiveness? Think now
> History has many cunning passages. . . .

It is futile to try to analyse the meaning of these two poems, because they are so deeply rooted in the meaning of an historical period. Baudelaire's voyager is the man who sets out for the pure joy of leaving his familiar world, and he is also the child who does not leave, who is in love with maps and pictures: 'l'enfant, amoureux de cartes et d'estampes'. The character in Eliot's poem, 'An old man in a draughty house', finds it difficult to return to former experiences and to comprehend them. But the minds of Eliot's old man and of Baudelaire's voyager contain the universe. There is a moment at the end of each poem when the protagonist experiences the intoxication and the exaltation of the infinite:

> Gull against the wind, in the windy straits
> Of Belle Isle. . . .

> *Nos cœurs que tu connais sont remplis de rayons!*

Each of these poets has sung of the aridity of contemporary life, and each one also has sung of the same aspiration toward purity, the same search for humility. Baudelaire's influence was double, as Eliot's is double today. Each offers us the example of the creative and the critical intelligence. In reading the measured verses of these two poets we become accomplices of extreme sentiments. This poetry does not reassure us. It does not engulf us with illusions.

In one of his earliest essays, 'Tradition and the Individual Talent', Eliot taught two generations that it is impossible to evaluate a poet by himself. In order to understand him in a true sense, for the purposes of comparison and contrast, he has to be situated in relationship with the dead. This is an entire programme, an elaborate principle of literary criticism in which Eliot affirms the solidarity of the centuries. Baudelaire, who possessed far less culture than Eliot, emphasized his belief that all great poetry must have a moral basis, that all great poetry must reflect the problem of good and evil.

Many scholars have pointed out themes common to Baudelaire and Eliot: the strong attraction to the sea, an obsession with the city and its populous quarters, spleen, a tone of derision, and especially perhaps the theme of anguish, comparable to the anguish studied by Jean-Paul Sartre in *La Nausée*. But no one has yet studied an art, specifically Baudelairian, which Eliot learned from the French poet and perfected in accordance with his own aptitude and talent. It is the art of evoking a memory, and often a distant memory, deliberately and wilfully, the art of associating the sensation of this memory with the spirit and the intellect, and at the same time excluding all sentimentality. . . .

SOURCE: extracts from 'Baudelaire and Eliot', in *T. S. Eliot: The Man and His Work*, ed. Tate, pp. 304–5, 310–13.

J. Grover Smith   'Preludes', 'Rhapsody' and Bergson (1956)

. . . The 'Preludes' are better unified than Eliot's method of composing them might seem to have permitted. Indeed, the first and second, written in close succession, not only complement each other but together lead into an epistemological concept entertained in the third and fourth; and all four agree in imagery. They illustrate a practice tested in 'Prufrock' and followed again in the 'Rhapsody', namely, of depersonalizing character by talking about bodily members such as feet, hands, eyes, fingers. Eliot's imagism was of his own contriving, for he was not in touch with the contemporary experiments of T. E. Hulme and F. S. Flint. The first 'Prelude' begins with winter nightfall in an urban back street; from indoor gloom and the confined odor of cooking it moves outside into the smoky twilight where gusts of wind whip up leaves and soiled papers, and a shower spatters the housetops. Such adjectives as 'burnt-out', 'smoky', 'grimy', 'withered', 'vacant', 'broken', and 'lonely' carry the tone. Reversing the direction, the second 'Prelude' begins in the street, as morning (with a hang-over, one might almost say) 'comes to consciousness' of stale-beer smells and coffee fumes; and the piece ends in contemplating house windows where, 'With the other masquerades / That time resumes', hands are 'raising dingy shades'. The third 'Prelude' exposes one of the 'thousand furnished rooms' where a not overclean woman, sluggishly struggling awake and preparing to get out of bed, starts her own return to consciousness for resumption of life's masquerade. Since this masquerade (a 'thousand sordid images') constitutes the woman's soul, just as in the fourth 'Prelude' the transitory show of fingers, newspapers, and eyes constitutes the soul of the personified street, the hidden human reality it masks is itself neither soul nor 'conscience' but a kind of register upon which the images have impinged as upon a *tabula rasa*. At the same time both woman and street are individual substances, so that each peculiarly registers the images they share. The woman can accordingly have 'such a vision of the street / As the street hardly understands' – an intuition contrasted with the street's assurance 'of certain certainties', equated somewhat ungrammatically in the fourth 'Prelude' with a cocky masculine readiness 'to assume the world'. Woman and street alike are earthbound: she supine in bed, 'he' trampled under foot; and in their hypothetical aspirations upward, when her soul's images flicker overhead and his soul is 'stretched tight across the skies', they but mirror the degraded nature of their conscious selves.

Eliot's virtual repetition, in the fourth 'Prelude', of the imagery from the opening lines of 'Prufrock' supports this renewed treatment of the ideal and the actual or, rather, this review of the Prufrockian problem; for here his premise is not that these personages are spiritually superior to external actuality but rather that they have no images distinguishable from it. Prufrock, while cringing immobilized before the actual, does not relinquish the preferable ideal; but the woman and the street not only do not have any such ideal in reserve but, indeed, cannot have – for their consciousness and the external scene are identical. In other words, they cannot be, in the manner of Prufrock, romantic idealists because their consciousness embraces only what their senses can confront. There may be something illogical in Eliot's having endowed the woman with a 'vision', though not if this means only experience or perception; clearly, while aware of the images making up her soul, she need not divine her lack of images more attractive.

One may surmise a partial debt to Bergson, whom Eliot had been reading at Paris. In Bergson's *Matter and Memory* an 'image' is indifferently definable as a perception or as the perceived thing itself, so that subject and object merge. The perceiver, by coming into contact with the material world, absorbs images into his consciousness, where they persist as memories. In the aggregate, memories thus form a *durée*, considered by Bergson to be creative, since, as he explains in *Creative Evolution*, they affect the perception of things in the perceiver's future. Eliot's poem, however, holds up to view a set of images so disagreeable; or at any rate so empty of charm, that an optimism like Bergson's must appear implausible: what vital impulse can animate either the woman or the street, however impatient for creative action, if the consciousness of each is downtrodden and spiritless? Thus the fourth 'Prelude' turns to pity, to a 'notion of some infinitely gentle / Infinitely suffering thing' incarnate in these depersonalized images and, therefore, in the souls comprising them. But at once it shows cynical revulsion from sentimental fancies ('Wipe your hand across your mouth, and laugh'), as much as to say that such an existence is contemptible.

> The worlds revolve like ancient women
> Gathering fuel in vacant lots.

The plight of the woman and of the street collectively – the people whose souls are mere congeries of fugitive appearances – points up the meaninglessness of the universe, no living entity proceeding by instinct toward an appointed goal but a worn-out mechanism with parts stiffly toiling as, without destination, it moves in endless epicyclic paths. And yet, of course, this closing image intensifies that pity against which the spectator has been warned. For the 'ancient women' are not to be derided; if perhaps in one moment they seem ludicrous, they seem in the next distressed with the bleakness of destitute old age, ignorantly condemned to privation. With the pathos of 'brightness falls from the air', there lingers in the poet's mind the memory of an ancient golden age. Seeing the world as tragic in its very meanness, he manages to suggest, in retrospect, some pity even for the woman and the street.

. . . there remains the Bergsonian philosophy which may have influenced the rationale of the poem. The 'lunar incantations', or nocturnal voices that in the 'Rhapsody' ensorcell the stroller's midnight ramble while the moon hypnotizes the deserted street, are Laforguian; but the dissolution of orderly thought into an irrational, almost surrealistic collage of discontinuous mental impressions obeys the laws of instinctive consciousness according to Bergson. Mingling as fluid perceptions, kaleidoscopic images pour into memory, the organ of time, the 'floors' of which break down to enable their total synthesis. This dreamlike process, the quintessence of the non-intellectual, works by free association rather than by logic. From the meanings borne by the word 'rhapsody', the reader of this poem might pick out several appropriate to an understanding of its title; perhaps the most suggestive meaning is the musical one, implying here the irregularity and diversity attendant on the principle of association. On the other hand, Eliot's images are not altogether random.

The 'Rhapsody' has for speaker a man who, experiencing a 'vision of the street', soliloquizes in response to visual images. His is the consciousness, corresponding to that of the woman in the 'Preludes', which marshals the flickering images into a pattern of subjective *durée*. In the poem there is also, it is true, a clock-time structure (or, as Bergson would say, a 'spatial' structure), divided by the hours announced at the beginning of the strophes – 'Twelve o'clock', 'Half-past one', and the rest. This structure is spatial more particularly because the times are synchronized with the speaker's pauses at street-lamps. But as each lamp mutters an 'incantation' to direct his gaze toward new spatial images, these pass into his memory and unite with memories already there to make up subjective time where space is non-existent. The rhapsody of consciousness moves like a musical composition by introducing, abandoning, and returning to set themes scattered in time. Among its recurrent motifs are *irrationality* (the dissolving of 'divisions and precisions', the madman shaking the geranium, the lapping tongue of the cat, the automatic gesture of the child, the vacancy behind the child's eye, the instinctive reflex of the crab, the moon's loss of memory) and *decay* or *inanimation* (the dead geranium, the pin, the twisted driftwood and the rusty spring, the mechanical toy, the paper rose, the reek of airless places, the bed waiting for its occupant). Depressing images besiege the speaker's consciousness, for he cannot evade them: what is more dismaying, they constitute his soul, for he is similar to the woman in the third 'Prelude'. It is not surprising therefore, in view of the 'Preludes' and 'Prufrock' as well, that the 'Rhapsody' ends bleakly. The withdrawal of the speaker into his solitary room, as the last lamp shows him the way, furnishes no escape from a world within. 'Memory!' the lamp reminds him: 'You have the key'; and memory *is* the 'key' to the imprisoning life for which his repose shall prepare – not the memory of what the intelligence can learn, like the number on the door, but the memory of what arbitrarily exists, the unalterable reality. And so the pity that in the fourth 'Prelude' can be diverted to the slums and their creatures comes back to the poet, or to the mask through which he speaks, in the shape of terror for his own trapped human situation, and the knowledge pierces him with a 'last twist of the knife'. . . .

SOURCE: extracts from *T. S. Eliot's Poetry and Plays* (Chicago and Cambridge, 1956) pp. 21–3, 24–5.

Gertrude Patterson   'Preludes' and 'Rhapsody' (1971)

. . . We [should discern] the cinematic-type images of the first Prelude, where a succession of cinematic-type shots are 'worked up' into a complex montage. Whether or not Eliot was consciously using the technique of cinematic assemblage is perhaps doubtful, but it is perhaps not unreasonable to view the structure of 'Preludes' with this in mind since he makes allusion to the cinema in Prelude III. The woman is seen here, lying on her back, 'watching' the thousand sordid images of her soul as they flicker in cinematic-type projection on the ceiling overhead.[1] Applied to Prelude I we can see how the camera moves with the observer through the dirty littered streets at evening, picking out 'grimy scraps', bits of newspaper, showers beating on chimney-pots, broken blinds and a solitary cab horse, steaming and stamping. Eisenstein spoke of working up a montage from a series of varying shots by which, 'combining these monstrous incongruities, we newly collect the disintegrated event into one whole'.[2]

The first Prelude is fused into unity by the line: 'The burnt-out ends of smoky days'. Here we have two distinct images fused into one in typical Imagist manner. We see a dark evening. We see perhaps a cigarette end finished, burnt out. The two act together and the poetic image 'happens'.[3] The connotations of the fragments are clearly defined. Night is the burnt-out end of a day which smouldered, a 'smoky day' which never burst forth into living flame. A useless end to a useless day is suggested, and an emotion of despondency is worked up.

In the second Prelude the camera moves to day and picks out the 'masquerade' which people resume in a typical, 'smouldering', damp day. With the mention of the 'furnished rooms' – which connotatively suggest all the loneliness and dinginess not associated with 'home' – the camera moves inside and gives a 'close-up' of a Berthe-type creature of Charles-Louis Philippe's novel *Bubu de Montparnasse*,[4] alone, 'clasping' her yellow feet, and then, 'curling' the papers from her hair, after the 'masquerades' of the night before – presumably these are the images which 'flickered against the ceiling'. This woman knows the life of the 'inside' as the street comprehends the sordid life of outside. The images which she sees flickering overhead do not form any revitalizing vision. 'Clasping' and 'curling' are verbs which suggest no action. And here the camera comes to rest. So far we have fragments. In Prelude IV they act together and add up to form something like artistic 'empathy'. The soul of the street and the souls of the passers-by are fused into a single dominant image. Eliot, we remember, was concerned with the Bradleyan philosophy of 'finite centres' at this time, which stated that the private feeling is continuous with, even identical to, the objective material that has provoked it. Subject and object become one in a pure contemplation. Here we have artistic presentation of it. Vital art is opposed to abstract art, as Worringer puts it, where there is a 'feeling of separation in the face of outside nature'.[5] 'In empathizing . . . into another object, however, we *are* in the other object. We are delivered from our individual being as long as we are absorbed into an external object, an external form, with our inner urge to experience.'[6]

In Prelude IV, the previous Preludes are fused into a whole to become an instance of art. In this Prelude, associations of despondency, suffering, along with the grim impatience of the passers-by to assume the daily 'round', are identified with the soul of the suffering, 'trampled' street. Written after Eliot's return from Paris where he heard Bergson's lectures on art, it is not surprising that we have here an illustration of his idea – the idea of the later Imagists – that

many diverse images borrowed from very different orders of things may, by the convergence of their action, direct the consciousness to the precise point where there is a certain intuition to be seized. By choosing images as dissimilar as possible, we shall prevent any one of them from usurping the place of the intuition it is intended to call up.[7]

The intuition is obvious, but Eliot expresses it:

> I am moved by fancies that are curled
> Around these images, and cling:
> The notion of some infinitely gentle
> Infinitely suffering thing.

The emotion of pity in the face of suffering humanity is not allowed to dominate, however. This feeling may be the personal reaction of the poet, but to conclude the poem here would be to indicate a singleness of attitude which is not compatible with the impersonal, comprehensive art which Eliot advocates. Hence he goes on:

> Wipe your hand across your mouth, and laugh;
> The worlds revolve like ancient women
> Gathering fuel in vacant lots.

Here we have two clear-cut reactions to the same scene, two ways that the reader might look at it. The emotion which the poem evokes is therefore comprehensive and not single. The end of the poem thus completes a circle. The poet has circled an object, a single scene of degradation and misery, and 'worked up' a comprehensive emotion in the reader from it.

Gertrude Stein perhaps sums up the structure of the poem best. She sees that art must 'live in the actual present' and describes all modern art as a cinematic 'series production'. In describing her own work, she describes Eliot's: 'I was doing, what the cinema was doing, I was making a continuous succession of the statement of what that person was until I had not many things but one thing.'[8] The poem is an excellent example of how a new art-emotion is worked up from a series of images articulating the simple, undramatic emotion of disgust, an 'ordinary' emotion which the poet experiences, or in the case of Prelude III – where Grover Smith points out an obvious source in a passage from Charles-Louis Philippe's novel *Bubu de Montparnasse* – an objective equivalent of it which he has found. The group assembled forms a connotative structure. If we applied the mathematical formula to it: $I + II + III = IV$. The comprehensive art-emotion of Prelude IV is worked up from the individual emotions of the first three.

'Rhapsody on a Windy Night', belonging to the same period as 'Preludes', has been variously described as a 'sick version of life'[9] or, in Maxwell's terms, a poem which 'does not mean "anything"', anything more, that is, than 'the translation of a mood': 'a conscious attempt to do in English what the symbolists had done in French to mirror a mood by a selection of images which have in common subservience to that mood, and hence act as symbols for it'.[10] Grover Smith speaks in more specific terms of its connotational structure whereby

the dissolution of orderly thought into an irrational, almost surrealistic collage of discontinuous mental impressions obeys the laws of instinctive consciousness according to Bergson. Mingling as fluid perceptions, kaleidoscopic images pour into memory, the organ of time, the 'floors' of which break down to enable their total synthesis. This dreamlike process, the quintessence of the non-intellectual, works by free association rather than by logic.[11]

The analogy which Grover Smith makes to painting is perhaps a more useful one to examine than the musical, rhapsodic structure which he himself goes on to describe in his examination of the poem. 'Free association' was the battle-cry of the Collage group of painters, working at the same time as Eliot was writing 'Rhapsody'. These painters introduced into the texture of their 'painting', objects and materials which they found in the world of their immediate experience, rather than use the 'pure' colours of more traditionalist media. Found objects were presented in the Collage structure in the recognisable and concrete form in which the artist found them, retaining 'marks of their previous form and history':

When paper is soiled or lacerated, when cloth is worn, stained, or torn, when wood is split, weathered, or patterned with peeling coats of paint, when metal is bent or rusted, they gain connotations which unmarked materials lack. More specific associations are denoted when an object can be identified as the sleeve of a shirt, a dinner fork. . . . In both situations meaning and material merge.[12]

Perspective is abandoned in this type of art and its 'communication' depends on the imaginative sensibility of the spectator, that is, on his ability to perceive the same areas of connotation as those which the found objects held for the artist. The success of these structures demanded from the artist the task of defining these connotations . . ..

What we are presented with in 'Rhapsody on a Windy Night' is the observer's (the 'I' of the poem) immediate experience of the real world, the immediacy of which is emphasized by a clock-time progression from midnight until four o'clock. Juxtaposed with it is the world of the past, a Bergsonian *durée*, a subjective time, measured out here by street lamps which illuminate visually the 'memories' which are the assembled subconscious 'self' of the observer. Kristian Smidt in *Poetry and Belief in the Work of T. S. Eliot* quotes Bergson's own definition of *durée* from 'Essai sur les données immédiates':

La durée toute pure est la forme que prend la succession de nos états de conscience quand notre moi se laisse vivre, quand il s'abstient d'établir une séparation entre l'état présent et les états antérieurs. . . il suffit qu'en se rappelant ces états il ne les juxtapose à l'état actuel comme un point à un autre point, mais les organise avec lui, comme il arrive quand nous nous rappelons, fondues pour ainsi dire ensemble, les notes d'une mélodie.[13]

The remembered things of this poem are as real as the immediate things, and are pressed into the foreground, so that what we are confronted with is a perspective-less collage structure. Writing of Picasso and Braque, Seitz says: 'The objects they depicted no longer diminished in size or disappeared in light and atmosphere. Immediate and tangible, their subjects were pressed forward by the advancing rear wall of the picture, so that cubism became an art of the close-up, that dealt with what was, literally as well as figuratively, "close at hand".'[14]

This simultaneous existence of past and present becomes an increasingly important element in Eliot's poetry. Its implications are obvious here: Eliot does away with 'perspective' in this poem, in the sense that for the observer past and present coexist. Both worlds present equally abhorrent, equally useless images of life. Hence Rosenthal can say of the poem: 'we cannot ignore the possibility. . . that the night-time world may be the real world'.[15]

A passage from Conrad's 'Heart of Darkness' provides an interesting background against which we may view the connotations of the fragments of the poem. It is the passage where Marlowe sits brooding in the darkness falling over the Thames and remembers that his experiences with Kurtz are like a dream: 'To him the meaning of an episode was not inside, like a kernel, but outside, enveloping the tale which brought it out only as a glow brings out a haze, in the likeness of those misty haloes that sometimes are made visible by the spectral illumination of moonshine.'[16] When we remember how the wilderness whispered things to Kurtz in 'the heart of darkness' and that Marlowe listened to drums beating in the night, we may well here have found one possible source of 'Rhapsody'. In Eliot's poem too, the moonlight and the misty haloes of the lamplight throw up images and objects from the world of memory, which likewise illuminate the present:

> Every street lamp that I pass
> Beats like a fatalistic drum,
> And through the spaces of the dark
> Midnight shakes the memory
> As a madman shakes a dead geranium.

Each image in this structure is precise and its connotations clearly fixed. Only the word 'memory' is released with its full connotations, and it is the object of the poem to define the specific associations which it has for the observer. From the first fragment, memory is suggested as a storehouse. Genesius Jones gives us the full connotations of this image:

Platonic speculation on memory as a sort of broken bridge between the soul and the divine Ideas was kept alive throughout the Hellenic world by the neo-Platonists, and realised in a Christian context by St. Augustine. From his time Christian thinkers saw the memory as an image in the human soul of the creative *Ars Aeterna* in the Trinity. . . . But memory has not been regarded merely as a still storehouse. From the time of Plato onwards, this storehouse has presented a scene of intense activity as its contents were pressed into service by the mind of man. Medieval thinkers, especially Hugo of St. Victor and St. Bonaventure saw it as a medium where the *umbra, vestigia, imagines* and *similitudines* of the Divinity were to be sought as the soul led the world of its apprehending back to God.[17]

The floors of this storehouse dissolve and, from the third fragment, we see the 'objects' which pour out: 'a crowd of twisted things', 'a twisted branch', 'a broken spring' – rusty, useless, lifeless objects. The associations of these objects are juxtaposed with those of the objects from the immediately perceived world, experienced in the image of the torn, stained dress of the woman, whose eye is also twisted. The two sets of images share the connotations which useless, lifeless, 'junkyard' objects present.

The nausea which the observer senses in the immediate world is presented in the quick action-image of the cat, lapping up 'rancid butter' – a useless gesture, contrasted with the automatic grabbing action of a child at a toy, connotatively useless, since it has been discarded and runs along the quay. 'Memory' presents a similar picture, now of a crab clutching the end of a lifeless stick; but a crab will clutch at anything, so this too is a futile gesture. The common associations of present and past experience are obvious. Clearly, 'memory' in this poem only serves to make the present more sordid, more meaningless; this is the only 'illumination' which it can offer: it can urge the observer to no meaningful activity since its contents are useless to him.

The attention of the observer is drawn to the moon, queen of the night world, whose light *could* illuminate the uselessness of the world, and inspire the observer to use his memory in more useful ways. But the moon who sees everything has also lost her faculty for remembering better things. She is identified with a woman 'twisting a paper rose' – another futile gesture. The part she plays in the kingdom of the night is therefore a passive, indifferent one: 'La lune ne garde aucune rancune'.

Memory throws up further images, now of dry geraniums – flowers which we associate with city window boxes, which here suggest the neglect they have suffered in the hands of city dwellers – and nauseating 'female smells', 'cigarettes in corridors'. It is obvious that 'memory' has no Platonic associations in this poem.

And so the observer is led 'home'. His only useful memory is the number on his door. The door is opened and a small ring of light is cast on the stairway, illuminating the bed where sleep will prepare the observer for 'life'. But if past memories are of useless things and the present is equally sordid, life ahead has little potential. Hence the irony of the last line: 'The last twist of the knife'.

The poem, therefore, as we can see, is not an exercise in completely 'free' association. The connotations of

> Midnight shakes the memory
> As a madman shakes a dead geranium

are painfully clear. The 'memory' is simply a still storehouse for sordid impressions. The faculty of remembering is a useless one.

Graham Hough has perhaps been harsh in attacking Eliot for his lack of 'logical' progression. In his view, 'an order of emotions' such as we have in these poems, is only possible in short lyrics. He points out that 'classical poetic theory' – and it is with this he points out that Eliot would identify himself – 'was not deduced from brief lyrics'. He goes on:

One does not insist on Aristotelian rigour of construction; but even in the looser forms the sense of a syntax of events of a syntax of thoughts is preserved; and criticism insisted on it. Emotions are not capable of such a syntax. A pattern can be made of them, by simple juxtaposition, but it will hardly be an integrated pattern, unless there runs through it the thread of narrative or logic.[18]

One could not say that the juxtaposition of the poems I have dealt with so far is simple. Nevertheless, I have attempted to point out that the juxtaposing of fragments is a procedure capable of giving unity to a connotative structure. The emotions juxtaposed in 'Rhapsody' are simple, however, in that they illustrate a consistent disgust at the life of the city. Grover Smith has pointed out that Eliot's poetry goes on to deal with more complex emotions: 'Squalor itself was not his bane; he did not aspire to found a "junkyard" school of poetry. What perturbed him was the helplessness of sensitivity and idealism against matter-of-factness.'[19] It is true that from 'Rhapsody' onwards, the poetry presents a conflict of emotions, where 'Preludes' and 'Rhapsody' each articulated a 'sick' vision of life. The poet rendered this vision artistically comprehensive, however, by providing, in the case of 'Preludes' for example, two ways for the reader to view the sordid aspects of life which it presented. In 'Rhapsody' the same sick vision is made comprehensive, by being illuminated from the past as well as being contemplated in the present. Whatever way it is viewed, however, the emotions which the individual parts of both these poems represent are simple, in that they indicate no conflict in the emotions of the 'I' of either poem. The poems which follow, however, present a struggle between conflicting emotions and for this reason mark an advance in comprehensiveness and dramatic technique. These emotional conflicts are now given names, which set the poems at a greater distance from the poet than the 'I' of 'Preludes' and 'Rhapsody'. Prufrock, the Lady, Sweeney and Gerontion are the recognizable concrete forms in which emotions, the subject matter of the poems, are embodied. These emotions will therefore be expressed most accurately when the 'persona' is shown as realistically as possible.

I have already mentioned Eliot's belief that even lyric poetry involves a 'praxis' of the Aristotelian theory and quoted the passage from the *Poetics* which illustrates what Aristotle meant by it: 'All human happiness or misery takes the form of action; the end for which we live is a certain kind of activity, not a quality. Character gives us qualities, but it is in our actions – what we do – that we are happy or the reverse.' The same thought is echoed by G. T. Wright who gives an interesting historical interpretation of the 'personae' of modern poetry in general, in *The Poet in the Poem*. In his introductory remarks, Wright sums up what I believe the intention of Eliot is, in his use of dramatic personae to give shape and order to the conflict of emotions which he wishes to present: 'the person *is* what he *does*; his actions define him. But as soon as we begin to interpret those actions, we begin to lose our objectivity in observing him'.[20] A dramatic poet, Eliot wrote, must 'take genuine and substantial human emotions, such emotions as observations can confirm, typical emotions, and give them artistic form'.[21]

This concern for accuracy in the presentation of dramatic characters has its background in twentieth-century philosophy. In Bergson's terms, similar to the notion of personality articulated by Bradley, we cannot 'think' of ourselves, we can only *live*; hence our being can only be found amidst the shifting currents of our most immediate experience. We cannot even conceive of ourselves as having a single clear identity; when we do, we are translating our experiences into logical reconstructions of them, or in other words, transposing the data of experience into concepts that are extraneous to the data themselves. Hence Eliot presents emotions in personae most concretely and accurately, by confining his descriptions of them to perceived, significant acts, illustrating Pound's remarks: 'I catch the character I happen to be interested in at the moment he interests me, usually a moment of song, self-analysis, or sudden understanding or revelation'.

SOURCE: extract from *T. S. Eliot: Poems in the Making* (Manchester, 1971) pp. 94–103.

NOTES

1. It is interesting to note that 'Prufrock' also contains a similar allusion:

It is impossible to say just what I mean!
But as if a magic lantern threw the nerves in patterns on screen. . . .

2. Wylie Sypher, *Rococo to Cubism in Art and Literature* (1960) p. 283.
3. Herbert Read, *The True Voice of Feeling* (1953) p. 115.
4. See J. Grover Smith, *T. S. Eliot's Poetry and Plays* (1956) pp. 20–1.
5. See Herbert Read, *The Philosophy of Modern Art* (1951) p. 218.
6. F. Worringer, *Abstraction and Empathy* (1953) p. 24.
7. Henri Bergson, *Introduction to Metaphysics*; quoted in William Seitz, *The Art of Assemblage* (New York, 1961) p. 83.
8. Quoted in Sypher, *Rococo to Cubism*, p. 267.
9. M. L. Rosenthal, *The Modern Poets* (1960) p. 7.
10. D. E. S. Maxwell, *The Poetry of T. S. Eliot* (1952) pp. 65–6.
11. Grover Smith, *T. S. Eliot's Poetry and Plays* [See preceding extract in this Casebook – Ed.].
12. Seitz, *The Art of Assemblage*, pp. 17, 84–5.
13. Kristian Smidt, *Poetry and Belief in the Work of T. S. Eliot* (1961) p. 163.
14. Seitz, *The Art of Assemblage*, p. 22.
15. Rosenthal, *The Modern Poets*, p. 7.

16. Quoted in Wylie Sypher, *Loss of Self in Modern Literature and Art*, 1964 edition, pp. 60–1.

17. Genesius Jones, *Approach to the Purpose: a Study of the Poetry of T. S. Eliot* (1964) pp. 169–70.

18. Graham Hough, *Image and Experience* (1960) p. 18.

19. Grover Smith, *T. S. Eliot's Poetry and Plays*, p. 29.

20. G. T. Wright, *The Poet in the Poem* (1960) p. 1.

21. T. S. Eliot, 'Rhetoric and Poetic Drama', *Selected Essays* (1934) p. 41.

C. K. Stead 'Gerontion' (1964)

. . . In 1919 Eliot's brief period as a conscious manipulator of elegant satiric verse ended with the writing of 'Gerontion'. 'Gerontion', like 'Prufrock', is an expression of something which has its genesis at a deeper level than that of the conscious will – and here, for the first time, the 'psychic material', 'the octopus or angel with which the poet struggles', takes on the dark stain of some intense suffering which carries over into *The Waste Land*. The gentle youthful aspirations of 'Prufrock' have passed through fulfilment into some unimagined horror in which all desire that issues in action is seen as destructive. In the passionate pursuit of some essential quality – beauty, or truth, or merely 'life' itself – beauty turns to terror and passion destroys itself:

> I that was near your heart was removed therefrom
> To lose beauty in terror, terror in inquisition.
> I have lost my passion. . . .

Whatever is attained in the pursuit, and possessed, loses the quality which encouraged the pursuer – 'Since what is kept must be adulterated'.

The 'house' of which Gerontion speaks seems variously his own (rented) house, turned brothel; his body, the decaying house in which his soul is prostituted; and the body of a woman turned prostitute.

> Think at last
> We have not reached conclusion, when I
> Stiffen in a rented house.

Here 'stiffen', like some Elizabethan puns on 'die', compresses sexual intercourse and death into a single corruption. Again in the lines

> And an old man driven by the Trades
> To a sleepy corner

'Trades' suggests more than the winds which blow incessantly through the poem. The word seems to carry something of the meaning it has in *Measure for Measure*,[1] which provides the poem's epigraph:

> How would you live, Pompey? by being a bawd?
> What do you think of the trade Pompey? is it a lawful trade?

The wind is an image of time. It is the consciousness of time (History) and hence of death that drives us ('driven by the Trades') towards sexual experience which is another kind of death ('a sleepy corner'). So all who are alive are old like Gerontion, close to death; 'stiffen in a rented house'. Everything must be borne away on the wind –

> Beyond the circuit of the shuddering bear
> In fractured atoms.

Finally the poem leaves us only the image of the Gull – innocence, imagination, spirit – fighting its battle with time ('against the wind'), both raped ('running on the Horn') and seduced ('the Gulf claims'):

> Gull against the wind, in the windy straits
> Of Belle Isle, or running on the Horn,
> White feathers in the snow, the Gulf claims,
> And an old man driven by the Trades
> To a sleepy corner.

Some such feeling as I have outlined here seems to lie behind 'Gerontion', but Eliot, I think, fails to project it into a coherent poem. Only a pattern imposed by a critic willing to do some of the poet's structural work for him will give the poem an appearance of completeness. The mixture of images from Eliot's current reading, together with what seem to be echoes of contemporary events, form a rich and varied condensation of experience which fails in this case to

hold together as a coherent poem. 'Gerontion' has been found by
various critics to contain echoes from Henry Adams's *Education*, H. C.
Benson's *Edward Fitzgerald*, Lancelot Andrews's *Sermons*, Joyce's *Ulysses*,
Bussy D'Ambois, *Measure for Measure*, and *The Changeling*. No doubt there
are other sources yet undiscovered. Hugh Kenner suggests further that
the 'wilderness of mirrors' and History's 'contrived corridors' have their
genesis in news of Versailles and the Polish Corridor. And I add a
suggestion: that the phrase 'fractured atoms' would not have occurred
to Eliot a year earlier – since it was June 1919, at the time of the
Versailles conference, that the first splitting of the atom (by Ernest
Rutherford) was announced. More significant, of course, if such source
hunting were important, would be phrases which could be found to
establish direct links with events in the poet's private life. In 'Gerontion'
Eliot fulfils his own description of the poet as a man in whom, by a
strange chemical process, 'disparate experiences . . . are always forming new wholes'. But the poem shows, I think, that the sorting out of
these private experiences is no aid to our understanding. The concern of
criticism is not these experiences, but the emotional unity and depth of
the 'new whole'. In 'Gerontion' coherence is not fully achieved.

Eliot perhaps felt this incompleteness himself. The writing of
'Gerontion' seems to have precipitated a number of ideas in his three
1919 essays . . ., one of which contains the theory of the 'objective
correlative'. *Hamlet*, like the sonnets, he writes in his essay, 'is full of
some stuff the author could not drag to light, contemplate, or
manipulate into art.' The 'stuff' which fails to find expressive form is
described as 'intense feeling, ecstatic or terrible, without an object or
exceeding its object'; and Eliot adds that such a feeling 'is something
which every person of sensibility has known'. We may take it, then, that
he is speaking of his own experience, and it is likely, I think, that such a
feeling as this failed to find a satisfactory 'correlative' in the persona of
Gerontion. Eliot's own realization of this failure would account for the
attempted self-explanation of the concluding lines of the poem –

> Tenants of a house,
> Thoughts of a dry brain in a dry season

which stand out as an obvious and unsatisfactory attempt to cast order
and meaning back over the whole poem.

SOURCE: extract from *The New Poetic* (1964) pp. 157–60.

NOTE

1. Just as 'kept' and 'adulterated' in the line quoted above suggests perhaps the shadowy figure of a 'kept' woman and an 'adultress'.

John Crowe Ransom 'Gerontion' (1966)

When Mr Eliot's death was announced, I think the news did not wholly discomfit us on his physical account. It was our understanding that he had been seriously ill, and suffering pain. How natural and merciful that his mortal turn had come; and we knew as well as he that his literary testament was finished and secure. Still we were greatly moved. We had now acquired a responsibility which it would be difficult to discharge. We must re-read him, and think a long time about his achievement, and about how the parts cumulated into a whole; thinking as precisely as we could possibly think about something intangible, in order to say what he had meant to English letters. His writings had already been committed to the public domain, but suddenly we had become the executors who must appraise the estate.

A special burden rested upon me, from which I am sure the other tributaries in this collection of essays have been exempted. Twice only have I written pieces about Eliot, and now I have to make two recantations. The first time I scolded him for *The Waste Land*, with what I took to be its academic trick of recondite allusions on the one hand, and on the other hand its want of a firm and consistent prosody, such as I seemed to require. I was mistaken about the allusions. It turned out quickly, and increasingly, that they meant a great deal to the members of a very important public. These were the remarkably bright young scholars and critics who aspired in that age to a complete learning, including the precise identification of original texts which might be referred to, even if ever so slightly. They were as tough-minded as they were competent, and when they succeeded they were elated like professional sportsmen over their triumphs. But they were most challenged when Eliot gave them sly literary allusions from which some religious or moral faith depended, and over which hovered the sense of a secret passage from Eliot's mind to theirs. Eliot was always a religious poet, though he never propounded the dogmas of his faith, which evidently was rather eclectic; it could be Hebraic, or Christian, or Greek, or even Oriental. But those sturdy people who studied his *Waste Land* felt the passion which he had put into the transaction. They must have had a feeling of having been starved of something or other in the poverty of their intellectual interests, and now of knowing that what they had missed was the religious sense in which they had been reared. (I am afraid it becomes less and less in the rearing of our successive modern generations.) Their vague uneasiness in their occupation became a good plain nostalgia when they saw what it had meant. Eliot gave back their old world to them. It was a beautiful predicament, and repeated many times.

As to the prosody, it took me rather longer to repent. But by the time when the *Four Quartets* was finished, I had come to think that, of all the pioneers who had looked for a suitable modern prosody, Eliot was the best. He favoured a profusion of new rhythms replacing the steady old rhythms, which seemed worn to death; or keeping more or less the iambic pentameters of the blank verse he needed by 'counterpointing' them with smaller cross-rhythms. Somebody, by precept and example, had to bring into the music of poetry the grace and freedom which had arrived in the art of pure music many years before. Eliot was the man.

My other unfortunate estimate of Eliot came when I wrote a harsh review of *Murder in the Cathedral*. I read the play at one sitting, and wrote my piece the next day at another sitting. The trouble was that in that period I was studying my Milton, and had a special liking for *Samson Agonistes* over all his other works. The *Murder* like the *Samson* was in the Greek form of drama, but it seemed to me that the *Murder* was always running wild, and rejecting its form. I disliked the Interlude containing the Becket sermon, the language of the poor old women employed in the Chorus, and especially the speeches of the silly young royalists who tried to justify themselves for murdering an archbishop. But I was able after a little while to be reasonable, and to reflect that the form of drama is subject to changes as soon as a new and able dramatist wants it so, and that as a rule the new wine tastes better to his own public than the old.

I have chosen to write something about 'Gerontion', a very important poem in the Eliot canon; and besides that, the particular poem in which Eliot first worked out to his own satisfaction that brisk prosody which was to be his staple thereafter. Allen Tate wrote approving my choice, and saying that he liked this poem better than any of Eliot's except the *Quartets*. It is he that should be writing up my topic; but his job of collecting and editing all these essays was prior, and prohibitive.

The man of the poem in this dramatic monologue is in that final stage of human misery when there is nothing to do but brood over what little remains of a life that came rather early to have no principle of direction except its worldly interests; and to wish and wait for death, which is imminent, as its perfect ending. The poet does not name him as Geron, who is any old man, but as Gerontion, a little old man, shrunken in body and soul. But we must say emphatically, not in the force of his intellect. When characters are obliged by their poet to speak for themselves, they have to be supplied with a suitable poetry, and a great poet may bestow upon an important character a poetic immortality. Gerontion is still in complete possession of intelligence and wit, but the wit is as acrid as the substance, and the whole of the monologue is as magnificent as it is tragic.

But I must digress for a few minutes. Is there any critic who tries to see this poet whole, yet never looks away from the particular poem in question to the analogies and differences that exist in the other poems? Here we are reminded inevitably of the poem about Prufrock, five years earlier. He and Gerontion are two of the living dead who abound in Eliot's verse, especially in *The Waste Land*. Prufrock is of middling age, though grown too lean, and balding; perhaps a rather charming man and still an eligible bachelor; but fatally divided between his amours and his morals. He is given to citing Scripture, at least to his better self, his conscience or Superego to whom his words are spoken; and surely is acquainted with the letter of Paul to the Church at Corinth, where in the seventh chapter Paul proposes a way of life whereby married partners may keep their chastity, then adds a few words to help the unmarried and the widows: 'But if they cannot contain, let them marry; for it is better to marry than to burn.' And indeed it may seem that Prufrock has found his woman; if it is really she who is twice referred to as 'one', among the women in the drawing-room about whom with some contempt he makes the refrain,

> In the room the women come and go
> Talking of Michelangelo.

How could they have had any inkling of that glory which Michelangelo had put into his marbles and his paintings? And a more pointed question: Was there in the special woman's head any possible cranny into which the sense of divinity could find an entry?

His name is Prufrock, and to the women that sounds like the name of a man both 'prudish' and 'preachy'. He may have looked the part, and perhaps he has incautiously spoken once or twice in that character, this being the real reason they look upon him as a laughing-stock. It makes him extremely self-conscious in their presence. Perhaps Prufrock is the most sensitive and self-depreciating of all dramatic heroes. He cannot bring himself to speak up for Christ; so far from being an intellectual that he does not know how, and so afraid that he will not try. He says he is no prophet like John the Baptist, 'Though I have seen my head (grown slightly bald) brought in upon a platter.' It might have been easier to say he had walked the narrow streets of the poor quarter,

> And watched the smoke that rises from the pipes
> Of lonely men in shirt-sleeves, leaning out of windows

which would have been a Christian's way of raising the social issue. Here is the latest and longest of these key passages:

> And would it have been worth it, after all,
> After the cups, the marmalade, the tea,
> Among the porcelain, among some talk of you and me,
> Would it have been worth while,
> To have bitten off the matter with a smile,
> To have squeezed the universe into a ball
> To roll it towards some overwhelming question,
> To say: 'I am Lazarus, come from the dead,
> Come back to tell you all, I shall tell you all' –
> If one, settling a pillow by her head,
>   Should say: 'That is not what I meant at all.
>   That is not it, at all.'

I have belaboured the poem to this length because I think too many critics who are generally admirable have not seen it in a very clear perspective. They may have been deceived by its full title: 'The Love Song of J. Alfred Prufrock'. And Eliot may have gleefully expected them to be. At one period I always knew a few of my students would write in their examination papers something like this: 'The poem therefore means to say that Prufrock was too cowardly to pop the question to his lady.' Critics whom they had read had said as much, with more vocabulary and circumstance. And certainly that question is in Prufrock's mind. But another question has to come first: How does she feel about religion? If he asked it, and she was displeased with him for asking it, he would be displeased with her for not answering it, and they could reject each other simultaneously.

Prufrock's indecision is finally decisive; he returns to his mermaids, and that is the moral end of him. We are not obliged to see the physical end of him, but the moral crisis has been fully resolved, and it is downhill for him all the rest of his life. The pleasures of the body, however, have a high rating in most societies, as they should, and at the moment of his final surrender the actuaries could probably read off their tables for him a generous 'life-expectancy'. We must define the dramatic mode of this poem as tragi-comedy. But 'Gerontion' is pure tragedy.

We have been given to know that Eliot intended the 'Gerontion' of 1920 to be part of *The Waste Land* of 1922, which was already in preparation, and that Pound dissuaded him. But I cannot remember knowing Pound's objection. Eliot would have told him of his plan to write the book in the form of a poetic symphony having five movements; and Pound was by long odds the most knowledgeable adviser to poets that Eliot could have found. May not Pound have told him that 'Gerontion' was already a sort of symphony having five movements, or at least the perfect miniature of one; and that Eliot could not reduce a symphony of five movements to a single movement in another symphony? It happens that 'Gerontion' is about the length of the average of the five movements in *Waste Land*; and that the second of the movements of 'Gerontion' has three parts, though they are perfectly consecutive, and only the third part ends with a period stop. But all its five movements are as distinct from one another as the five in *Waste Land*, and the six movements in *Ash Wednesday*, and the five movements in *Four Quartets*. I think it is generally agreed that in music proper the particular symphonic form is subject to the composer's will; and why may we not extend the same privilege to the poet? It is true that the movements in *Waste Land* and *Ash Wednesday* and *Quartets* are announced by title at the top, or by Roman numerals, or by both. But to deny 'Gerontion' because it does not exercise that privilege would be pettifogging; we may insert our own numerals in our copies. If

nevertheless 'Gerontion' is probably the littlest symphony ever published, in pure music or in poetry, it becomes all the more prodigious. It
has everywhere in it all the wealth of detail and imagery that we could
ask, but compacted; and I have come to think that nothing else in Eliot
fills us with such an awe of his power.

[1]

Here I am, an old man in a dry month,
o   – –   o   –   –   o o –   –   /

Being read to by a boy, waiting for rain.
o o   –   o o o –   – o   o   – /

I was neither at the hot gates
o o   –   o o o   – –

Nor fought in the warm rain
o   –   o o   –   – /

Nor knee deep in the salt marsh, heaving a cutlass,
o   –   –   o o   –   –   / – o o – o

Bitten by flies, fought.
– o   o – / –   /

My house is a decayed house,
–   –   o o o   –   – /

And the jew squats on the window sill, the owner,
o   o –   –   o o – o   – / o   – o/

Spawned in some estaminet of Antwerp,
–   o –   o   – o – / o – o /

Blistered in Brussels, patched and peeled in London.
– o   o – o   –   o   –   / o – o /

The goat coughs at night in the field overhead;
o   –   –   o – / o o – oo – /

Rocks, moss, stonecrop, iron, merds.
–   –   – o   –   – /

The woman keeps the kitchen, makes tea,
o   – o –   o – o / –   –

Sneezes at evening, poking the peevish gutter.
–   o o – o   – o o – o / – o /

                                    I an old man,
                                    o o   – –

A dull head among windy spaces.
o –   –   oo   –   o – o/

This movement stands in sixteen lines, and is very slightly longer than the average of the five. Nine of the lines could be considered pentameters: Lines 1-2 and 8 14. But rarely does the old iambic rhythm hold up; that rule has been discarded; in the interest of fresher and more spontaneous rhythms for the modern ear. Can we imagine a symphonic poem whose rhythms are otherwise? The long lines mean mostly to be broken up into rhythms corresponding to their phrase-units. This movement starts by identifying the man, and the man's age and helplessness, then the man's house, and household, and landscape. The whole movement gives us Gerontion exactly as he is, and leaves it to the later movements to identify his intentions.

Let us look closely at a sufficient number of passages both as to their substance and as to their rhythms. Lines 1-2 are a model of introduction, brief without a wasted word or syllable. The rhythm which appears three times in line 1 ends with a spondee (containing two adjacent stresses) preceded by one or two unstressed syllables which I shall call unstresses. Line 2 has two rhythms which match sufficiently, each showing two stresses of which one is final, and a swarm of unstresses to be distributed. But in lines 3-6 the fireworks begin. Lines 3 and 4 are phrases in rhythms which match each other almost precisely; there are three stresses, of which the concluding two make a spondee, with unstresses preceding the first stress and the final spondee. In both lines the theme is the valour of soldiers in combat; it is repeated in line 5 by another pair of two-stress rhythms; and again, beginning towards the close of line 5 and continuing into line 6, by a still fiercer pair of two-stress rhythms in which the first word has one stress and the last word has the other. But it could hardly have been expected that Gerontion would take such an honest care as, at the very beginnings of the first three lines, to deny that such valour had ever been his own. The four lines end with the powerful monosyllable 'fought'. It stands independent of any rhythmic pattern, but is a heavy and important word that refers back to the whole passage about soldiery, like a final chord of music in the right key that is held for a moment after a rhythmic passage.

In line 7 we have another introduction which concerns Gerontion's house and uses a pair of rhythms which show again the spondaic structure. Then we pass to the household, and it appears that the owner of the house is himself a resident, like Gerontion who rents it. He is described by his tenant with lordly contempt in three lines which rival for poetic supremacy lines 4-6. But Gerontion is a lord of language, like

Virgil in Tennyson's poem, and prepared to turn on his full power even when he speaks evil. The tone-quality is very crisp and beautiful, and the rhythms especially decisive. Without dwelling unnecessarily upon them – they are marked if the reader wants to consult my text – I wish to notice what happens rhythmically if my readers will agree with me about the status of those three phrases which stand at the ends of lines 8–10. They read respectively: 'the owner', 'of Antwerp', and 'in London'. The first of these phrases is isolated completely by the final punctuation mark and also the one which preceded it; the others have punctuation after them but not before. But why not treat them all as unnecessary excrescences upon the preceding rhythms, language-wise, perfectly agreeing with each other rhythmically? By these considerations I felt entitled to think of the three rhythms as echoing one another and composing a valid rhythm, though widely separated.

Two other remarks may be made about the prosody of Movement I. First, there is the memorable line 12, which we might have said was a pentameter making a single rhythm of five bare monosyllables. But I have taken the extra syllable of the third one as important because of its addition of an unstress, and as perhaps our cue to look closely and see if we may not suppose a strong caesura at that point, dividing the pentameter into a pretty trimeter and a crushing dimeter. The words 'Rocks, moss, stonecrop' make just such a series of detail as Wordsworth might have employed lovingly in one of his listings of the features of a fair landscape. But the landscape in question is only 'the field overhead', where the goat ranges; and the dimeter gives it quite another status. We may take the 'iron' to mean the scrap-iron of used-up metal gadgets tossed from the passing cars, and composing not a landscape but a litter; and merds are merds. There could not be terms terser and more euphemistic at the same time, but they have their savagery.

Finally we have to concern ourselves with that last sentence of the movement, lines 15–16. It is set away and Southeast from the body of the movement, but it recapitulates the theme in terms and rhythms somewhat like the first two lines. We may call it a coda, as according to the style of symphony.

But perhaps now we are entitled to a sort of inkling of what this symphonic poem is going to mean to our old castaway, whose power of poetry is his only possession.

The soft reader, because he is a sentimentalist, may not care much for this movement. It has a very homely theme, upon which it expends very little latinity, and has for its biggest word the French *estaminet*. But the poetry seems to be redeemed at least twice by gorgeous passages, in lines 3–6 and 8–10. How melancholy it may appear that the heroic martial strain of the first passage should be repudiated three times, and at the very beginning of the lines, as having nothing to do with his own history. And it must be equally sad that he should compose so grand a passage as the second one about an unsavoury person. But we must concede them, and be glad of them. Gerontion knows that valour always deserves the grand style though he has not personally experienced it; and as to the disreputable theme of the second passage he knows that in proportion to its own excess it too must be treated extravagantly.

Must we not subscribe to Kant's definition of the famous pleasure which is unique in poetry, and other arts? Aristotle must have been the first theorist who proposed this association, but apparently it is going to last for all the eternity which poetry may expect. Kant did not reject it, but he defined it, by means of certain exclusions which did not contain it; and his definition-by-exclusion satisfied Hegel, who commended it as the first rational word that had been spoken in aesthetics. Kant was bold enough to say that the pleasure of poetry (and of every other art) did not consist in the pleasures of the greedy body, nor the pleasure of the understanding (or science) when it succeeded in its purpose whether as theory or as utility, nor even in the noble pleasure of a good conscience; and capped all these exclusions by remarking that it did not matter to poetry whether the world it set up had real existence or was only imaginary. Let us keep Kant's doctrine in mind throughout 'Gerontion', to see what the outcome will be. But not without knowing well that Eliot was accomplished in philosophy, and would have agreed with this Kantianism.

[II]

Signs are taken for wonders. 'We would see a sign!'
–   o   – o o   – o / o o   – o – /

The word within a word, unable to speak a word,
o   –   o   – o –   o – o o –   o – /

Swaddled with darkness. In the juvescence of the year
–   o   o   – o / o o o   – o o o – /

Came Christ the tiger
o   –   o –o /

In depraved May, dogwood and chestnut, flowering judas,
o o –   –   – o   o – o – oo   – o /

To be eaten, to be divided, to be drunk
o o – o o o o –o   o o –

Among whispers; by Mr Silvero
o o   –   o / o – o – o

With caressing hands, at Limoges
o   o – o   –   / o o –   /

Who walked all night in the next room;
o   –   – – o o   –   – /

By Hakagawa, bowing among the Titians;
o – o – o / – o o –   o – o /

By Madame de Tornquist, in the dark room
o o –   o –   – / o o –   – /

Shifting the candles; Fraulein von Kulp
– o   o – o / – o o –

Who turned in the hall, one hand on the door.
o   –   o o – / – – o o – /

    Vacant shuttles
    – o – o

Weave the wind. I have no gh sts,
–   o – / o o   – –   /

An old man in a draughty house
o – – o o –   o –

Under a windy knob.
– o o – o – /

The second movement may be regarded as the most lyrical of the five. Musically, the quick two-stress rhythms are preponderant, numbering twenty-five by my count; and the range in the substance of these combinations is wide, so that sometimes we have trouble finding it, though at least we are always assured that it will be fresh and vivid. Do such properties not testify to the lyrical mode; and in the strictest sense, which means that the poem is like the song which the Greek poets sang to the rhythms of the plucked strings of the lyre?

Let us think of the poet in the act of composing such a movement. His head is full of many important ideas which have to find their images, and often the first image that comes is so bold that he refuses to change it, expecting us to grasp it if we can. Probably words came quickly and easily in this movement, and did not have to be so laboured as we imagine the first movement to have been.

The introduction to this movement requires four lines which come in the fourth to a climax of the first order: 'Came Christ the tiger'; the passage is left open without punctuation for immediate development in the second part and half of the third. And as to the three lines of preparation for it, Gerontion would have been well educated in religious as well as secular learning, and would have been acquainted with Bishop Lancelot Andrewes's sermon about the *infans*, the infant Christ who was a Word that could not speak a word. He employs Andrewes's phrases, and it is well. But Christ acquired at a prodigious rate the Word for his mission; that was well known everywhere in Gerontion's time, and to that faith Gerontion committed himself. Yet after some years, how many we do not know, Gerontion fell into a neglect of Christ. This Christ had appeared originally and officially on earth as the Lamb of God who by the sacrifice of his own body would take away the sins of the world. But now he appeared to come in the menacing image of Christ as tiger.

What is the significance of 'in the juvescence of the year'? The nearest analogue in Eliot's work is the opening passage of *Waste Land*, where 'April is the cruellest month' because it arouses us from the dull peace of the winter. But it suits the opening line of the second movement, where the trees appear sensuous – and even sexual, if we consider sexual function – as they come into luxuriant blossom. Its purport there is that Eliot is asking, Are we to conduct ourselves after the fashion of trees?

A small aside. Eliot in the 'Gerontion' has brought into the language three new though classical words. The first is the title word, straight from the Greek. The second is 'juvescence', supposedly from the Latin, but incorrect. The proper word was 'juvenescence'; and it may be that Eliot changed it because it would have given two stresses instead of the one he wanted. But if the Romans had wished to contract the long word, they would have made it *junescence*; for they really did contract the comparative adjective *juvenior* to *junior*. The third word is 'concitation' in Movement IV; it is as close to the Latin *concitatio* as our language permits. So much for the poet's versatility, which embraces so many kinds of linguistic device.

Coming now to line 5, we should know, perhaps, that the tree which we call dogwood was called by the Greeks 'dog's-tongue'; they would have meant the red-blossoming dogwood, thinking the petals were like the tongues of dogs in the chase. In that sense the blossom is menacing, and I cannot tell in what sense it is sensual. It is like the 'judas tree' which we associate with the unfortunate betrayer of Christ. But only the critics of this poem have made me think back upon my youth when we knew all the big chestnut trees as bearers of blossom and fruit, and never thought of the blossoms as other than specially handsome. We did not notice its spike as sensual association. But I cannot risk disagreeing with a symbolism which Eliot, like all his critics, may have observed.

We must admit anyway the 'depraved May' as a symbol of evil; and Fräulein von Kulp in line 12 bears a name related to *culpa*, guilt, and moves furtively in the hall as if up to mischief. My own conclusion would be that Gerontion had his degree of promiscuity, which may have contributed to his apostasy. But I cannot see in this movement, any more than in Movement I, any evidence that Gerontion has not now arrived at a point far beyond the possibility of dishonest representations, or that his great fault was not as he represents it in Movement I and in movements later than this one: to put the world before Christ.

The four persons recalled in the second and third parts of Movement II are offered as not being Christians. It must be Gerontion's understanding that Christ came 'to be eaten' and 'to be drunk', but that these persons either had not undertaken that in the first place, or had backslidden if they had. But they make a rich context of sad meaning.

In line 14 the conclusion approaches: 'Vacant shuttles / Weave the wind. I have no ghosts.' The shuttles of the mind move busily, but they accomplish nothing; they have no threads to weave. Gerontion has known many people, including foreign people, but he shared no great friendship with them, nor thinks of them as faithful ghosts to be summoned up in his memory and held again in affection. The opposite of having no ghosts in this sense is the illusion of meeting again a wise and cherished ghost, as Eliot does in the second movement of the fourth *Quartet*; that ghost is W. B. Yeats, who had died three years before; and that passage has no superior even in Eliot's ripest verse.

Immediately after these rhythms we have, for conclusion, the coda again, resembling that added to Movement I. I have marked the seven stresses, but not divided them in any way. They compose a perfect line in the ballad form. It is in the Common Metre, as the hymn-books have it; the stresses are not eight, nor six, as they might have been in Long

Metre or Short Metre, but seven. The instrumental music would have
to hold the final stress for another full bar, and the reader's voice would
have to make a full-stress pause after it.

[III]

After such knowledge, what forgiveness? Think now
o o -   -   o   -   o - o / -   - /

History has many cunning passages, contrived corridors
- o o / o   - o   - o   - o o o -   - o o

And issues, deceives with whispering ambitions,
o   - o   o -   o   - o o   o - o

Guides us by vanities. Think now
-     o o - o o / -   -

She gives when our attention is distracted
o   - o   - o- o o o - o

And what she gives, gives with such supple confusions
o   -   o - / -   o o   - o o - o

That the giving famishes the craving. Gives too late
o   o - o   - o o o   - o / o   -   -

What's not believed in, or is still believed,
o   -   o - o / o o - o -

In memory only, reconsidered passion. Gives too soon
o _ oo   - o / - o - o   - o / o   -   -

Into weak hands, what's thought can be dispensed with
o o -   -   / o   -   o o o -   o /

Till the refusal propagates a fear. Think
o   o o - o - o-   o - / -

Neither fear nor courage saves us. Unnatural vices
o o - o   - o   - o / o - o o - o

Are fathered by our heroism. Virtues
o   - o   o o - o- / - o

Are forced upon us by our impudent crimes.
o   -   o - o o o   - o o   - /

These tears are shaken from the wrath-bearing tree.
-     -   o - o o o -   - o - /

In Movement III we may identify for the first time the silent auditor to
whom the monologue is addressed. Line 1 puts a question; and then an

imperative: 'Think now'. The imperative is repeated twice more, and is made urgent by coming awkwardly at the end of the lines. The auditor is Christ, who in Movement IV will become the definitive 'you' and 'your'.

Four arguments are uttered in lines 2–11; they try to justify Gerontion's rejection of Christ. Fortunately they do not take an academic or intellectual form of expression. The deceitful temptress who causes Gerontion's apostasy is perhaps associated in his imagination with Fate, with Lachesis herself, the middle Fate, who was supposed by the Greeks to appoint the destiny of every mortal man; and to bring it to pass by circumstances which are wholly adventitious so far as he can tell, and not to be countered. But Gerontion is a modern, and he calls the woman 'History'. She arranges those 'cunning passages' which lead to doom. But suddenly the 'passages' cease to be generalized when they are translated into 'contrived corridors / And issues', a physical image. Then she 'gives with such supple confusions / That the giving famishes the craving', which is marvellous; and we admire those 'supple confusions', which means that they are not confusions at all in those exact designs appointed by History. The third argument has her giving back his faith, but it comes too late. And finally he refers again to her first giving, but that came too soon; he had neglected it, and then been filled with fear. Beginning with the end of line 11 and continuing through line 14, he talks with great pith about courage and fear as producing each other, in alternation.

We must surely remark, I think, that 'what's thought can be dispensed with' contains a logical error. The 'what's' is wrong for 'what it's'. Possibly Gerontion preferred the wrong version because it would not require a stress on 'what' and spoil a five-stress line. At least half the lines can be counted as having nine stresses each. In this modern verse we may not exercise our old privilege of stressing in any line a weak word, or two or three, in order to fill up the blank verse; nor refuse to stress a strong word when it would make the line spill over with stresses. Eliot in his blank verse generally preferred to make his stresses sound loud and clear, and to let his weak syllables remain weak and manage for themselves. But I hold him in grateful memory because he hailed the ghost of Yeats, in that final *Quartet*, as both 'master' and friend; and because three years before he had presented himself in person in Ireland, at the tomb prepared for Yeats's body, and made a public speech in which he declared Yeats the greatest poet of his time and perhaps of all time. This last tribute I take from Joseph Hone's literary biography, *W. B. Yeats*; but it may have been on Eliot's part a little too generous, as according to the conventions of panegyric. Yet Yeats had used the old privileges of English prosody, and permitted himself to strengthen the weak words when necessary and slide over the strong words which could not keep their stresses in order to hold to the effect of a pure and prevailing form, a continuous bed of rhythm, such as ordinary language would never have worried into existence. Nevertheless, it does not appear even today that anybody has complained about this convention in Yeats. The voice of his great lines is that of an impassioned oracle. And doubtless we have observed that there has already been a partial return to the old metres, in reaction against the modern rhythms, among many of those fine poets who have established themselves in the generation now in middling age; they keep pretty well to their count of stresses and are rather indeterminate about the unstresses. A poet may still suit himself; but the better poets will keep some measure of control over their prosody.

After the four arguments we find three short sentences about fear and courage, virtues and crimes, alternatively producing each other. These observations are as accurate psychologically as they are untechnical and terse.

Line 15 concludes the movement with what we may call a coda: 'These tears are shaken from the wrath-bearing tree.' For Gerontion is of the seed of Adam, and was doomed to offend.

[IV]

The tiger springs in the new year. Us he devours. Think at last
We have not reached conclusion, when I
Stiffen in a rented house. Think at last
I have not made this show purposelessly
And it is not by any concitation
Of the backward devils.
I would meet you upon this honestly.
I that was near your heart was removed therefrom
To lose beauty in terror, terror in inquisition.
I have lost my passion: why should I need to keep it
Since what is kept must be adulterated?

> I have lost my sight, smell, hearing, taste and touch:
> How should I use them for your closer contact?

. . . the text of this movement and of the one following [is inserted] for the reader's convenience; though I have not marked the prosodies.

There are only thirteen lines in this movement; which is not to say that it conforms to the rule of *The Waste Land* and *Four Quartets*, where the fourth movement in Eliot's five symphonic poems must be much shorter, and more lyrical, than the other movements. Here the fourth movement is only a little shorter.

'The tiger springs . . . .' We know by now that the lamb who came to be devoured turns into the tiger when Gerontion has forgotten the lamb. And so with other people, such as the acquaintances he mentioned in Movement II; 'Us he devours.' The pronouns are inverted.

Gerontion uses language here which would fall a little short if he were a lesser poet. 'Reached conclusion' is a scholarly phrase, but how well he redeems himself at once by 'Stiffen in a rented house'; the scholar would never have thought of 'stiffen' as an image which would make words such as 'age' or 'grow old' seem stale; or may we say the phrase is 'jejeune'? The noun in that Latin family of words referred to a meagreness or poverty in one's vocabulary. 'Purposelessly' is a grammarian's cacophony, twice compounded of sibilants too difficult to pronounce briefly before the following l's. And it stands just over the word 'concitation' in the following line, a philologist's word, though novel to the English language. Does Gerontion propose not only to tell Christ of his final rejection, but to do it rather bookishly? But he concludes the sentence with some straight talk of the 'backward devils', who are probably the evil spirits prompting him to backslide. He takes care to profess his honesty, and considering his merciless self-exposure previously we like to believe him. All the same, we cannot but feel a satiric quality in his language now. We remember that Eliot, his author, was just coming out of a period of poems, some of them in savage satire against the religious institution, and others in which he was nostalgic for it. He had been one of those who blow hot and blow cold; one of the Laodiceans. He permitted the honest Gerontion to exhibit a trace of hostility to his auditor.

But the sentence of the last two lines is a crushing rejection. Its first line contains a top-grade hyperbole he has lost every bit of every one of his five physical senses. He lists them scrupulously as if he were preparing an official document showing all the specifications of his ground for asking to be relieved of a contractual obligation. But perhaps we would do better to call it a perfect litotes rather than a hyperbole. His senses have attenuated to zero; they have not increased to the point of maximum capacity.

We can do without the final coda we may have expected. We have at least the perfect phrase of conclusion.

[v]

These with a thousand small deliberations
Protract the profit of their chilled delirium,
Excite the membrane, when the sense has cooled,
With pungent sauces, multiply variety
In a wilderness of mirrors. What will the spider do,
Suspend its operations, will the weevil
Delay? De Bailhache, Fresca, Mrs Cammel, whirled
Beyond the circuit of the shuddering Bear
In fractured atoms. Gull against the wind, in the windy straits
Of Belle Isle, or running on the Horn.
White feathers in the snow, the Gulf claims,
And an old man driven by the Trades
To a sleepy corner.
                    Tenants of the house,
Thoughts of a dry brain in a dry season.

I think we must take this last movement, this grand finale, as the great one of the five. In its mastery of the vocabulary and the music of language, of course; and even in its high spirits, because Gerontion rejoices in having settled and dismissed an old uneasiness of conscience. It is like a little Ode on the Prospect of Death, exultant because he has brought to completion the best work of his whole lifetime, so that his going will be not with a whimper but a bang.

Gerontion is one of those men in whom we may say there has been a kind of displacement of their youthful and instructed faith by their increasing passion for an art. We are told nothing about his occupation. But seven of his acquaintances have been named, four in Movement II, and three more in this last movement. They all have foreign names, though Mr Silvero and Mrs Cammel had evidently come to live in England; and what is more significant, two of them, Mr Silvero and Hakagawa, were connoisseurs of porcelain and painting respectively; with Mr Silvero caressing his prizes and in his excitement walking all night in his room, and Hakagawa bowing before his Titians. Perhaps Gerontion, whatever his means of livelihood, had been an art-lover too, unable to make the grade as an artist himself; but late in life, when he could no longer travel, had found his true gift as a poet, just in time. Here I am trying to imagine the image which Eliot would have had of him; though Eliot characteristically had preferred to let the reader make his own image.

In the late twenties Eliot returned to the Church; and from that moment on he laboured diligently in the vineyard. It must have taken a monumental strength and patience to keep up at the same time his profession as poet and critic; and especially to protect the independence of his poetry as keeping to its aesthetic form. Now, to use Aristotle's valuable terms, the material cause (or medium) of poetry is the words, whether common or uncommon; the efficient cause is the poet (having both reason and imagination); the final cause is to give a unique pleasure, which may amount to ecstasy. But there is also a formal cause, without which a poetry is not formed; and that is the adaptation of the words to the rhythms of a music. Of course there are many excellent words and systems of words, as for example in theology and religious experience, which need not bother with this formal requirement and are content to remain other than poetry. But Eliot took care to hold all his religious verse strictly to the formal standard; his darting eye throughout the *Quartets* may have liked to hit upon moral and religious behaviours, as constituents of poetry especially dear to his heart; but they had to take a shape subordinated to the rhythmic form.

Eliot gave many examples of those special moments when something natural takes on a look of the supernatural; and many times defined these moments as the intersection of time with the timeless. But let us see something of the range they took in the *Quartets*. The best one is surely the first one, in the first movement of 'Burnt Norton', where the bird in the rose garden prompts the guests to look quickly before the vision is gone. On other occasions he would catalogue a whole set of moments in one passage. In the last movement of 'The Dry Salvages', for example:

> The distraction fit, lost in a shaft of sunlight,
> The wild thyme unseen, or the winter lightning
> Or the waterfall, or music heard so deeply
> That it is not heard at all, but you are the music
> While the music lasts.

All these, except the last, are natural images actually perceived by our senses, but supernatural too, as we feel in our moment of ecstasy. The shaft of sunlight perhaps comes sloping through a murky air and is apprehended by vision; the wild thyme is unseen but known by its fragrance; the winter lightning is like a light from heaven, totally unexpected and vanishing quickly; the waterfall is perhaps heard rather than seen, and imagination plays with it better than if it were seen. But finally there is music, made with instruments, and heard in our deepest being where we are not tempted to analyse it. Up to the point when this music occurs, all the presentations are actual, as the senses attest. But with the utterance of the formal music we are in the domain of artistic imagination, where the actual senses cannot testify to the fictions of art. That is an important distinction in the Kantian aesthetics. Perhaps I need to explain that I am taking the bare listing of the occasions for the special moments as being merely the poet's pointing, slightly in the didactic manner; as if saying, Watch out for occasions of that sort. But the heard music is more than recommendation; it is art itself, 'imitating reality'; not the presentation but the 'representation', as Kant put it.

The movement ends with this passage:

> We, content at the last
> If our temporal reversion nourish
> (Not too far from the yew-tree)
> The life of significant soil.

This means, we are obliged to think, that Eliot had no special fixation upon the resurrection of the body after death according to orthodox principle.

But in 'Little Gidding', the first movement, there is a passage about prayer; for in the offices of the Church there are many provisions made for the special moments of ecstasy:

You are here to kneel
Where prayer has been valid. . . .
Here, the intersection of the timeless moment
Is England and nowhere. Never and always.

And finally there is conclusion of 'Little Gidding' and the whole book of
Quartets:

And all shall be well and
All manner of thing shall be well
When the tongues of flame are in-folded
Into the crowned knot of fire
And the fire and the rose are one.

Eliot was very well acquainted with Dante's visions, and they deserved
it; but they were representations, not presentations. And may a later
poet with another language use Dante's vision of the rose of Heaven?
That would require a re-representation. I think one of Eliot's aims in
'Little Gidding' was to harmonize within himself the poet and the
churchman, and at the end he fell back too easily upon Dante. It is not
in Eliot's own voice, and I wish it were.

And now, for my own conclusion, a few remarks upon the final
movement. We must recognize exactly what Gerontion has been doing
in the whole monologue. He lives with impoverished senses and
pocketbook, but there is no poverty in his imagination or in his
vocabulary. The first sentence (lines 1−5) has three beautiful pre-
dicates: 'Protract the profit' and 'Excite the membrane' and 'multiply
variety / In a wilderness of mirrors'. The 'mirrors' are probably the most
wonderful. Gerontion is not afraid of a few latinisms if they are choice,
and in the image I have of him he started to say 'reflections', to pair with
the 'deliberations' above. But imagination quickly got the better of
reason, saying 'reflectors' would have more character, looking backward as they did; but why not 'mirrors'? How much better is the
metaphor of the physical instruments, any number of them, searching
into his past. And with that he has finished his confessions and turns to
the future, which is now secure.

We could count all of lines 1−6 as being blank verses, if only Eliot had
permitted him to stress a little *of* in line 2; and to bring the first word of
line 7 back into its place in line 6, so that both 6 and 7 would be norms.

But the modern prosodist is greatly prejudiced in favour of open-ended lines in this measure, and 'Delay?' would have brought line 6 to a full stop. As the text stands, there are two sentences, no line having a full stop.

It is when Gerontion asks the question about the spider and the weevil that he comes into his real theme; the first sentence is his repudiation of something that is finished. His author has not allowed him – but that is redundant and gratuitous; let us say he has not allowed himself to say in so many words what his theme is about. But we know now that he is his own man and is talking about death. The spider and the weevil are hateful creatures, but they work in their respective occupations till they collapse and are dead. But what of those men and women, people of distinction, who die by cataclysm and destruction, and have their bodies annihilated and scattered into fractured atoms? That is a heroic sort of death which Gerontion abhors, though the press will play loudly upon it. Then there is the gull's death, leaving his white feathers to be claimed by the Gulf; which is probably the Abyss, or Bottom of the World as the Greeks called it. These two sentences are the work of a master of his art, being so wildly beautiful.

But the second of these sentences is not quite finished; just here, in the most dramatic place possible, comes the old refrain or coda, about the humble old man in his corner. But there is a variation; it is a sleepy corner. He is thinking about that last sleep. Probably he will spend the last wakeful days reciting his own poem. Sometimes perhaps (but with his fingers crossed) he will cite the Scripture which follows the account of the six Days of Creation: 'And God saw every thing that he had made and, behold, it was very good.'

The two final lines, separated a little from the main text, do not repeat the coda; they recapitulate the theme of the whole poem; that is, they make a kind of epilogue to a dramatic work. They begin with a nice metaphor, 'Tenants of the house', which are translated back into reality in the concluding line. The two lines together form a full ballad line having four pairs of stresses making the rhythm, and it again is in Common Metre. It would have been read like this:

> Tenants of the house,
> Thoughts of a dry
> Brain in a dry
> Season.

He is playing with this irony again, as always. But after the one stress of the final rhythm the reader must make a full stop to fulfil the movement.

SOURCE: essay in *T. S. Eliot: The Man and His Work*, ed. Tate, pp. 136–60.

2. THE QUATRAIN POEMS

Robert Graves and Laura Riding 'Burbank' (1927)

. . . A poem by Mr Eliot may be quoted to show how limited the humorous appeal of modernist verse may become. The extreme particularity of some of the references may be called the teasing element of modernist wit. We do not pretend to see all the jokes in Mr. Eliot's poem; literary specialists will be able to follow the scent farther than we have done, and of course Mr. Eliot himself could, if pressed, make everything clear:

BURBANK WITH A BAEDEKER

BLEISTEIN WITH A CIGAR

Tra-la-la-la-la-la-laire – nil nisi divinum stabile est; caetera fumus – the gondola stopped, the old palace was there, how charming its grey and pink – goats and monkeys, with such hair too! – so the countess passed on until she came through the little park, where Niobe presented her with a cabinet, and so departed.

> Burbank crossed a little bridge
>   Descending at a small hotel;
> Princess Volupine arrived,
>   They were together, and he fell.

> Defunctive music under sea
>   Passed seaward with the passing bell
> Slowly: the God Hercules
>   Had left him, that had loved him well.

> The horses, under the axle-tree
>   Beat up the dawn from Istria
> With even feet. Her shuttered barge
>   Burned on the water all the day.

This is modern Venice visited by two American tourists, one, who may or may not be called Burbank after Luther Burbank the horticulturist famous for his 'crossings' of fruits and plants, the other a caricature Jew. The Latin quotation means: 'Nothing is lasting unless it is divine: the rest is smoke.' The remainder of the introduction, with the exception of 'with such hair too!' mischievously borrowed from Browning and a little snippet from Henry James, may be anyone, even by Mr. Eliot himself: we do not know.[1]

The old palace is one of the many show-places on the Grand Canal: possibly the one where Lord Byron's intrigue with the Countess Guiccoli took place. The goats and monkeys may be relics of the zoo which Lord Byron kept there; but they may also symbolize lechery. Not only are monkeys permanent features of Venetian palaces, but they paly a symbolic part in *The Merchant of Venice*; and *The Merchant of Venice* is a suppressed *motif* in the poem. Jessica, it will be remembered, turned her back on Jewry, took up with Christians and at once bought a pet monkey. The little parks are features of some of these Venetian palaces. Niobe is the Greeks symbol of sorrow: her children were slain as a punishment for her pride in them. The cabinet is a memorial of Niobe's sympathy with Venice, whose pride has also been brought low. Princess Volupine evidently represents the degenerate aristocratic romanticism of Venice: she has an intrigue with Burbank, who stands for the sentimental element in modern civilization – a sort of symbolical 'decent chap'. 'Defunctive music' comes from Shakespeare's 'The Phoenix and the Turtle'. The last line of the first stanza is possibly also a quotation, like the last two of the second and the first two of the third, but here again we leave pedigrees to more reference-proud critics than ourselves. Burbank's power leaves him. (Hercules is the Latin god of strength, and also the guardian of money.)

The third stanza marks an increase from the second in the mock-grandeur of the writing: it almost threatens to become serious. This in turn demands the sudden bathetic drop of the fourth stanza. The manner of the third stanza accounts for the artificiality of the symbols used: their grandiosity and the obscurity of their source throw a cloud over their precise significance. The horses under the axle-tree may be the horses of the sun under the axle-tree of heaven; but they may also suggest the little heraldic horses fixed at the side of every Venetian gondola, which may be said to be under the axle-tree of the gondola, i.e. the oar. So this may be a conceit which amounts to calling the sun a sky-

gondola rather than a chariot. Or it may not. Istria lies east from Venice
on the road to Vienna. Princess Volupine's shuttered barge burns on the
water all day, a sign that she is now closeted with someone else. There is
an echo here from *Antony and Cleopatra*:

> The barge she sat in, like a burnished throne,
> Burned on the water. . . .

At this point the other member of the cast enters the poem: Bleistein the
Jew. Burbank walks through Venice with a Baedeker, that is to say with
a melancholy respect for the past; Bleistein, on the contrary, walks
through Venice with a cigar, a symbol of vulgar and ignorant self-
enjoyment. The name Bleistein is a caricature of the common Goldstein
or 'Goldstone': it means 'Leadstone'.

> But this or such was Bleistein's way:
> A saggy bending of the knees
> And elbows, with the palms turned out,
> Chicago Semite Viennese.

> A lustreless protrusive eye
> Stares from the protozoic slime
> At a perspective of Canaletto.
> The smoky candle end of time

> Declines. On the Rialto once.
> The rats are underneath the piles.
> The jew is underneath the lot.
> Money in furs. The boatman smiles. . . .

Burbank sees the strength and wealth of Venice departed, the
remnants of her glory enjoyed by an upstart Chicago Jew who
probably started life as a furrier's apprentice in Leopoldstadt, the
Jewish quarter of Vienna. Canaletto was an eighteenth-century painter
whose aristocratic pictures of Venice lie at a long remove from
Bleistein's world – though Bleistein may one day carry Venice to the
United States by presenting the Chicago Art Institute with an
authenticated Canaletto in evidence of his good citizenship. The smoky
candle end recalls the Latin motto: 'The rest is smoke.' Burbank

sorrowfully pictures the Rialto of other days. The rats are underneath
the piles now, and the Jew (the eternal Shylock) is the rat of rats. The
jew (Jew is written with a small initial letter like rat) is a rat because he
has made money and because for some reason Jewish wealth, as
opposed to Gentile wealth, has a mystical connexion with the decline of
Venice. This may not be Burbank's private opinion, or even Mr. Eliot's.
It at any rate expresses for Burbank and Mr. Eliot the way Venice at
present feels, or should feel, about the modern Jew strutting through her
streets. 'Money in furs' refers not only to the fact that the fur trade is
largely in Jewish hands and that this is how Bleistein made his money,
but also to some proverbial witticism, perhaps about the ability of a Jew
to make money even out of rats' skins, out of the very instruments of
decay.

The smiling boatman, who has for centuries seen everything, stands
as an ironic fate between Bleistein and Princess Volupine.

> Princess Volupine extends
>   A meagre, blue-nailed, phthisic hand
> To climb the waterstair. Lights, lights,
>   She entertains Sir Ferdinand

> Klein. Who clipped the lion's wings
>   And flea'd his rump and pared his claws?
> Thought Burbank, meditating on
>   Time's ruins, and the seven laws.

Venice, in the person of Princess Volupine (is this another French
comic-opera character? Or a coined word compounded of the Latin for
'pleasure', *voluptas*, and the name of a play of Ben Jonson's, *Volpone, the
Fox*? Or a character from one of the obscurer dramatists of the Mermaid
Series? We do not pretend to know), has now sunk so low that, no longer
content with Byronic intrigues, she actually admits the Jew (in the
person of Sir Ferdinand Klein, a British financier) to her embraces. Sir
Ferdinand's name is an epitome of contempt and pathetic comedy: the
Jew, having made money, has similarly conquered and corrupted
English society; his noble Christian name is purloined from the very
country which most persecuted him (now also in decay); his family
name means 'little' and is, appropriately enough, from the
German – there is no sentimental condolence with the Germans

because, presumably, they do not suffer from this peculiarly Mediterranean type of decay. Thus, in the person of Sir Ferdinand Klein, Bleistein succeeds where Burbank fails; the implication being that the Jew is not an individual but an eternal symbol, each Jew being the entire race. 'Lights, lights!' is a Shakespearianism further evoking *The Merchant of Venice* atmosphere, though it is the cry which usually goes up just before the *dénouement* of a tragedy, not a comedy. The lion is the winged lion of St. Mark, the patron saint of Venice; but also, in a secondary sense, the British lion whose wings have been clipped by the Jew. What the seven laws are in the Venetian context will probably be found in Baedeker, or in the Classical Dictionary, or in *The Merchant of Venice* along with rats, the Rialto, cabinets and pet monkeys.

This is not, of course, popular writing. It is aristocratic writing, and its jokes are exclusive; but only exclusive if the reader has neither capacity nor interest for sharing in them: the Baedeker is common to all men, so are the Classical Dictionary and Larousse and the plays of Shakespeare. The jokes are against modern civilization, against money, against classicism, against romanticism, against Mr. Eliot himself as a tourist in Venice with a Baedeker. One of the few privileges of the comedian is to have prejudices for which he cannot be held morally accountable; and the modernist poet, taking full advantage of this privilege, indulges his caprices without feeling obliged to render a rationalistic report on them. The anti-Jewish prejudice, for instance, occurs frequently in modernist poetry; and the anti-American prejudice also. It is part of the comedy that a Jew or an American may equally express these prejudices. . . .

SOURCE: extract from *A Survey of Modernist Poetry* (1927) pp. 154–8.

NOTE

1. Now we do know: See p. 182.

F. W. Bateson   'Burbank' (1970)

. . . The role of learning – or what looks like learning – in *The Waste Land* has already received a more than sufficiently detailed treatment elsewhere. An earlier and less familiar example of the same technique is Eliot's 'Burbank with a Baedeker: Bleistein with a Cigar', a poem that has never in my opinion had proper critical justice done to it. Its technical interest is the dual function, private as well as public, to which the not inconsiderable learning packed into it is put. It is also the last and perhaps the best of Eliot's exercises in semi-comic satire. I will confess to greatly preferring its verbal concision and poker-face gaiety to the hysterical sublime of *The Waste Land* and 'The Hollow Men'.

'Burbank' was printed with 'Sweeney Erect' in the same issue of *Art and Letters*. Like its companion-pieces, an epigraph precedes the poem, but instead of the customary extract from some Elizabethan play we are provided with a passage of amusing almost nonsensical prose which proves on inspection to be a cento of phrases from Gautier, St Augustine, Henry James's *The Aspern Papers*, *Othello* ('goats and monkeys'), 'A Toccata of Galuppi's' ('with such hair too') and a masque by John Marston. The key to a method in the confusion is that most of the extracts are from English literary classics that are sited in Venice. Burbank, it is clear, has brought more than a Baedeker with him to Venice.

On the surface the poem itself is a miniature comic drama describing Burbank's brief love affair with the Princess Volupine and his displacement in her favours first of all by his compatriot Bleistein ('Chicago Semite Viennese') and then by Sir Ferdinand Klein, a knight-errant presumably of Lloyd George's creation. But this simple story of feminine infidelity is narrated in the poetic diction of high ironic scholarship. The members of the Shakespeare Association would have been delighted no doubt to meet in the second verse 'defunctive music' from 'The Phoenix and the Turtle', which is followed by two passages from *Antony and Cleopatra*, one diverted to Burbank and the second to the Princess, a familiar scrap from *The Merchant of Venice* and another from *Hamlet*. There is also – a more recondite allusion – an echo of a line in Chapman's *Bussy D'Ambois* which is itself an imitation of an image in

Seneca's *Hercules Furens*. Finally, the poem's fourth line, ('They were together, and he fell') is a comic reversal of the fourth line in Tennyson's 'The Sisters': 'They were together, and she fell.'

Eliot's use of familiar, or reasonably familiar, literary allusions in 'Burbank' gives the poem its special mock-heroic effect. As in such Augustan mock-heroics as *MacFlecknoe* and *The Rape of the Lock*, the reproduction of a sordid or trivial modern incident in the magnificent phraseology of the literature of an earlier age diminishes the modern participants without in any way degrading the classic models. (Burbank is equated with Shakespeare's Antony and Bleistein with Shylock for the light it throws on them, not on their models.) But the total effect of Eliot's poem is very different from that of the Augustan mock-heroics. The learning to which it appeals, for one thing, is not public in the sense in which the conventions of classical epic were public in Pope's time. In spite of occasional suggestions of Pound's *Mauberley*, 'Burbank' is very much Eliot's poem and one concerned with Eliot's own personal predicament.

Negatively, then, Pound was certainly right when he wrote to William Carlos Williams in 1920, 'Eliot is perfectly conscious of having imitated Laforgue, has worked to get away from it, and there is very little Laforgue in his Sweeney, or his Bleistein Burbank, or his "Gerontion"'. 'Burbank' is *not* Laforgue in English. The self-pitying irony of Laforgue is completely absent from it. But Eliot's positive poetic achievement is not defined in Pound's letter.

A detail that may assist such a definition is a sentence in the *Athenaeum* review of Henry Adams's *Education* already referred to. Eliot wrote in the course of this review that 'Henry Adams in 1858 and Henry James in 1870 . . . land at Liverpool and descend at the same hotel'. 'Burbank', which must have been written within a few weeks of the *Athenaeum* review, begins, it will be recalled:

> Burbank crossed a little bridge
> Descending at a small hotel. . . .

To 'descend', in its special nineteenth-century sense, was to step down from a carriage or cab – a physical impossibility in the Venice of 1919 as the *carrozza* did not ply there. For this brief moment, however, Burbank has ceased to be an American tourist arriving by gondola in Venice and has become the young Henry Adams, or the young Henry

James, who is about to spend his first night in Europe. The allusion or error is private to Eliot, but it helps to give the poem a public context. Burbank, who is Adams, James and Eliot, is also a more representative figure – the young American intellectual of Anglo-Saxon stock with the whole of New England culture symbolized in his name and his guidebook.

The poem, therefore, is a sort of Henry James novel in miniature. Its essential subject is the relationship of the American intelligentsia to Western Europe. But its date is 1919; Europe is now in ruins after the First World War; America has passed out of its Burbank phase to a domination by men like Bleistein ('Money in furs'). And so this wry international comedy ends on an almost serious note with the question that is raised by Burbank in the last verse:

> . . . Who clipped the lion's wings
> And flea'd his rump and pared his claws?
> Thought Burbank, meditating on
> Time's ruins, and the seven laws.

If, as seems likely, the seven laws are Ruskin's *Seven Lamps of Architecture*, an element of satire re-enters with them. And the pseudo-scholar is again in evidence here, though for the only time in the poem. The work of Ruskin's that Burbank would have been much more likely to pack with his Baedeker is surely *The Stones of Venice*.

The critical conclusion to which I have been leading is that the 'learning' in Eliot's earlier poems must be seen as an aspect of his Americanism. As scholarship it is wide-ranging, but often superficial and inaccurate. At one level, indeed, the enjoyment that he and Pound found – and successfully communicated to their readers – in exploiting their miscellaneous erudition is the same in kind, if not in degree, that every American pilgrim of our cathedrals, galleries and museums experiences. The appearance of literary scholarship parallels the tourist's apparent acquistion of 'culture'. When Eliot in 1920 prefixed to *The Sacred Wood* – facing the title-page – the phrase 'I also like to dine on becaficas', he was merely showing off. Why should the reader recognize this line from Byron's *Beppo*? Why should he be expected to know that 'becaficas' – which both Byron and Eliot misspell – are Italian birds that make good eating? In any case what is the relevance of this particular line of Byron's on the attractions of Italy as a place to live in to a collection of critical essays? This is tourist-erudition. Such frivolities can be disregarded. Their interest – like that of 'Burbank' (which has other interests too, as I have argued) – lies in the evidence they supply of a certain gaiety of spirit that Eliot never fully recovered after his nervous breakdown in 1921. For the poetry the significance of the 'learning' is that it was an American supplement to the various attempts made by the best European poets of the time to escape from the *impasse* of Pure Poetry. In the end, of course, the expatriate American intellectuals – with the eccentric exception of Pound – had either to adapt themselves to their European surroundings or to return to America. Eliot gradually merged into the Anglo-French literary establishment, though with the poetic consequence that when (in and after 1927) he had formally become an English citizen the 'learning' had lost most of its aesthetic *raison d'être*. He was no longer an American poet with a revolutionary new technique – as Poe and Whitman in their different ways had been before him. After *The Waste Land*, therefore, the learned allusions tend to persist only as a matter of literary habit. In *Four Quartets* (composed 1935–42) in particular it is noticeable how functionless most of the allusions, quotations and plagiarisms now are. The impression one has is of an essayist in the Lamb or Hazlitt manner eking out material that is subjectively and emotionally decidedly 'thin'. The one exception that occurs to me is the half-translation from Mallarmé in the beautiful Dantesque episode in 'Little Gidding'.

The unconscious reminiscences, on the other hand, especially in *Four Quartets*, are not from European literature at all but, as far as I have been able to detect them, from Whitman's *Leaves of Grass*. Pound's curious poem beginning

> I make a pact with you, Walt Whitman —
> I have detested you long enough

and ending

> We have one sap and one root –
> Let there be commerce between us

might also have been written, whether Eliot was fully aware of it or not, by the author of *Ash Wednesday* and *Four Quartets*. The anomalies of attitude and subject-matter should not be allowed to obscure the fact that in a final analysis Eliot was an American poet of enormous talent who happened to live in England – as James was a great American novelist who too happened to prefer living in England.

It is in such a context that the 'learning' of Eliot has ultimately to be explained and justified. In the earlier poems the plagiarism-quotations and the whole façade of erudition are part of the poetry as well as biographically a stimulus to its composition. They make a contribution peculiar to American intellectuals – where a great university still has something of the sanctity of a medieval monastery – to the revival of modern poetry. . . .

Source: extract from 'The Poetry of Learning', in *Eliot in Perspective*, ed. Graham Martin (1970) pp. 39–43.

Ernest Schanzer 'Mr Eliot's Sunday Morning Service' (1955)

The perusal of the recent correspondence in *Essays in Criticism* about the meaning of 'A Cooking Egg' has left us sadder and wiser men. For it startlingly revealed the complete lack of agreement among trained critics about even the most general meaning of one of Mr. Eliot's less difficult poems. While divided on whether to blame the poet or his critics for this breakdown in communication, most of us are probably agreed on the usefulness of such an occasional co-operative attempt at elucidation. I propose to take what seems to me a much more difficult poem from the same collection as 'A Cooking Egg', 'Mr. Eliot's Sunday Morning Service', hoping that some of its perplexities may be resolved by means of a similar discussion.

The poem's setting is indicated by its title. It is Sunday morning and a service is in progress in what must be either a High Anglican or a

Roman Catholic church, for religious paintings are found within its walls. The poem's outward unity is supplied by the wandering eye and mind of Mr. Eliot. While he sits in the church his eye strays along the stained glass windows depicting various early Church Fathers, among them presumably Origen, so that the figures appear to drift past him in procession.

> Polyphiloprogenitive
> The sapient sutlers of the Lord
> Drift across the window-panes.

They make him reflect on the ironic contrast between the Word of God and the wordiness of the controversialists of the early Church. 'In the beginning was the Word', the poet comments sarcastically. At the very beginning of our Church history came the copious flow of words from the pens of the learned theologians, the 'sapient sutlers', with a pun on 'sutlers' and the ironic implication that 'the hungry sheep look up and are not fed'. For instead of feeding the army of the Church Militant with the Word of God the sutlers provide an abundant diet of subtle, abstract, and barren arguments.

> In the beginning was the Word.
> Superfetation of τὸ ἕν,
> And at the mensual turn of time
> Produced enervate Origen.

The wordiness of some of the early theologians is described as a 'superfetation', a second conception, of God, following upon the initial conception of the Word of God (the repetition of the last line of the preceding stanza is probably meant to underline this). Eliot chooses Origen as representative of this group of theologians. For not only was he one of the most voluminous of all the Church Fathers (St. Epiphanius in an exaggerated estimate puts the number of his writings at 6000), but he was particularly famed for his lengthy commentaries on the Scriptures. His comments on St. John's 'In the beginning was the Word' alone 'furnished material for a whole roll' (*Catholic Encyclopaedia*). In the spectacle of Wordiness commenting on the silent Word the ironic contrast is crystallized for us. Origen is also chosen because, as the word 'enervate' reminds us, he committed self-castration as a youth of

seventeen. We have thus the further contrast between his verbal fertility
and his sexual sterility, a contrast which is also enforced by the poet's use
of words of primarily sexual connotation, such as 'superfetation' and
'polyphiloprogenitive', in a non-sexual context. The essential sterility of
Alexandrian theology is thus suggested to us. The poem's rather
ludicrous opening word with its suggestion of both the prolificity and
the prolixity of the writings of the Alexandrian school at once sets the
tone of the whole poem and adumbrates its main satiric theme: the
remoteness of the Alexandrian theology from simple Christian sentiment and belief.

In the third stanza the poet turns from the wordiness of Origen to the
Word become Flesh, the Logos in its illuminative and redemptive
activity. His eyes wander from the stained glass figures of the early
Fathers to an Umbrian painting of the Baptism of Christ.

> A painter of the Umbrian school
> Designed upon a gesso ground
> The nimbus of the Baptized God.
> The wilderness is cracked and browned
>
> But through the water pale and thin
> Still shine the unoffending feet
> And there above the painter set
> The Father and the Paraclete.

With its *Waste Land* symbolism and its sensuous simplicity the
description admirably suggests the feeling of primitive Christianity as
well as of primitive Italian painting, and as a contrast to what precedes
it needs no comment, except for the reminder that Origen was famous
for his voluminous speculations on the nature of the Trinity.

An interval of time seems indicated by the dotted line which divides
the poem into two halves of equal length. The poet's eye now fastens on
the officiating priests and on members of the congregation.

> The sable presbyters approach
> The avenue of penitence;
> The young are red and pustular
> Clutching piaculative pence.

The next, grammatically incomplete stanza appears to contain the description of another religious painting that has caught the poet's eye. It depicts the tortures of purgatory.

> Under the penitential gates
> Sustained by staring Seraphim
> Where the souls of the devout
> Burn invisible and dim.

Eliot's choice of Seraphim for its guardian angels may be due to their association with purgation of sins through the Seraph that in Isaiah's vision touches his lips with a live coal, and perhaps also to the fact that, according to the *Encyclopaedia Britannica*, representations of such figures as the Seraphim seen by Isaiah 'were to be found at the entrance to oriental temples, where they served as guardians of the gate'. But it may well be that in his choice of Seraphim Eliot was also guided by memories of Dante, who in the *Convivio* declares that the Seraphim are supreme in their comprehension of God the Father ('li serafini che veggiono più della prima Cagione, che alcun' altra natura' – *Conv.* II, 6). The Seraphim with their intuitive understanding of God may thus be seen as providing a further contrast to the Alexandrian theologians with their elaborate and arduous reasoning about His nature. The description of the Seraphim as 'staring', though perhaps entirely due to some pictorial impression, may also owe something to memories of the lines in the *Paradiso* (XXI, 91–2) in which the Seraph is described as

> quell' alma nel ciel che più si schiara,
> Quel serafin che'n Dio più l'occhio ha fisso.

It is of course possible to interpret the sixth stanza as describing the continued approach of the presbyters through the chancel arch into the nave. But though this makes better syntactic sense it seems to me to raise more difficulties than it solves; above all it leaves the last two lines of the stanza excessively obscure. As I see it stanzas 5 and 6 stand in clear contrast to each other. The true purgation of sinful man in purgatorial flames, as depicted in the religious painting, is contrasted with the easy penance by means of 'piaculative pence' of the modern churchgoer. Yet the very fact that two such utterly divergent interpretations of stanza 6 should be conceivable points to one of the serious flaws in the poem.

The poet's eye next drifts through the open window out into the churchyard.

> Along the garden-wall the bees
> With hairy bellies pass between
> The staminate and pistillate,
> Blest office of the epicene.

The blest office of the epicene bees is here contrasted with the office of the epicene priests which, to the poet, lacks the blessing of fruitfulness. The quotation from *The Jew of Malta*, 'Look, look, master, here comes two religious caterpillars', which forms the poem's epigraph, being clearly inapplicable to the 'sapient sutlers', who are marked by excessive industry rather than sluggishness, seems intended for application to the sable presbyters. While the sapient sutlers fail in their function by providing a barren fare of words, the sable presbyters fail more completely still, and merely feed themselves. They possess not even the industry which links the Alexandrian Fathers with the bees, while both are sterile, incapable of fertilizing and feeding the life of the spirit.

The poem's unity of setting is abandoned in the last stanza, where Eliot introduces his Irish-American voluptuary and vulgarian, Sweeney.

> Sweeney shifts from ham to ham
> Stirring the water in his bath.
> The masters of the subtle schools
> Are controversial, polymath.

The description of Sweeney in his bath helps to knit up the poem by providing a threefold contrast by means of surface parallels with other parts of the poem: that between Sweeney and the masters of the subtle school, stirring the waters of controversy, and shifting their argumentative positions; that between Sweeney's 'hams' in the bath-water and Christ's 'unoffending feet' in the river Jordan; and that between Sweeney's voluptuous wallowing in his hot bath and the tortures of the elect in the flames of purgatory.

The poem is clearly carefully constructed. Its final two lines closely correspond to the two opening lines. At the centre of the poem are two religious paintings, suggesting the true Christianity from which both the Alexandrian Fathers and the modern priests and congregation seem to the poet to have strayed. The poem is held together by a series of simple contrasts, or by surface parallels with underlying oppositions. The first four stanzas seem to me an unqualified success. But with the introduction of the sable presbyters and the theme of purgation the satiric focus of the poem is dispersed, much to the detriment of its unity and the bewilderment of the reader. There seems to be an insufficient connection between the satire directed against the sable presbyters, which, much as in 'The Hippopotamus', appears to be essentially an attack on the church of the Laodiceans, and that directed against the Alexandrian Fathers, and the stitching together of the two themes by means of the references of the last two stanzas seems to me insufficient to overcome the poem's lack of thematic unity. The abandonment of the unity of setting by the introduction of Sweeney in the last stanza, whatever the compensations it brings with it, still further lessens the coherence of what has always seemed to me one of Mr. Eliot's most bewildering and most fascinating poems.

Source: *Essays in Criticism*, v (1955) 153–8.

David Ward 'Mr Eliot's Sunday Morning Service' (1973)

. . .'Mr Eliot's Sunday Morning Service'. . . is built upon an ironic conflict between the ordinary sensual life and the life of *askesis*. The underlying debate is, I believe, entirely serious, but it is expressed in this poem, as in all the other quatrain poems, in a game of ideas; the kind of over-clever play which often is the signal of a delicate and very active mind driven close to desperation by unresolved conflicts. The tone is quite different from that of the seventeenth century Metaphysical poets; Eliot's poems are more purely metaphysical in their natures than most of the poems of Donne, Marvell or Herbert, in whom the metaphysics is only one aspect of a very complex blend of idea and feeling, while in

Eliot the metaphysical anxiety overrides everything else and controls the whole world of poetic feeling. The quatrain poems express a metaphysical and therefore a personal sickness, whereas poems such as 'To His Coy Mistress' or Donne's 'Third Satire' or Herbert's 'The Collar', for all their troubled concern with time and death, with truth and with faith, point with assurance towards solutions in living; the quatrain poems remain imprisoned in terrible doubt and uncertainty.

The final stanza of 'Sunday Morning Service' introduces Sweeney, a figure who becomes of some importance in the image structure of Eliot's verse. He is the ordinary sensual man, the focus of all metaphysical and theological problems; mortal in flesh, yet the figure without whom the thousands of years of debate about the spirit, the sacrifice of Christ, the elaborate theology of the Trinity, would all be meaningless. He shifts from ham to ham in his bath, mimicking with his fleshy indolence the chop and change of the austere and abstract metaphysical dialectic of the schoolmen, and at the same time parodying the awful significance of the sacrament of baptism. The whole poem focuses upon this absurd forked naked creature, just as does the whole theological and metaphysical tradition which the poem plays with in its teasing and deliberately blasphemous way.

The doctrine of the Trinity has been at the centre of the belief of many millions of men, and yet it is a curious and irrational doctrine (which is perhaps its great strength). Like the doctrine of the Incarnation, with which it is bound in a subtle complex of mysterious paradoxes, it is an attempt to express and explain the impossible by equally impossible means. Belief in the oneness of God is central to the Christian faith, and so is belief in the divinity of Christ. But so also is the belief that Christ, though divine, became human as well; and since the oneness of God implies His freedom of space, time and mortality, the notion of the Divinity of the Christ who submitted to space, time and mortality raises certain insoluble problems of logic. The Gospel of St John complicates the problem by applying the ancient Greek concept of the *logos* to Christ, and insisting on the co-eternality and consubstantiality of Christ the Word and God the Father: 'In the beginning was the Word, and the Word was with God, and the Word was God' (John 1:1).

Christ, therefore, exists in a timeless unity. But through the incarnation He also exists in Time and Space. This duality parallels the duality of man, who through the sacraments is able to become part of the mystical body of Christ while mysteriously remaining in his natural body.

St John is also responsible for the further complication of the Paraclete, or Comforter. He makes Christ promise: 'And I will pray the Father, and he shall give you another Comforter, that he may abide with you for ever; Even the Spirit of truth; whom the world cannot receive, because it seeth him not, neither knoweth him: but ye know him; for he dwelleth with you, and shall be in you' (John 14:16).

The language of this clearly suggests a division between the Christian and the world, and a unity of a kind between the Christian and God, a suggestion which is strengthened by: 'Yet a little while, and the world seeth me no more; but ye see me: because I live, ye shall live also. At that day ye shall know that I am in my Father, and ye in me, and I in you' (John 14:19–20).

The Comforter, the Holy Ghost, thus enters as the third person of the Trinity, but paradoxically in a passage which stresses the unity of the Father with the Son, the Christian with Christ, and the unity of the Holy Ghost with all these. The doctrine of the Trinity is therefore in one way an assertion of unity; a unity in which man shares, through the magic of the sacraments.

We have already seen how Eliot, though attracted strongly by the elegant and supple reasoning of Bradley, began to feel dissatisfied with him. The Christian theological tradition offered something much more substantial and much less abstract in terms of philosophic myths embodying the endless puzzles which are involved in the condition of humanity. There remains for Eliot a feeling of the absurdity that these elaborate and beautiful puzzle-games of unreason should be developed for phallic Sweeney in his bath, and delight in the absurdity combines with the fascination of the problem, and the fear of it, in 'Mr. Eliot's Sunday Morning Service'. So:

> In the beginning was the Word.
> Superfetation of τὸ ἕν,
> And at the mensual turn of time
> Produced enervate Origen.

As in many of the other quatrain poems sexual metaphors are used for spiritual matters. The Word is one with the Father and yet begotten by Him; therefore by an inescapable blasphemous logic begotten upon

Himself. The Incarnation expresses in worldly form the creativeness of the Father; the sexual metaphor is carried over to describe the 'polyprophilogenitive' priests, fecund in proselytes but barren in body. The tragi-comedy that the propagation of the Word should be entrusted to those who deny their own sexual creativity is sharpened by the reference to Origen, who took Paul's injunction to mortify one's members all too literally and castrated himself in the service of God. The phrase 'mensual turn of time' is a problem: the word mensual is not in the English dictionary, though it must mean monthly, and must carry some association with 'menstrual'. Perhaps 'the mensual turn of time' suggests an onset of barrenness in the world of time analogous to the female change of life; the magnificent creativeness of God becomes represented by a Church and priests who choose sterility as a pledge of dedication.

The painting of the Umbrian school is an icon which compactly symbolizes the whole pattern of doctrine. The beginning of Christ's ministry on earth, and thus the opening of all the problems implicit in the new covenant, was at His baptism. He is represented as half in, half out of the water; as it were half in, half out of this world and that. Above Him are the dove of the Holy Ghost and God the Father enthroned in majesty; pure spirits in a timeless world, but in His baptism Christ links the timeless world and the waters of time. The world is a wilderness against which the cloud of light around His head glows; it is pale and thin like the water through which the divine feet shine. Baptism is the sacrament which joins man with Christ. Thus the baptized God represents Christ, and in doing so represents man in Christ; represents man, and thus represents Christ in man. So Sweeney, at the end of the poem, in his baptismal bath, is in a bizarre way the imitation of Christ; hippopotamus that he is, he is nearer salvation than the neuter worker-bees of the Church.

'The sable presbyters', sombre with all the mournfulness of Scots dissenting religion, as well as the sombre celibacy of the Roman dispensation, approach divine truth through ascetic discipline; they are compared to the angels who swarm about the white heavenly rose of sanctified spirits in Canto XXIII of Dante's *Paradiso* like bees around an earthly flower. The celibate priests, like worker bees or like angels in the convention of mediaeval angelology, are neuter, yet busy themselves in the reproductive processes of the spirit, cross fertilizing the male stamen and the female pistil with love. With somewhat cruel satirical humour the priests neutered by their vows are made hairy-bellied bees rather than the angels of Dante, with their faces of living flame and golden wings, and Sweeney, who is no angel, but yet the essential subject of the incredible theological drama, soaks in comfort containing it all. . . .

SOURCE: extract from chapter 2 of *Between Two Worlds: A Reading of T. S. Eliot's Poetry and Plays* (1973) pp. 31–5.

Hugh Kenner 'Whispers of Immortality' (1960)

. . . [The quatrain] poems constitute an attempt to create a satiric medium for twentieth-century usage, nurtured by the perception that satire in verse works by assembling a crazy-quilt of detail, each detail an unchallengeable fact (everything in 'Mr. Eliot's Sunday Morning Service', from the sable presbyters to the bees' hairy bellies, exists on the plane of fact). The satiric decasyllabic couplet, of course, implies a mock-heroic convention. Eliot, reversing the telescope, manufactures in octosyllabic quatrains a convention of mock-casualness. The method of 'Whispers of Immortality', the most celebrated of the quatrain poems, is to shift at mid-point from one historic limit of the quatrain to the other; from the grave meditative idiom of Donne or Lord Herbert of Cherbury –

> Webster was much possessed by death
> And saw the skull beneath the skin

– to a brave *fin-de-siècle* smartness:

> Grishkin is nice; her Russian eye
> Is underlined for emphasis.

The 'Whispers' in the title effects a sinister inflection of Wordsworth's bucolic 'Intimations'; located midway in time between Webster and Grishkin, between a world dead and one powerless to be born, Wordsworth contrived cosmic exhilarations ('Everything that is is blest') out of the undeniable fact that he didn't, in middle life, feel as blest as he believed he once had. If he refused to consider 'the skull beneath the skin', neither would he have known what to make of Grishkin. In the ages of metaphysical intuition, however, 'Webster was much possessed by death' – possessed as by a lover, or by a devil? –

> And breastless creatures under ground
> Leaned backward with a lipless grin

adopting postures of compliant sexuality in

> a fine and private place,
> But none, I think, do there embrace.

His morbid delectation – thought clinging round dead limbs – was but a perversion of a fact, that the vehicle of thought is the corrupting body; lusts and luxuries, however cerebral, are 'tightened' with a sensation of physical tension. Webster was the contemporary of Donne, who preached in his shroud and imagined his own skeleton exhumed with 'a bracelet of bright hair about the bone'; but the living body, however puzzling its role, is never for Donne an occasion of morbidity or an impediment to spiritual joys. ('They are ours, though they're not wee, Wee are / The intelligences, they the spheare.')[1]

> Donne, I suppose, was such another
> Who found no substitute for sense,
> To seize and clutch and penetrate. . . .

The three sequential verbs create their predicate; but the predicate, not being specified, may as well be metaphorical as personal; Donne's understanding came through his sense, though it ached to transcend the senses; he was not 'controversial, polymath', a 'religious caterpillar' beclouding himself with a cocoon of deductions or (though a preacher) an 'enervate Origen' doing the 'blest office of the epicene'.

> He knew the anguish of the marrow
> The ague of the skeleton;
> No contact possible to flesh
> Allayed the fever of the bone.

The bone's fever is to know; as the finite centres cry out from their blood heat for union and communion. Donne dared more than Prufrock, but (except as an artist) accomplished no more; his words 'suggest unmistakably the awful separation between potential passion and any actualization possible in life. They indicate also the indestructible barriers between one human being and another'. Eliot wrote those sentences about Stendhal and Flaubert; but his preamble makes it clear that he means them to be of general application to any artist honest enough to 'dispense with atmosphere' and 'strip the world', any man of 'more than the common intensity of feeling, of passion'.

It is this intensity, precisely, and consequent discontent with the inevitable inadequacy of actual living to the passionate capacity, which drove them to art and to analysis. The surface of existence coagulates into lumps, which look like important simple feelings, which are identified by names as feelings, which the patient analyst disintegrates into more complex and trifling, but ultimately, if he goes far enough, into various canalizations of something again simple, terrible and unknown.

The second half of the poem, consequently, brings us to Grishkin, a world that awaits stripping;

> Uncorseted, her friendly bust
> Gives promise of pneumatic bliss.

'Pneumatic', of course, evokes by its etymology the things of the spirit, though it is unlikely that Grishkin is one of the 'martyr'd virgins'. And her presence reduces those 'important simple feelings' which coagulated on the surface of existence to baffle Prufrock, into something 'simple, terrible and unknown':

> The couched Brazilian jaguar. . . .

She is an opportunity for a Donne; her charms defy indifference; they abound, tightening lusts and luxuries into a concreteness to which Abstract Entities are merely external, circumambulant; 'one might

almost say her body thought', if any thought is indeed to be predicated.
But her superior corporeality polarizes the superior delicacy of such
people as we are, of a legation of Prufrocks (inheritors of Wordsworth's
poetic chastity), which 'crawls between dry ribs'[2] as between dry sheets,
or as a spider in a rib-cage, the bone feverless, 'To keep our metaphysics
warm'. For Grishkin abolishes that which is beyond the physical, and
'our lot' prizes nothing else. A passage from Bradley's *Principles of Logic*
which Eliot quoted in a *New Statesman* review the year before this poem
was published may be invoked as its unofficial epigraph. 'That the glory
of this world is appearance leaves the world more glorious if we feel it is a
show of some fuller splendour; but the sensuous curtain is a deception
and a cheat – if it hides some colourless movement of atoms, some
spectral woof of impalpable abstractions, or unearthly ballet of
bloodless categories.' . . .

SOURCE: extract from *The Invisible Poet: T. S. Eliot*, pp. 76–9.

NOTES

1. [Donne, 'The Extasie' – Ed.]
2. Le squelette était invisible
   Au temps heureux de l'Art païen.

P. G. Mudford   'Sweeney among the Nightingales' (1969)

The version of 'Sweeney among the Nightingales' in Eliot's *Poems*
(1919) and *Ara vos Prec* (1920) was preceded by two quotations:
ὤμοι πέπληγμαι καιρίαν πληγὴν ἔσω, and 'Why should I speak of
the Nightingale? The Nightingale sings of adulterate wrong.' The
second (from the anonymous *Edward III*, II 109–10) did not appear

either in *The Little Review* for September 1918, where the poem was first printed, or in the *Poems 1909 – 1925*. But together they associate the title of the poem with the *Agamemnon* and the tale of Tereus and Philomela in Book VI of Ovid's *Metamorphoses*, as well as providing a signpost to the landscape of the poem, which Eliot may well have felt to be necessary after its first appearance. No doubt the obvious weakness of the second quotation in comparison to Agamemnon's single line played some part in its disappearance; and anyway after *The Waste Land* the association of nightingales, in Eliot's mind, with the *Metamorphoses* needed no underlining. The point, though, is worth raising, I think, because the second quotation does have its uses in interpreting a poem which continues to raise difficulties. Hugh Kenner, for example, writing in *The Invisible Poet*, remarks, ' "Sweeney among the Nightingales" . . . is deliberately involved in Eliot's besetting vice, a never wholly penetrable ambiguity about what is supposed to be happening'.[1] Grover Smith comments, 'In plot, setting and characters this poem is opacity itself', an opacity that he goes on to thicken by telling us that the nightingales migrated into Eliot's concluding stanzas from the grove of the Furies ('bloody wood') in Sophocles's *Oedipus at Colonus*, and then continues, 'Eliot really brought in the Nightingales from Sophocles by mistake'.[2] This kind of truffle-hunting attitude towards literary criticism, which ends in displaying the truffle and destroying the poem, really will not do.[3]

While Grover Smith and Kenner both charge Eliot with violations of poetic decency, F. R. Leavis confines himself to an admission that the problem is of a subtler kind, involving something possibly recondite that it may be necessary to struggle with a bit to gain a glimpse of: 'In "Sweeney among the Nightingales" . . . the contrast is clearly something more than that between the sordid incident in a modern brothel and the murder of Agamemnon'.[4] I wish here to suggest by means of an interpretation of the poem what this something more may conceivably involve; and in doing so to indicate a way of avoiding the flight in which Professors Kenner and Grover Smith have taken refuge.[5]

The line from the *Agamemnon*, which stands at the head of the poem, conveys the power of its feeling, to a considerable degree, from the emphasis which falls on the adverbial ἔσω, at the end of the line. And one does not need either to be a Greek scholar, or to turn up the various translations of this line, to respond to its ambiguity: Agamemnon has been struck down within the palace; he has also been struck down

within the House of Atreus, by his own wife, in fulfilment of the doom
that has fallen upon it. And this gives us a clue to the kind of relationship
that we may expect between Sweeney and his nightingales. At the same
time it suggests an important difference: the murder of Agamemnon
violated a rigid bond between husband and wife which the more flexible
associations of Sweeney do not seem to include. The significance of this
last point I hope to make clear when I come to discuss the last six lines of
the poem.

The poem begins with Apeneck Sweeney alone; and he at once
confronts the reader with the question of how he is intended to be taken.
The problem becomes more pressing when the first two verses have
made apparent the remoteness of the Sweeney from that of 'Sweeney
Erect', behind whom the figure of the Boston pugilist, Steve O'Donnell,
is easily and closely felt. The Sweeney of this poem embodies a different
kind of force which is suggested by the central metaphor that the first
verse contains. His nickname, Apeneck, is taken up in the simian
suggestiveness of 'letting his arms hang down to laugh', and is extended
in the metaphorical use made of the 'zebra' and 'giraffe'. By means of
these animal metaphors Sweeney is identified in name, personality, and
appearance with the instinctive 'primitive' man; and Sweeney's
landscape or environment, typified in the next verse, is conveyed in
images appropriate to a figure of that imaginative level, ritualistic and
hierarchical:

> The circles of the stormy moon
> Slide westward toward the River Plate,
> Death and the Raven drift above
> And Sweeney guards the hornèd gate.

The moon, death, and the river of silver, named after Spanish fantasies
of fabulous wealth in the South American continent, are at the same
time richly suggestive and naturally associated; and they form an
appropriately numinous landscape for the Sweeney of the first four
lines. One important problem, however, remains: the significance of the
fact that Sweeney guards the hornèd gate? It means literally, of course,
that he guards the gate through which true dreams pass; and the rest of
the poem may most easily be taken, I think, as an amplification of what
it means to say that Sweeney guards this particular gate. On a tiny scale,
it will be seen, the structure of the poem can be compared to the circles

of descent in Dante's *Inferno*. Sweeney represents a personification of the animal instinct inside us; and this ritualistic figure is established in the first two verses. In the third, we pass through the hornèd gate to get a glimpse of his soul within the house. And what we find there, as in the descent of Dante's *Inferno*, is not something radically different, but the projection of a more complex darkness, through the harmonisation of landscape with the emotions of particular individuals.

On the other side of the gate, the landscape, appropriately, does not change much at first; as the moon is stormy outside, so here the stars are veiled (a fact that sets off an echo of Macbeth's 'Stars hide your fires, let not your light see my black and deep desires') and the seas are shrunk. Here, though, a reduction in 'poetic' intensity occurs; the focus of the poem turns from the numinous landscape to the more active social world of people, but people whose primary purpose is still to amplify the significance of Sweeney as guardian of the gate.

It is at this point that Eliot's comment upon the poem, quoted by F. O. Matthiessen, becomes useful: 'All that I consciously set out to create in "Sweeney among the Nightingales" was "a sense of foreboding".'[6] By means of the shadowy silent figures who surround Sweeney, Eliot fulfils his conscious intention: the person in the Spanish cape thought to be in league with Rachel *nee* Rabinovitch of the murderous paws, the silent vertebrate in brown, the indistinct figure with the host by the door, and the man with the heavy eyes and a golden grin (who suggests in a menacing way the daylight crime that is anticipated and unprevented) accumulate the atmosphere that Eliot aims at – and in close imaginative consistency with the kind of figure that we know Sweeney to be. The eye of the poem moves – and I think this is all that needs to be said about these central verses – between these shadowy figures, as the visual eye moves through the prisons of Piranesi – with similarly disturbing effects. It is an environment in which things (the various fruits and the wistaria), not people, possess an overabundant clarity that once again recalls the ambiguity of objects in dreams. And this physical clarity contrasts effectively with the psychological shadows in the behaviour of people.

But the sense of foreboding is not consummated in any act of violence, because the poem is not concerned with an event, but a state (another way of explaining why the last eight verses are an amplification); and this state is summed up and commented on in those six lines of very remarkable intensity with which the poem ends:

The Nightingales are singing near
The Convent of the Sacred Heart,
    And sang within the bloody wood
When Agamemnon cried aloud,
And let their liquid siftings fall
To stain the stiff dishonoured shroud.

The nightingales that sing near the convent of the sacred heart remind
us both of the nightingales that hover near Sweeney physically and of
Philomela who sings of her violation – and was referred to in the
abandoned quotation. But stating this does not account for the kind of
effect that these lines achieve. In one sense they can, no doubt, not be
interpreted, except in different terms by psychology; but they can be
illuminated by comparison with passages whose intensity is of a similar
kind. And one of these occurs, I think, in the *Agamemnon*, not very far
from the line which Eliot quotes.

After Clytemnestra has led her husband away to be killed in his bath,
Cassandra is left outside with the Chorus, and she sees, as in a
hallucination, what is happening within. At this point the Chorus
compare her, in her prophetic lamentation, to Philomela, in a passage
that I quote here from Louis MacNeice's translation:

You are mad, mad, carried away by the god,
Raising the dirge, the tuneless
Tune, for yourself. Like the tawny
Unsatisfied singer from her luckless heart
Lamenting 'Itys, Itys', the nightingale
Lamenting a life luxuriant with grief.[7]

The Chorus, by its association of the prophetess carried away by the
god, with the nightingale luxuriant with grief, underlines the intense
communication between the mind of Cassandra and the events that are
taking place inside the palace. She has become for them, as for us, a
figure of horror, as well as a provider of information. In short, she
simultaneously symbolises the murder by her immersion in it, and
proclaims it. So here, in Eliot's poem, the nightingales of Sweeney's
landscape proclaim a threat that is all too near the convent of his sacred
heart, and at the same time symbolise its nature, through their
mythological role as birds luxuriant with grief at the knowledge of a
desecration performed.

But Eliot communicates an important difference (which I mentioned earlier) between the crimes of which these nightingales know, and that against Agamemnon: the voice of Philomela recalling an incestuous violation has become liquid excreta falling upon the stiff dishonoured shroud. And this underlines a degradation in the historical process, a dissolving of the clear definitions in human relationships which gave to the crimes of Tereus and Clytemnestra a part in the pattern of sacred events. The stiff dishonoured shroud acts as a metaphor for the violation that exists in Sweeney's dream-world (one might compare the 'corpse in the garden' of *The Waste Land*); and the liquid excreta that fall upon it not only provide a comment upon its dishonour, but communicate the poem's grasp of that area of the mind where the sacred and the profane touch each other closely – in a form that would now find plenty of corroboration in the annals of psychoanalysis and criminal pathology.

Any whole response to the poem demands, then, a recognition of the different levels of intensity that the verse achieves: the first ten and the last six lines are remarkable for their appeal to what W. H. Auden has defined as the primary imagination: 'The concern of the Primary Imagination, its only concern, is with sacred beings and sacred events. . . . The response of the imagination to such a presence or significance is a passion of awe.'[8] Apeneck himself, and the nightingales, like Cassandra in that particular scene of the *Agamemnon*, seem to demand that we respond to them as Sacred Beings of this sort. And one of the weaknesses in the poem is perhaps that the transitions in it involve the leaping of imaginative gulfs that are more personal than the brilliant surface of the poem at first suggests. The achieved objectivity was not – and could not be – at the beginning of the twentieth century of the same order as Eliot's poetic forebears had achieved in the seventeenth. And this no doubt was one of the things to which he was pointing, in his now largely discredited dictum about the 'dissociation of sensibility'. Nevertheless, the power and the suggestiveness of the poem is extraordinary; it succeeds in making concrete that area of the mind where the sacred and profane are uneasy companions of everyday affairs; and communicates how the appearance of this conflict is transformed by the social context into which it erupts. What in the world of Greek tragedy meant the fall of a royal house had become by the end of the First World War a chimerical and pervasive darkness that menaced a man from within.

Source: *Essays in Criticism*, xix (1969) 285–91.

NOTES

1. Hugh Kenner, *The Invisible Poet* (1960) p. 79.
2. J. Grover Smith, *T. S. Eliot's Poetry and Plays* (Chicago, 1956) pp. 45–6.
3. Eliot stated in a letter to the *Sunday Times* of 6 April 1958 that 'the wood I had in mind was the grove of the Furies at Colonus; I called it "bloody" because of the blood of Agamemnon in Argos'. This remark not only shows up the confusion in Grover Smith's argument, but makes clear his failure to consider (before condemning the poem) what Eiot had said much earlier about poetic borrowing – i.e. that good poets make what they borrow into something better, or *at least something different.*
4. F. R. Leavis, *New Bearings in English Poetry*, 1954 edition, p. 88.
5. The view I am putting forward here is not inconsistent, I think, with admitting that the 'feeling' of the poem has the directness of something seen in a music-hall or a 'saloon'. But one can get no further along those lines.
6. F. O. Matthiessen, *The Achievement of T. S. Eliot* (1958) p. 129.
7. Aeschylus, *Agamemnon*, trans. Louis MacNeice (1936) pp. 51–2.
8. W. H. Auden, *The Dyer's Hand* (1963) pp. 54–5.

3. 'THE HOLLOW MEN', *ASH WEDNESDAY* AND THE ARIEL POEMS

Allen Tate   Ash Wednesday (1931)

Every age, as it sees itself, is peculiarly distracted: its chroniclers notoriously make too much of the variety before their own eyes. We see the variety of the past as mere turbulence within a fixed unity, and our own uniformity of the the surface as the sign of a profound disunity of impulse. We have discovered that the ideas that men lived by from about the twelfth to the seventeenth century were absolute and unquestioned. The social turmoil of European history, so this argument runs, was shortsighted disagreement as to the best ways of making these deep assumptions morally good.

Although writers were judged morally, poets purveyed ready-made moralities, and no critic expected the poet to give him a brand-new system. A poem was a piece of enjoyment for minds mature enough – that is, convinced enough of a satisfactory destiny – not to demand of every scribbler a way of life.

It is beyond the scope of this discussion, and of my own competence, to attempt an appraisal of any of the more common guides to salvation, including the uncommon one of the Thirty-nine Articles, lately subscribed to by Mr. T. S. Eliot, whose six poems published under the title *Ash Wednesday* are the occasion of this review. For it is my belief that, in a discussion of Eliot's poetry, his religious doctrines in themselves have little that commands interest. Yet it appears that his poetry, notwithstanding the amount of space it gets in critical journals, receives less discussion each year. The moral and religious attitude implicit in it has been related to the Thirty-nine Articles, and to a general intellectual position that Eliot has defended in his essays. The poetry and the prose are taken together as evidence that the author has made an inefficient adaptation to the modern environment; or at least he doesn't say anything very helpful to the American critics in their struggles to adapt themselves. It is an astonishing fact that, near as we are to a decade obsessed by 'aesthetic standards', there is less discussion of poetry in a typical modern essay on that fine art than there is in Johnson's essay on Denham. Johnson's judgment is frankly moralistic;

he is revolted by unsound morals; but he seldom capitulates to a moral sentiment because it flatters his own moral sense. He requires the qualities of generality, copiousness, perspicuity. He hates Milton for a regicide; but his judgment of *Paradise Lost* is as disinterested as any judgment we should find today; certainly no more crippled by historical prejudice than Mr. Eliot's own views of Milton. Yet Eliot's critics are a little less able each year to see the poetry for Westminster Abbey; the wood is all trees.

I do not pretend to know how far our social and philosophical needs justify a prejudice which may be put somewhat summarily as follows: all forms of human action, economics, politics, even poetry, and certainly industry, are legitimate modes of salvation, but the historic religious mode is illegitimate. It is sufficient here to point out that the man who expects to find salvation in the latest lyric or a well-managed factory will not only not find it there; he is not likely to find it anywhere else. If a young mind is incapable of moral philosophy, a mind without moral philosophy is incapable of understanding poetry. For poetry, of all the arts, demands a serenity of view and a settled temper of the mind, and most of all the power to detach one's own needs from the experience set forth in the poem. A moral sense so organized sets limits to human nature, and is content to observe them. But if the reader lack this moral sense, the poem will be only a body of abstractions either useful or irrelevant to that body of abstractions already forming, but of uncertain direction, in the reader's mind. This reader will see the poem chiefly as biography, and he will proceed to deduce from it a history of the poet's case, to which he will attach himself if his own case resembles it; if it doesn't, he will look for a more useful case. Either way, the poem as a specific object is ignored.

The reasoning that is being brought to bear upon Mr. Eliot's recent verse is as follows: Anglo-Catholicism would not at all satisfy me; therefore, his poetry declines under its influence. Moreover, the poetry is not 'contemporary'; it doesn't solve any labor problems; it is special, personal; and it can do us no good. Now the poetry *is* special and personal in quality, which is one of its merits, but what the critics are really saying is this – that Eliot's case-history is not special at all, that it is a general scheme of possible conduct that will not do for them. To accept the poetry seems to amount to accepting an invitation to join the Anglican Church. For the assumption is that the poetry and the religious position are identical.

If this were so, why should not the excellence of the poetry induce writers to join the Church, in the hope of writing as well as Eliot, since the irrelevance of the Church to their own needs makes them reject the poetry? The answer is, of course, that both parts of this fallacy are common. There is an aesthetic Catholicism, and there is a communist-economic rejection of art because it is involved with the tabooed mode of salvation.

The belief is that Eliot's poetry – all other poetry – is a simple record of the responses of a personality to an environment. The belief witnesses the modern desire to judge an art scientifically, practically, industrially – according to how it works. The poetry is viewed first as a pragmatic instrument, then examined 'critically' as a pragmatic result; neither stage of the approach gives us 'useful' knowledge.

Now a different heredity – environment combination would give us, of mechanical necessity, a different result, a different quantity of power to do a different and perhaps better social work. Doubtless that is true. But there is something disconcerting in this simple solution to the problem when it is looked at more closely. Two vastly different records or case histories might give us, qualitatively speaking, very similar results: Baudelaire and Eliot have in common many *qualities* but *no history*. Their 'results' have at least the common features of irony, humility, introspection, reverence - qualities fit only for contemplation and not for judgment according to their utility in our own conduct.

It is in this, the qualitative sense, that Eliot's recent poetry has been misunderstood. In this sense, the poetry is special, personal, of no use, and highly distinguished. But it is held to be a general formula, not distinct from the general formula that Eliot repeated when he went into the Church.

The form of the poems in *Ash Wednesday* is lyrical and solitary, and there is almost none of the elaborate natural description and allusion that gave to *The Waste Land* a partly realistic and partly symbolic character. These six poems are a brief moment of religious experience in an age that believes religion to be a kind of defeatism and puts all its hope for man in finding the right secular order. The mixed realism and symbolism of *The Waste Land* issued in irony. The direct and lyrical method of the new poems is based upon the simpler quality of humility. The latter quality comes directly out of the former, and there is an even continuity in Eliot's work.

In *The Waste Land* the prestige of our secular faith gave to the style its special character. This faith was the hard, coherent medium through which the discredited forms of the historic cultures emerged only to be stifled; the poem is at once their vindiçation and the recognition of their defeat. They are defeated in fact, as a politician may be defeated by the popular vote, but their vindication consists in the critical irony that their subordinate position casts upon the modern world.

The typical scene is the seduction of the stenographer by the clerk, in 'The Fire Sermon'. Perhaps Mr. J. W. Krutch has not discussed this scene, but a whole generation of critics has, and from a viewpoint that Mr. Krutch has recently made popular: the seduction betrays the disillusion of the poet. The mechanical, brutal scene shows what love really is – that is to say, what it is scientifically, since 'science' is truth: it is only an act of practical necessity for procreation. The telling of the story by the Greek seer Tiresias, who is chosen from a past of illusion and ignorance, permits the scene to become *a satire on the unscientific values of the past*. It was all pretense to think that love was anything but a biological necessity. The values of the past were pretty, absurd, and false; the scientific truth is both true and bitter. This is the familiar romantic dilemma, and the critics have read it into the scene from their own romantic despair.

There is no despair in the scene itself. The critics, who being in the state of mind I have described are necessarily blind to an effect of irony, have mistaken the symbols of an ironic contrast for the terms of a philosophic dilemma. It is the kind of metaphorical 'logic' typical of romantic criticism since Walter Pater. Mr. Eliot knows too much about classical irony to be overwhelmed by a popular dogma in literary biology. For the seduction scene shows, not what man is, but what *for a moment* he thinks he is. In other words, the clerk stands for the secularization of the religious and qualitative values in the modern world. And the meaning of the contrast between Tiresias and the clerk is not disillusion, but irony. The scene is a masterpiece, perhaps the most profound vision that we have of modern man.

The importance of this scene as a key to the intention of *Ash Wednesday* lies in the moral identity of humility and irony and in an important difference between them aesthetically. Humility is subjective, a quality of the moral character: it is thus general, invisible, and can only be inferred, not seen. *Irony is the visible, particular, and objective instance of humility*. Irony is the objective quality of an event or situation which stimulates our capacity for humility. It is that arrangement of experience, either premediated by art or accidentally appearing in the affairs of men, which permits to the spectator an insight superior to that of the actor; it shows him that the practical program, the special ambition, of the actor at that moment is bound to fail. The humility thus derived is the self-respect proceeding from a sense of the folly of men in their desire to dominate a natural force or a situation. The seduction scene is the picture of modern and dominating man. The arrogance and the pride of conquest of the 'small house agent's clerk' are the badge of science, bumptious practicality, overweening secular faith. The very success of his conquest witnesses its aimless character; it succeeds as a wheel succeeds in turning: he can only conquer again.

His own failure to understand his position is irony, and the poet's insight into it is humility. But for the grace of God, says the poet in effect, there go I. This is essentially the poetic attitude, an attitude that Eliot has been approaching with increasing purity. It is not that his recent verse is better than that of the period ending with *The Waste Land*. Actually it is less spectacular and less complex in subject matter; for Eliot less frequently objectifies his leading emotion, humility, into irony. His new form is simple, expressive, homogeneous, and direct, and without the early elements of violent contrast.

There is a single ironic passage in *Ash Wednesday*, and significantly enough it is the first stanza of the first poem. This passage presents objectively the poet *as he thinks himself for the moment to be*. It establishes that humility towards his own merit which fixes the tone of the poems that follow. And the irony has been overlooked by the critics because they take the stanza as a literal exposition of the latest phase of the Eliot *case history* – at a time when, in the words of Mr. Edmund Wilson, 'his psychological plight seems most depressing'. Thus, here is the vain pose of a Titan too young to be weary of strife, but weary of it nevertheless.

> Because I do not hope to turn again
> Because I do not hope
> Because I do not hope to turn
> Desiring this man's gift and that man's scope
> I no longer strive to strive towards such things
> (Why should the agèd eagle stretch it wings?)
> Why should I mourn
> The vanished power of the usual reign?

If the six poems are taken together as the focus of a specific religious emotion, the opening stanza, instead of being a naïve personal 'confession', appears in the less lurid light of a highly effective technical performance. This stanza has two features that are necessary to the development of the unique imagery which distinguishes the religious emotion of *Ash Wednesday* from any other religious poetry of our time. It is possibly the only kind of imagery that is valid for religious verse today.

The first feature is the regular yet halting rhythm, the smooth uncertainty of movement which may either proceed to greater regularity or fall away into improvisation. The second feature is the imagery itself. It is trite; it echoes two familiar passages from English poetry. But the quality to be observed is this: it is secular imagery. It sets forth a special ironic situation, but the emotion is not identified with any specific experience. The imagery is thus perfectly suited to the broken rhythm. The stanza is a device for getting the poem under way, starting from a known and general emotion, in a monotonous rhythm, for a direction which, to the reader, is unknown. The ease, the absence of surprise, with which Eliot proceeds to bring out the subject of his meditation is admirable. After some further and ironic deprecation of his worldly powers, he goes on:

> And pray to God to have mercy upon us
> And pray that I may forget
> These matters that with myself I too much discuss,
> Too much explain.

We are being told, of course, that there is to be some kind of discourse on God, or a meditation; yet the emotion is still general. The imagery is even flatter than before; it is 'poetical' at all only in that special context; for it is the diction of prose. And yet, subtly and imperceptibly, the rhythm has changed; it is irregular and labored. We are being prepared for a new and sudden effect, and it comes in the first lines of the second poem:

Lady, three white leopards sat under a juniper-tree
In the cool of the day, having fed to satiety
On my legs my heart my liver and that which had been contained
In the hollow round of my skull. And God said
Shall these bones live? shall these
Bones live?

From here on, in all the poems, there is constant and sudden change of rhythm, and there is a corresponding alternation of two kinds of imagery – the visual and tactile imagery common to all poetry, without significance in itself for any kind of experience, and the traditional religious symbols. The two orders are inextricably fused.

It is evident that Eliot has hit upon the only method now available of using the conventional religious image in poetry. He has reduced it from symbol to image, from abstraction to the plane of sensation. And corresponding to this process, there are images of his own invention which he almost pushes over the boundary of sensation into abstractions, where they have the appearance of conventional symbols.[1] The passage I have quoted above is an example of this: for the 'Lady' may be a nun, or even the Virgin, or again she may be a beautiful woman; but she is presented, through the serious tone of the invocation, with all the solemnity of a religious figure. The fifth poem exhibits the reverse of the process; it begins with a series of plays on the Logos, the most rarefied of all the Christian abstractions; and it succeeds in creating the effect of immediate experience by means of a broken and distracted rhythm:

> If the lost word is lost, if the spent word is spent
> If the unheard, unspoken
> Word is unspoken, unheard;
> Still is the unspoken word, the word unheard,
> The word without a word, the Word within
> The world and for the world . . ..

SOURCE: essay in *Hound and Horn*, IV (1931) 129–35.

NOTE

1. Mr. Yvor Winters would doubtless call this feature of the poem 'pseudo-reference'.

F. R. Leavis   Ash Wednesday and Marina (1932)

... The epigraph of 'The Hollow Men' – *Mistah Kurtz – he dead* – coming from *The Heart of Darkness*, suggests a dissolution of all the sanctions of life; and the tailing off of the poem into

> This is the way the world ends
> Not with a bang but a whimper

so completely justifies itself that it does not appear the audacity it is: 'audacity' suggests too much vigour. The poem develops certain elements of *The Waste Land* in a kind of neurasthenic agony. Yet this evocation of

> Shape without form, shade without colour,
> Paralysed force, gesture without motion

is a marvellously positive achievement, and if we should be tempted to relate too crudely the 'mind that created' with 'the man who suffered'[1] we have the various drafts[2] to remind us that it is after all a poem that we are dealing with. The terrible closing section, with its nightmare poise over the grotesque, is a triumph of aplomb. The three middle sections begin that exploration of 'the dreamcrossed twilight'[3] which (in a different spirit) is to be pursued in *Ash Wednesday*.

Between 'The Hollow Men' and *Ash Wednesday* come three poems published separately in the Ariel series. These show a curious change. We find in them, instead of the fevered torment of 'The Hollow Men', a kind of inert resignation. The movements are tired and nerveless; they suggest marvellously the failure of rhythm. If the extreme agony of consciousness has passed, so has the extraordinary vitality that went with it. But the change has another aspect. These three poems reveal a significant preoccupation; they have a direction, and they all point the same way. *Journey of the Magi* and *A Song for Simeon* deal dramatically with their religious theme, the promise of salvation, but the dramatic

form amounts to little more than delicacy in the presentment of
intimate personal issues:

> were we led all that way for
> Birth or Death? There was a Birth, certainly,
> We had evidence and no doubt. I had seen birth and death,
> But had thought they were different; this Birth was
> Hard and bitter agony for us, like Death, our death.
> We returned to our places, these Kingdoms,
> But no longer at ease here, in the old dispensation,
> With an alien people clutching their gods.
> I should be glad of another death.

The queer, essential equivocalness of this is the poet's, and the dramatic
theme, it becomes clear, is a means to the expression of it. The
ambivalence comes out still more strikingly in the end of *A Song for
Simeon*:

> I am tired with my own life and the lives of those after me,
> I am dying in my own death and the deaths of those after me.
> Let thy servant depart,
> Having seen thy salvation.

It is something very different from an affirmation that so transforms the
original theme: the air is 'thoroughly small and dry'.[4] And yet there is
something positive present, if only a direction of feeling and
contemplation – something specifically religious. At the end of *Animula*, the third Ariel poem, the liturgical note characteristic of *Ash
Wednesday* appears.

What seemed most to distinguish the first poem of *Ash Wednesday*
when, as 'Perch' io non spero', it appeared in *Commerce*,[5] from the Ariel
poems was the rhythm. The rhythm varies within the sequence from
part to part, but it is in general very much more nerved and positive
than that of the Ariel poems. In the comparison it is not extravagant to
speak of it as having certain qualities of ritual; it produces in a high
degree the frame-effect, establishing apart from the world a special
order of experience, dedicated to spiritual exercises. To discuss *Ash
Wednesday*, then, is a delicate business, incurring danger both of crudity
and impertinence. We remind ourselves of Mr Eliot's precept and

practice in criticism: the sequence is poetry, and highly formal poetry.
Yet it is impossible not to see in it a process of self-scrutiny, of self-
exploration; or not to feel that the poetical problem at any point was a
spiritual problem, a problem in the attainment of a difficult sincerity.
The poetry belongs to

> the time of tension between dying and birth
> The place of solitude where three dreams cross

and is a striving after a spiritual state based upon a reality elusive and
yet ultimate.

We cannot help recalling Mr Eliot's various observations about the
problem of belief. This, for instance, seems germane:

> I cannot see that poetry can ever be separated from something which I should
> call belief, and to which I cannot see any reason for refusing the name of belief,
> unless we are to reshuffle names together. It should hardly be needful to say that
> it will not inevitably be orthodox Christian belief, although that possibility can
> be entertained, since Christianity will probably continue to modify itself, as in
> the past, into something that can be believed in (I do not mean *conscious*
> modifications like modernism, etc., which always have the opposite effect). The
> majority of people live below the level of belief or doubt. It takes application,
> and a kind of genius, to believe anything, and to believe *anything* (I do *not* mean
> merely to believe in some 'religion') will probably become more and more
> difficult as time goes on.[6]

Mr Eliot's concern is specifically religious. Certain qualities of genius he
indubitably has, and *Ash Wednesday* is a disciplined application of them
to the realizing of a spiritual state conceived as depending upon
belief – belief in something outside himself. The result is a most subtle
poetry of great technical interest; and it is on the technical aspect that
critical attention must in any case focus.

For the poet 'technique' was the problem of sincerity.[7] He had to
achieve a paradoxical precision-in-vagueness; to persuade the elusive
intuition to define itself, without any forcing, among the equivocations
of 'the dreamcrossed twilight'. The warning against crude interpretation, against trying to elicit anything in the nature of prose
statement, is there in the unexpected absences of punctuation; and in
the repetitive effects, which suggest a kind of delicate tentativeness. The
poetry itself is an effort at resolving diverse impulses, recognitions and
needs.

Ash Wednesday is a whole. Faced with 'Perch' io non spero' as a separate poem, one might pardonably, perhaps, see an odd affectation in 'Why should the aged eagle stretch its wings?' But (though the criticism is still made[8]) in a reading of the whole sequence the ironical function of this self-dramatization becomes obvious. It is an insurance against the pride of humility; a self-admonition against the subtle treasons, the refinements, of egotism that beset the quest of sincerity in these regions. Again,

> And I pray that I may forget
> These matters that with myself I too much discuss
> Too much explain

intimates a capacity for a critical attitude towards the 'discussing' that the poetry is.

To take fragments separately at their face value is to misunderstand this poetry, which works by compensations, resolutions, residuums and convergences. What, we ask, does the poet resign and renounce in the first poem, and what is the nature of his renunciation? The line from the Shakespeare sonnet suggests that it is worldly ambition, personal glory, that he renounces. This becomes 'The infirm glory of the positive hour'; and 'The one veritable transitory power' together with the next lines –

> Because I cannot drink
> There, where trees flower, and springs flow, for
> there is nothing again

– seems to identify it with the vital illusion of youth. But, it next appears, what we have here is the sensory evocation of a spiritual state:

> Because I know that time is always time
> And place is always and only place
> And what is actual is actual only for one time
> And only for one place
> I rejoice that things are as they are and
> I renounce the blessed face
> And renounce the voice.

– This, with its bare prose statement, has the effect of a complete renunciation of supernatural assurance. And the general effect of the poem is negative. Yet the formula of renunciation –

> Teach us to care and not to care
> Teach us to sit still

– registers a positive religious impulse, which is confirmed by the liturgical close. And the positive element comes out more significantly in

> Consequently I rejoice, having to construct something
> Upon which to rejoice

– if the air is 'thoroughly small and dry' it is 'smaller and dryer than the will'. Not for nothing have the rhythms of *Ash Wednesday* so much more life than those of the Ariel poems. After this introduction, then, we know what are to be the themes of the following poetry, and what the mode of debate.

It is common to ask of the second poem, 'Who is the Lady, and what do the three white leopards stand for?' As for the first question, Mr Eliot in his 'Dante' writes: 'In the Earthly Paradise Dante encounters a lady named Matilda, whose identity need not at first bother us'; the identity of the Lady in this poem need not bother us at all. She reminds us not only of Matilda but of Beatrice and Piccarda too, and helps to define a mode of religious contemplation that characterizes the poem. The theme of the poem is death, and death is evoked as complete extinction:

> End of the endless
> Journey to no end
> Conclusion of all that
> Is inconclusible. . . .

ut the effect has extraordinarily little in common with that of the e theme in 'The Hollow Men' or *Journey of the Magi* or *A Song for* ?on. The desire for extinction ($\dot{\alpha}\pi o\theta\alpha\nu\epsilon\hat{\imath}\nu\ \theta\acute\epsilon\lambda\omega$)[9] – 'I should be glad of another death' and 'I am tired with my own life and the lives of those after me' – becomes curiously transmuted by association with something positive:

As I am forgotten
And would be forgotten, so I would forget
Thus devoted, concentrated in purpose.

The devotion and the concentration are represented by the Lady, who
serves to intimate the poet's recourse, in his effort 'to construct
something upon which to rejoice', to a specific religious tradition, and
they manifest themselves throughout in rhythm and tone. The 'burden
of the grasshopper' (a fine instance, this, of Mr Eliot's genius in
borrowing), though a burden, potently evoked, of annihilation, has
nevertheless its share of the religious emotion that pervades the poem.
The 'garden where all love ends' is associated with the garden in which
God walked 'in the cool of the day'. A religious sense of awe, an
apprehension of the supernatural, seems to inform the desert where the
bones are scattered.

As for the 'three white leopards', they are not symbols needing
interpretation; they act directly, reinforcing the effect of ritual that we
have noted in the verse and suggesting the mode of experience, the kind
of spiritual exercise, to which *Ash Wednesday* is devoted. They belong
with the 'jewelled unicorns' that have bothered some critics in the
fourth poem:

Redeem
The unread vision in the higher dream
While jewelled unicorns draw by the gilded hearse.

Perhaps in this last passage Mr Eliot has been too helpful and 'the
higher dream' is too like explicit elucidation. But it at any rate reminds
us conveniently of certain things that he says in his 'Dante'. He remarks
of the 'pageantry' of the *Paradise*: 'It belongs to the world of what I call
the *high dream*, and the modern world seems capable only of the low
dream.' And he says elsewhere:

Dante's is a *visual* imagination. It is a visual imagination in a different sense from
that of a modern painter of still life: it is visual in the sense that he lived in an age
in which men still saw visions. It was a psychological habit, the trick of which
we have forgotten, but as good as any of our own. We have nothing but dreams,
and we have forgotten that seeing visions – a practice now relegated to the
aberrant and the uneducated – was once a more significant, interesting, and
disciplined kind of dreaming.[10]

When Mr Eliot says that we have forgotten the trick he means it. He no more supposes that Dante's mode of vision can be recaptured than that Dante's belief can.[11] But his frequentation of Dante has its place in that effort 'to construct something' and that 'training of the soul' which he speaks of. And his leopards and unicorns seem to insist on the peculiar kind of 'disciplined dreaming' that he strives to attain in 'the dreamcrossed twilight' of *Ash Wednesday*. They go with the formal quality of the verse, in which we have already noted a suggestion of ritual, and with the liturgical element, to define the plane at which this poetry works. The spiritual discipline is one with the poetical.

The third poem of the sequence offers an admirable example of the way in which Mr Eliot blends the reminiscent (literary or conventional) in imagery with the immediately evocative. The 'stairs' of this poem (they have a 'banister') have their effect for a reader who recognizes no reminiscence. They concentrate the suggestion of directed effort that distinguishes this poetry from the earlier, and they define the nature of the effort. The poem epitomizes, as it were, a spiritual history, and records a sense of an advance and a hardly-dared hope of attainment (qualified by the humility that becomes explicit at the end). But the stairs also recall the stairs of the *Purgatorio* – a reminiscence that is picked up again in the next poem, in a further quotation from that Provençal passage of Canto XXVI which Mr Eliot has used so much:

> Ara vos prec, per aquella valor
> que vos guida al som de l'escalina
> sovegna vos a temps de ma dolor.[12]

This, in a new spirit, is the art that he practised in *The Waste Land*.

The opening of the fourth poem recalls a passage of the third, that giving the view through the 'slotted window':

> . . . beyond the hawthorn blossom and a pasture scene
> The broadbacked figure drest in blue and green
> Enchanted the maytime with an antique flute.
> Blown hair is sweet, brown hair over the mouth blown,
> Lilac and brown hair. . . .

This backward glimpse of youth 'where trees flower and springs flow' seems to be dismissed here as 'distraction'. But the sense of refreshment that distinguishes the fourth poem seems to owe something to the same source. The 'violet', the 'larkspur' and the 'varied green' have an effect like that of 'lilac', and she 'who walked' may well have had brown hair. But this imagery, which is directly evocative, also lends itself to symbolic associations – 'Going in white and blue, in Mary's colour' and 'In blue of larkspur, blue of Mary's colour' – and she who 'made strong the fountains and made fresh the springs' takes on a specifically religious significance. Is the poet remembering an actual religious experience, or is he using the memory of the time when the springs were fresh as a symbol? The case is subtler. The unspecified 'who' and the indeterminate syntax, together with the element of 'higher dream' that we have already discussed, and the 'White light folded, sheathed about her, folded', intimate that the process here is analogous to that represented by Dante's Beatrice.[13] The 'yews' again are directly evocative: they have current values; beneath them

> ghostly shapes
> May meet at noontide; Fear and trembling Hope,
> Silence and Foresight; Death and Skeleton
> And Time the Shadow

– though these yews, owing to the context, suggest a particular religious tradition.

A process analogous to Dante's; but the modern poet can make no pretence to Dante's certitude – to his firm possession of his vision. The ambiguity that constructs a precarious base for rejoicing in the fourth poem brings doubt and fear of inner treachery in the fifth. The breathless, circling, desperately pursuing movement of the opening, with its repetitions and its play upon 'word', 'Word', 'world' and 'whirled', suggests both agonized effort to seize the unseizable, and the elusive equivocations of the thing grasped. The doubts and the self-questionings are developed, and the poem ends with a despairing recognition of the equivocal that recalls, in a significant way, the second poem:

> In the last desert between the last blue rocks
> The desert in the garden the garden in the desert
> Of drouth, spitting from the mouth the withered apple-seed.

> O my people.

In the earlier poem the desert that the bones inherit – the 'garden where all love ends' – is associated with the garden in which God walked 'in the cool of the day'. The ambiguity is the condition of a poise between widely divergent impulses and emotions that produces a strange serenity. But here, in the fifth poem, we have instead an equivocation of experience that produces agonizing doubt: which is garden and which is desert?

In the last poem of the sequence the doubt becomes an adjuvant of spiritual discipline, ministering to humility. But an essential ambiguity remains, an ambiguity inescapable 'In this brief transit where the dreams cross'. To symbolize, to conceive for himself, the spiritual order that he aspires towards, the poet inevitably has recourse to his most vital mundane experience. But the memories of this present themselves also as temptation, as incitement to subtle treacheries:

> though I do not wish to wish these things
> From the wide window towards the granite shore
> The white sails still fly seaward, seaward flying
> Unbroken wings
>
> And the lost heart stiffens and rejoices
> In the lost lilac and the lost sea voices
> And the weak spirit quickens to rebel
> For the bent golden-rod and the lost sea smell. . . .

– The 'lost heart' is itself ambiguous: the heart is 'lost' because it succumbs to temptation and 'rebels'; but 'lost' also records a pang of regret, a rebellious questioning of the renunciation: the heart is 'lost' because it has lost the lilac and the sea voices. With 'merely vans to beat the air' the poet looks enviously at the unbroken wings that fly seaward, and prays: 'Suffer us not to mock ourselves with falsehood.'

In the Ariel poem that appeared after *Ash Wednesday* it is Marina, who was lost and found again, who becomes the symbol for the new realization striven after. But this is to simplify too much. *Marina* belongs, like *Ash Wednesday*, to 'the time of tension between dying and birth', and exhibits an even more subtle ambiguity than anything in the sequence. The liturgical note is absent, and one may indicate the change in rhythm by saying that it has about it nothing of ritual; yet the poem expresses something approaching nearer to assurance than anything in *Ash Wednesday*. Images like the things that the poet 'did not wish to wish' now 'return', bringing with them a sense of ineffable peace. The coming of 'this grace' by which the various forms of death

> Are become unsubstantial, reduced by a wind,
> A breath of pine, and the woodsong fog

is associated with the approach of a ship to 'granite islands'. The 'white sails' and the 'granite shore' of *Ash Wednesday* have taken another value here. The ship – 'I made this' – represents the effort 'to construct something upon which to rejoice'. Marina, the daughter lost and recovered, evokes the peculiar sense of victory over death that attends upon 'this grace':

> This form, this face, this life
> Living to live in a world of time beyond me; let me
> Resign my life for this life, my speech for that unspoken,
> The awakened, lips parted, the hope, the new ships.

Just what is the nature of the new life we cannot say. It is an elusive apprehension, conveyed poignantly, but in essential ambiguities. The poem is the resultant of diverse suggestions and orientations. The imagery belongs to the 'higher dream':

> What is this face, less clear and clearer
> The pulse in the arm, less strong and stronger –
> Given or lent? more distant than stars and nearer than the
>   eye. . . .

The indeterminate syntax intimates the kind of relation that exists between the various elements of the poem: one would not, to put it crudely, think of trying to relate Marina, her father, the ship and the islands in a story. And the elusiveness of the relations suggests at the same time the felt transcendence of the vision and its precariousness.

The poetry of the last phase may lack the charged richness and the range of 'Gerontion' and *The Waste Land*. But it is, perhaps, still more remarkable by reason of the strange and difficult regions of experience that it explores. Its association with Mr Eliot's explicit Anglo-

Catholicism has encouraged, in the guise of criticism, an extra-ordinarily crude and superficial approach. Critics speak of 'Pre-Raphaelite imagery' and a 'Pre-Raphaelite flavour' and deplore (or applaud) the return to the fold. But this poetry is more disconcertingly modern than *The Waste Land*: the preoccupation with traditional Christianity, the use of the Prayer Book, and the devotion to spiritual discipline should not hinder the reader from seeing that the modes of feeling, apprehension and expression are such as we can find nowhere earlier. If it is likely to be significant for young poets, that is not because of the intellectual fashions that attribute so much importance to T. E. Hulme, but because contemporary poets are likely to find that the kind of consciousness represented by *Ash Wednesday* and *Marina* has a close bearing upon certain problems of their own. It is not for nothing that in the field of critical thought – in the consideration of those general problems that literary criticism nowadays cannot ignore – Mr Eliot remains a directing influence.[14]

SOURCE: extract from *New Bearings in English Poetry* (1932) pp. 114–32.

NOTES

1. '. . . the more perfect the artist, the more completely separate in him will be the man who suffers and the mind which creates' – *The Sacred Wood* (1920) p. 48.

2. See *The Chapbook*, no. 39 (1924); and *Criterion*, x (Jan 1925) 170.

3. See *Ash Wednesday*, vi.

4. *Ash Wednesday*, i.

5. *Commerce*, xv (Spring 1928).

6. *The Enemy*, Jan 1927.

7. Cf. 'And this honesty never exists without great technical accomplishment' – T. S. Eliot on Blake in *The Sacred Wood*, p. 137.

8. Cf. Edmund Wilson, *Axel's Castle* (1931) p. 130: 'And I am made a little tired at hearing Eliot, only in his early forties, present himself as an "aged eagle" who asks why he should make the effort to stretch his wings.'

9. See the epigraph of *The Waste Land*.

10. 'Dante' (1929), in *Selected Essays*, 2nd edition (1934)

11. See 'A Note on Poetry and Belief', *The Enemy*, Jan 1927, p. 10

12. 'Now I pray you, by that goodness which guideth you to the summit of the stairway, be mindful in due time of my pain' – *Poi s'ascose nel foco che gli affina*.

13. See George Santayana, *Poetry and Religion* (1922) pp. 128–9.

14. See I. A. Richards, 'Review of *Science and Poetry*', *The Dial*, Mar 1927; and Eliot's 'A Note on Poetry and Belief', and 'Dante', note to ch. 2.

F. R. Leavis *Marina* (1942)

. . . The poetry from *Ash Wednesday* onwards doesn't say, 'I believe', or 'I know', or 'Here's the truth'; it is positive in direction but not positive in that way (the difference from Dante is extreme). It is a searching of experience, a spiritual discipline, a technique for sincerity – for giving 'sincerity' a meaning. The preoccupation is with establishing from among the illusions, evanescences and unrealities of life in time an apprehension of an assured reality – a reality that, though necessarily apprehended in time, is not of it. There is a sustained positive effort – the constructive effort to be 'conscious':

> Time past and time future
> Allow but a little consciousness.
> To be conscious is not to be in time
> But only in time can the moment in the rose-garden,
> The moment in the arbour where the rain beat,
> The moment in the draughty church at smokefall
> Be remembered; involved with past and future.
> Only through time time is conquered.

('Burnt Norton')

With these 'moments' is associated 'the sudden illumination':

> The moments of happiness – not the sense of well-being,
> Fruition, fulfilment, security or affection,
> Or even a very good dinner, but the sudden illumination –
> We had the experience, but missed the meaning,
> And approach to the meaning restores the experience
> In a different form, beyond any meaning
> We can assign to happiness.

('The Dry Salvages')

'Illumination', it will be seen, is no simple matter, and *Ash Wednesday*, where the religious bent has so pronounced a liturgical expression, is remarkable for the insistent and subtle scrupulousness of the concern manifested to guard against the possibilities of temptation, self-deception and confusion that attend on the aim and the method.

Perhaps the way in which the sense of an apprehended higher reality, not subject to the laws of time and mundane things, is conveyed is most simply illustrated in *Marina*, that lovely poem (a limiting description) with the epigraph from Seneca. There, in the opening, the enchanted sense of a landfall in a newly discovered world blends with the suggestions (to be taken up later on in the poem) of 'daughter' – the 'daughter' being associated by the title of the poem with the Shakespearean heroine who, lost at sea, was miraculously found again, for the father an unhoped-for victory over death:

> What seas what shores what grey rocks and what islands
> What water lapping the bow
> And scent of pine and the woodthrush singing through the fog
> What images return
> O my daughter.

The images that follow in the next paragraph bring in the insistently recurring 'Death' after each line, and they are evoked in order that we may find that they now

> Are become unsubstantial, reduced by a wind,
> A breath of pine, and the woodsong fog
> By this grace dissolved in place. . . .

It may be remarked that the mundane actuality, the world of inescapable death, is elsewhere in the poems of the phase less easily dismissed; its reduction to unreality is a different affair, having nothing of enchantment about it, and the unreality is not absence. And perhaps it should be noted too as an associated point that 'grace', in its equivocal way, is the one explicitly religious touch in *Marina*.

The evocation of the apprehended reality is now taken up, and is characteristic in method:

> What is this face, less clear and clearer
> The pulse in the arm, less strong and stronger –
> Given or lent? more distant than stars and nearer than the eye

Whispers and small laughter between leaves and hurrying feet
Under sleep, where all the waters meet.

The face, 'less clear and clearer', doesn't belong to the ordinary
experience of life in time, and the effect of a higher reality is reinforced
by the associations of the last two lines – associations that, with their
potent suggestion, characteristic of some memories of childhood, of a
supremely illuminating significance, recur so much in Eliot's later
work –

> We had the experience, but missed the meaning
> And approach to the meaning restores the significance
> In a different form, beyond any meaning
> We can assign to happiness.

The effect depends upon a kind of co-operative co-presence of the
different elements of suggestion, the co-operation being, as the spare
and non-logical pointing intimates, essentially implicit, and not a
matter for explicit development. What in fact we have is nothing of the
order of affirmation or statement, but a kind of tentatively defining
exploration.

The rest of the poem adds to the co-present elements the suggestion of
a constructive effort, which, though what it constructs is defective and
insecure, has a necessary part in the discovery or apprehension:

> I made this . . .

> Made this unknowing, half conscious, unknown, my own,
> The garboard strake leaks, the seams need caulking.
> This form, this face, this life
> Living to live in a world of time beyond me; let me
> Resign my life for this life, my speech for that unspoken,
> The awakened, lips parted, the new ships.

Thus, in the gliding from one image, evocation or suggestion to another,
so that all contribute to a total effect, there is created a sense of a
supreme significance, elusive, but not, like the message of death,
illusory; an opening into a new and more than personal life.

SOURCE: extract from a review in Scrutiny, XI (1942) 61–3.

Helen Gardner   Ash Wednesday (1949)

Although all Mr Eliot's poetry is the expression of a certain kind of apprehension, the change in his rhythms and style . . . and the change in his imagery, is the result of a profound change within this apprehension. In the earlier poetry the apprehension is a kind of glass through which he views the world; it is a dark glass through which life is seen with a strange clarity, but drained of colour and variety. In the poetry that follows *The Waste Land* the apprehension itself becomes more and more the subject. The poet's own image of a shadow can be used to define what is constant and what changes. At the beginning one is aware of life seen in shadow, a grey monotony. The shadow deepens, growing darker and darker, but up to *The Waste Land* the life it darkens is the subject. Now the shadow itself enters the poetry. Where before it was the shadow that was implied, and what we were given was its effect; now the shadow itself is the object of contemplation, and it is the light that casts it that is implied. Paradoxically the acceptance of the shadow lessens the darkness; the darkness of *The Waste Land* becomes a kind of twilight. From within that twilight the poet catches sight of brightness, far off perhaps, but still a brightness which is full of colour. The natural world, which is not looked at directly, has a beauty it did not have in his earlier contemplation of it. Instead of looking out upon the world and seeing sharply defined and various manifestations of the same desolation and emptiness, the poet turns away from the outer world of men to ponder over certain intimate personal experiences. He narrows the range of his vision, withdraws into his own mind, and 'thus devoted, concentrated in purpose' his verse moves 'into another intensity'. The intensity of apprehension in the earlier poetry is replaced by an intensity of meditation.

The withdrawal into the world of inner experience brings with it a new kind of imagery: an imagery deriving from dreams, not from observation, and retaining the inconsequence, the half-understood but deeply felt significance of dreams, their symbolic truth. The new imagery lacks the sharp precision as well as the realism of the earlier. The images are mostly beautiful and poetically suggestive in themselves, whereas the earlier imagery was more often grotesque. They are often drawn from nature, where the most characteristic of the earlier images came from human life lived in cities or, if from nature, from nature in its more sinister aspects. Many of the images are traditional, common symbols which have an age-old meaning: the rose, the garden, the fountain, the desert, the yew. The poet accepts this traditional imagery, and mingles it with images of natural beauty, and with more esoteric images: the white leopards, the jewelled unicorns, the agèd eagle, taken from medieval allegorical fantasy, and the flute-player in blue and green, and the 'silent sister veiled in white and blue', from the world of private myth-making. The figures in Ash Wednesday are not persons; they are like figures seen for a moment through the window of a swiftly moving train, where an attitude or a gesture catches our attention and is then gone forever, but remains to haunt the memory. Much of the imagery has this fleeting vividness; it is not fixed with the precision of the earlier poetry, and it is only occasionally that the brilliant exact wit of the earlier comparisons is found:

> the stair was dark,
> Damp, jaggèd, like an old man's mouth drivelling,
>   beyond repair,
> Or the toothed gullet of an agèd shark.

This, which has a particular purpose where it occurs, stands out as alien to the general tone of Ash Wednesday, where the poet seems not to wish to linger on any particular image, which might by its vividness, aptness, or unexpectedness interrupt the stream of meditation and distract us from his essential theme. Many of the images and symbols, unfixed by precise notation, recur with changing values and changing emphasis.

This recurring imagery, so suggestive, vague and poetic, when it is contrasted with the intensely particular, sharp and definite images of the earlier poetry, so traditional and archetypal in comparison with the realistic and highly original imagery of the first three volumes, expresses itself in new rhythms and a new style. Mr Eliot's most striking quality in the poetry that culminates in The Waste Land was an extreme power of condensation. Whether in free rhymed verse, or in quatrains, or in the blank verse of 'Gerontion' his poetry had a peculiar force of expression; it was economical of words, omitting the merely connecting phrase, elliptical and in the best sense rhetorical. The new style of Ash Wednesday shows an extraordinary relaxation; it is highly repetitive, and much of the repetition has an incantatory effect. It circles round and round certain phrases: 'Because I do not hope' or 'Teach us to care and not to care'; but it also plays with words, repeating them, where repetition is grammatically unnecessary:

> Because these wings are no longer wings to fly
> But merely vans to beat the air
> The air which is now thoroughly small and dry
> Smaller and dryer than the will
> Teach us to care and not to care
> Teach us to sit still.

To make a prose paraphrase of the earlier poetry one would have to expand, as one normally has to expand in paraphrasing poetry; here and in many places in *Ash Wednesday* one would have to condense. The poetic effect of this, and of passages such as the opening of section v, is very curious; it is as if the poet were not thinking of what he is saying. The constant internal assonance and internal rhyme have something of the same effect; they do not appear as if they were consciously meant. The poet's words seem to follow the laws of association rather than those of ratiocination.

> Will the veiled sister pray for
> Those who walk in darkness, who chose thee and oppose thee,
> Those who are torn on the horn between season and season, time and
>   time, between
> Hour and hour, word and word, power and power, those who wait
> In darkness? Will the veiled sister pray
> For children at the gate
> Who will not go away and cannot pray:
> Pray for those who chose and oppose. . . .

This style is the exact opposite of a rhetorical style, where we are delighted by our perception of the poet's exact placing of each word to give it its maximum force; where we are aware of the rightness of each word, and where sound and rhythm support and underline the sense. It is also wholly undramatic. Point is submerged in a musically flowing rhythm. It is a lyrical style, and in *Ash Wednesday* Mr Eliot reaches what he rarely attained before, the peculiar poignancy of lyric utterance. This lyrical note is sustained with particular beauty in the second and last sections but it is present throughout. The traditional symbols of fountains, springs, rocks, birds, flutes, belong to the world of lyric poetry, where feeling seizes on the first image that comes to the mind, and, not searching for the particular, finds itself employing stock images. Much of the poetry in *Ash Wednesday* reads as if it had simply come to the poet. One is hardly aware of the artist in control of his experience and shaping it into expression.

The change in Mr Eliot's poetry cannot be discussed without reference to the fact that the author of *Ash Wednesday* is a Christian while the author of *The Waste Land* was not. Nobody can underrate the momentousness for any mature person of acceptance of all that membership of the Christian Church entails. But the connection between his acceptance of the Christian Faith, and entry into the communion of the Church, and this change in the content and style of his poetry is a very complex one. Behind any such act of choice and affirmation of belief lie obscure experiences which the conscious mind has translated into intellectual formulas and the conscious will has translated into a decisive step. It is in these obscurer regions that the change in the poetry has its origins, not in the conscious act which is equally a result. Any such act, which makes an apparent break with the past, is itself the result of the past, and when it occurs makes the past assume a pattern not visible before. What is found is what was looked for, and since to look for anything is to act on the hypothesis that it exists, faith precedes faith in a regressive series. But the finding, the recognition of the assumption we have been acting on, which makes an alteration of our way of life, and makes imperative the acceptance of certain obligations, is profoundly mysterious. Nobody can explain why what seems at one time unbelievable, whether beautiful and attractive, or terrifying, comes to seem truth itself and the ground and test of all other truths. The Christian only gives the mystery a name when he speaks of grace; and must assent as he thinks of his choice to the words of the Lord: 'Ye have not chosen me but I have chosen you.' To Christian and non-Christian conversion is incomprehensible. This mystery lies behind *Ash Wednesday*, but the poem does not attempt to approach it. The discovery of faith is assumed. *Ash Wednesday*, as its title warns us, is a poem of purgation; it deals with the mortification of the natural man, the effort to conform the will. But the theme of penitence and the aspiration towards holiness, the acceptance of the Church's discipline of self-examination, contrition, confession and satisfaction, is crossed by another theme. It is clear that the poem springs from intimately personal experience, so painful that it can hardly be more than hinted at, and so immediate that it cannot be wholly translated into symbols. There is anguish both at the exhaustion of feeling and at its recrudescence, at loss and at feeling loss, at not desiring and at still desiring. The double theme: of Christian penitence and resolve, and of personal disaster, gives to almost every line a deep ambiguity which it is not the critic's business to remove. While the conscious mind is occupied with the effort to will what is, to be 'whole in the present', the almost unbearable sense of what was troubles its constancy and makes its affirmations and petitions seem ironic. The struggle between the effort to 'construct something upon which to rejoice' and the pain of existence, the distinction between what the poet wishes to wish, and what he does not wish to wish, but still wishes, gives to *Ash Wednesday* its peculiar intensity. The conscious effort of the will expresses itself in formulas; the movements of the mind and heart express themselves in symbols and visions and intense sense-impressions. The experience out of which the effort of the will arose is not itself approached.

SOURCE: extract from chapter 5 of *The Art of T. S. Eliot*, pp. 99–104.

Northrop Frye   Ash Wednesday (1963)

Eliot's later poems and the five plays, all of which are comedies or triumphant tragedies, belong to his 'purgatorial' vision. *Ash Wednesday* (in six parts, numbered here for convenience) presents us with a desert, a garden, and a stairway between them. The stairway is the *escalina* or winding mountain of Dante's purgatory. In St John of the Cross the 'dark night of the soul' is described as a spiritual dryness like that of a desert, and here again is a 'ladder', equated with the 'figure of the ten stairs' of St Benedict referred to in 'Burnt Norton'. St John also calls his purgation an 'ascent of Mount Carmel', adding that it could also be called a descent, a remark bringing us toward Heraclitus's 'the way up and the way down are the same'. The stairway appears in the 'infernal' vision in many ironic contexts, usually connected with failure in love. La Figlia Che Piange stands 'on the highest pavement of the stair'; the narrator in 'Portrait of a Lady' nearly loses his precious 'self-possession' at the top of his lady's stair; Prufrock wonders if there is time to turn back and descend the stair; the 'young man carbuncular' climbs a staircase to the typist's flat; the narrators of 'Rhapsody on a Windy Night' and '*The Boston Evening Transcript*' make their assignations with time and life at the top of steps: Princess Volupine climbs the water-stair to desert Burbank for Klein.

Desert and garden are central symbols in our literary and religious tradition, and a number of complexes of this symbolism have become so closely associated as to be readily identified. Seven of these, five from the Bible, one from Dante and one from the Church calendar, are identified in *Ash Wednesday*.

First, Adam, the 'ruined millionaire', is condemned to earn his living in the wilderness, but is ultimately to be led back to Eden and have the tree and river of life restored to him. Second, Israel wanders in the desert forty years trying to enter its Promised Land, the Canaan they finally conquered being more of a desert than a garden, as is indicated by the desert setting of the line: 'This is the land. We have our inheritance' (ii). Third, there is Israel in its later exile, urged by the prophets to return and rebuild its temple. Jeremiah, finding no one to listen to him, was forced to cry: 'O earth, earth, earth, hear the Word of the Lord.' In *Ash Wednesday* 'earth' is altered to 'wind' (ii), partly because the listening wind is associated with the Spirit inspiring the prophet. Isaiah speaks of the desert blossoming as the rose; Ezekiel in Babylon saw the valley of dry bones taking on the bodies of resurrection (ii); Micah speaks the reproaches of the Word to a disobedient people (v). A later rebuilder of the temple, Nehemiah, figures in *The Rock*, but not here, where building imagery is not wanted. Fourth, there is the contrast, in two books ascribed to Solomon, between the world of vanity with 'the burden of the grasshopper' in Ecclesiastes (ii), and the garden of the Bride and here sister in the Song of Songs. St John of the Cross wrote his treatise on the dark night as a commentary on a poem based on the Song of Songs. In Eliot's garden there is a 'Lady' (ii), later a 'veiled sister' (vi), who corresponds to Beatrice in Dante, besides the presence of the Virgin herself.

Fifth, the life of Christ is polarised between his temptation, where he wanders forty days in the desert, and his passion, which extends from the agony in the garden to his resurrection in another garden. In the Gospels, his ministry comes between these events, but in Biblical typology the temptation corresponds to the forty-year wandering of Israel in the desert under Moses, and the resurrection to the conquest of the Promised Land by Joshua, who has the same name as Jesus. Hence (sixth) the commemorating of the temptation by the Church in the forty days of Lent, which begins on Ash Wednesday, is immediately followed by the celebration of the resurrection in Easter. Finally, and seventh, Dante's *Purgatorio* takes us up a rocky mountain of penance into 'our first world' of Eden.

The desert of *Ash Wednesday* is the 'brown land' of the earlier poems, but, except for the references to 'noise' in v, it is conceived not as a sterile society but as a shrivelled individual spiritual life, a chapel perilous or house of the dead. Its main features parallel and contrast with those of the garden world above it. It is 'The place of solitude where three dreams cross' (vi), apparently the dreams of waking consciousness, memory, and dream proper, all of them animated by desire, all of them having no end but death. It is a place of thirst, in contrast to the fountains and springs of the garden, where water can only be miraculously provided, as it was to Moses and to Samson (the story of Samson's thirst may be glanced at in the line 'The broken jaw of our lost kingdoms' in 'The Hollow Men'). Above the desert, the inhabitants of the garden have abandoned the 'low dream' for the 'higher dream', and memory for a life 'In ignorance and in knowledge of eternal dolour' (iv). In Dante the river Lethe, which obliterates the memory of sin, and the river Eunoe, which restores unfallen knowledge, are in Eden. In Eliot's garden there can still be talk of 'trivial' things (iv), the word being an erudite pun on the three-way crossing of ordinary life.

The three dreams appear in the second section as three leopards eating the body and leaving only the dry bones. We are reminded of the three beasts encountered by Dante at the beginning of the *Inferno* and of the world, flesh and devil, symbolised as three beasts, in St John of the Cross. The contrasting image is that of the unicorns, emblems of chastity and of Christ, drawing the 'gilded hearse' of the body about to be glorified (iv). The limit of the desert is marked by two 'blue rocks' (v), suggesting the clashing Symplegades of the Argonautic voyage, and that in turn suggesting the open-mouthed monster of hell, mentioned earlier. The limit of the garden is marked by two yew trees(IV, VI), apparently representing the spiritual death of the first two sections and the physical death which follows it. At the same time the scene of the poem is 'The desert in the garden and the garden in the desert' (V); the two worlds occupy the same time and space.

The narrator is in middle life, beginning to realise that life is a parabola. He is not content however with the chagrin of ordinary experience: he wants to kill the ego, reduce it to scattered bones in a desert, pulverise it on Ash Wednesday into the dust from which it came. He descends from despair founded on disillusionment to despair founded on reality, the despair of finding anything in the past worth clinging to. The experiences worth clinging to are discontinuous, and pull one off the track of memory and desire. It is only when the narrator's very bones have stopped clinging together that he can become aware of any other reality, and his separating bones are in contrast to the prayer at the end: 'Suffer me not to be separated' (VI). The leopards, however terrifying, are really agents of redemption, an ambiguity which meets us often in the plays.

The poet, in climbing his stairway, looks down to see that he has been detached from his temporal self. The Jacob who dreamed of the ladder to heaven also wrestled with the angel, and the poet sees himself, 'the same shape' (III), in a lower world fighting the demon of hope and despair. He then sees more clearly that he is escaping from 'the toothed gullet of an agèd shark' (III), like Jonah, or Dante from hell. The glances are followed by a vision on his own level, where the world of memory and desire suddenly reappears in the form of a dancing Pan figure, and where the memories of 'Lilac and brown hair' (III) suggest that we are in the world of the hyacinth girl and La Figlia Che Piange. Finally we reach the garden, where Pan is reduced to a statue with a 'breathless' flute (IV), and where we meet the greater recognition scene hinted at in *Marina*:

> One who moves in the time between sleep and waking, wearing
> White light folded, sheathed about her, folded.

Ordinary consciousness reasserts itself, and we are back (V) in the desert, like Elijah, who sat down under a 'juniper tree' (II) and prayed to die. The juniper tree is also associated with a resurrection from bones

in a fairy tale of Grimm. Elijah, after earthquakes and thunder, heard
the still small voice of the Word, but the poet is in a world of constant
noise and distraction which is determined not to listen. So although the
poem begins with renunciation, 'Because I do not hope to turn again'
(I), it ends with the world of memory and desire stronger than ever:
'Although I do not hope to turn again' (VI). The 'unbroken wings' (VI)
of sailing ships mock the 'agèd eagle' (I) who cannot renew his youth,
and 'the empty forms between the ivory gates' (VI) of illusory dreams
come to him with the unbearable beauty of a lost paradise.

The experiences in *Ash Wednesday* take place on four levels: the level
of spiritual vision or high dream in III and IV; the level of nostalgic vision
in VI; the level of ordinary experience, of disillusionment and distraction, in I and V, and the level of ascesis or self-denial in II. The first level is
a world of identity, where the individual is identified with his
community, a member of one body, without losing his individuality:

> The single Rose
> Is now the Garden
> Where all loves end. . . . (II)

The second level is a world where experiences of peculiar intensity are
linked by memory and impose a pattern of greater significance and
sadness on ordinary life – very like the *temps retrouvé* of Proust. The third
level is ordinary experience, where the ego tries to achieve identity
through 'memory and desire' and the fourth level is the concentrating of
consciousness designed to break up the illusions of the ego. These four
levels rear in the *Quartets*. . . .

SOURCE: extract from chapter 5 of *T. S. Eliot* (Edinburgh,
1963) pp. 72–7.

B. Rajan   Ash Wednesday (1966)

... The thunder speaks from the horizon of *The Waste Land* because what it has to say is discerned rather than experienced. The break-out from sterility is no more than that; it is not a movement into fruitfulness. The poem is an advance from 'Gerontion', building on that poem's terrified recognitions and taking the vital step forward from a condition in which neither fear nor courage can save us. Its conclusion sets the arid plain behind and moves us to the fringe of a world which the poem can formulate but cannot enter. To make that entrance is the function of *Ash Wednesday*.

In *Ash Wednesday* the protagonist endures a death unlike those suffered by Prufrock, Gerontion, and Phlebas and climbs a stair, decisively unlike that climbed by Prufrock, to the threshold of the overwhelming question. He reaches a garden, a precarious state of enlightenment, only to realize that the place of understanding must be held in constant struggle against the persistent downward pull of the flesh. He looks out finally on that sea of doubt and renewal where all that he has learned must be revalidated. It is repetition with a difference, the difference marking, with such precision as is possible, the movement forward in the life of the whole work. The death by devouring in *Ash Wednesday* has a special place in this infrastructure. Unlike all previous dyings it is a dying into life; and its differences from Phlebas's death, which precedes it in the sequence, invite and respond to critical attention.

Phlebas too owes his place in the *œuvre* to Pound, and Pound, whether he knew it or not, was once again marking a turning-point. Phlebas's is the last of a series of old-style deaths, a warning of man's mortality, the inexorable reminder of the skull beneath the skin. Fear in a handful of dust is a step forward from the rather more animal fear of Gerontion, and the collocation of two mysticisms, as well as the play between purgatorial fire and the destructive fires of the flesh, points to the direction in which this fear can lead. It leads, in fact, to Chapel Perilous, but Phlebas's remains do not lie along this route. As a representative of that mercantile mentality for which the earlier poems preserve a special contempt, he is not permitted the consolation of any remains. De Bailhache, Fresca and Mrs Cammel are despatched into outer space and disintegrated into 'fractured atoms' in what seems a reasonably thorough process of destruction. But Phlebas has his bones picked for fourteen days by the mocking whispers of a current under sea and then enters a whirlpool, where he is presumably churned into a further refinement of non-being. In *Ash Wednesday* the death-rites may be superficially as gruesome, but the total effect is of a curious, limpid happiness. Despite its relevance, one would hesitate to use the word 'gaiety' if the voice of the thunder had not legitimized it. It is, in fact, something akin to Yeats's 'gaiety transfiguring all that dread' that lies on the other side of radical commitment, though to reach that other side one must pass through an experience, translatable only by the metaphor of death. The verse, by the manner in which its singing sweetness lives through and overrides the macabre narrative, embodies fully the elusive sense of metamorphosis into a higher reality. In what is later to be described as 'A condition of complete simplicity / Costing not less than everything' there is a kind of lucid, tranquil givenness, symbolized in the creative destitution of the landscape. To be aware of this it is not necessary to assign specific functions to the leopards; the number three is sufficiently evocative. As for the indigestible portions which the leopards reject, those may, as Unger indicates, represent a residue of the self which survives destruction, but they also surely stand for the difference between mere dying and dying into life. Two significant links in the chain remain to be added. First, the prison of the self is broken – the bones are united by their forgetfulness of themselves and each other. Second, the protagonist's cry in *The Waste Land* – 'Shall I at least set my lands in order?' – is answered by: 'This is the land. We have our inheritance.' As understanding passes into experience the ruined tower becomes the tradition redeemed.

Man's mind was not born for peace. It inhabits a time of tension and a place of twilight. To die into life, it renounces everything, including renunciation. Then, reborn, it must climb a stairway, along which the process of struggle and rejection is once again enacted. The higher reality may be given to us eventually, but it is not given for settlement. The desert is in the garden and the garden in the desert. The withered apple-seed of our failing may be spat out but there is every possibility that the seed will flourish again. In the story of the quest, the chapter called *Ash Wednesday* has a certain stubborn honesty because of its quiet demonstration that the only end to the quest is its renewal. . . .

SOURCE: extract from 'The Overwhelming Question', in *T. S. Eliot: the Man and His Work*, ed. Tate, pp. 372–4.

Herbert Read
'The Hollow Men' (1966)

. . . The most significant of all Eliot's poems, from a confessional point of view, is 'The Hollow Men'. It was written in 1925, the year of religious crisis, and apart from some minor poems, it is the last example of what I would call his *pure* poetry. *Ash Wednesday*, which followed in 1930, is already a moralistic poem, especially in the last two sections. All the poetry that follows, including the *Four Quartets*, is, in spite of flashes of the old fire, moralistic poetry.

There are no strict rules for the creation of poetry, but nevertheless a poem is neither an arbitrary nor a deliberate event. As critics we must act on the assumption that a correspondence exists between the shifting levels of consciousness and what we call moments of vision or flashes of inspiration. One of the critic's tasks is to survey the devious intercommunications between these various levels of consciousness. So long as the lines of communication are open, inspiration, as we say, *flows*. For a time, for a year or perhaps five years, rarely more than ten, the divine madness, as Plato called it, descends on a mortal and then burns out. 'The Hollow Men' is a celebration of this incineration. *'Mistah Kurtz – the dead. A penny for the Old Guy.'* But Mistah Kurtz, though he may have been a bad man, a corrupt man, a suffering man, saw visions that were splendid. Even when, as in this poem, he is evoking 'death's other Kingdom', he does so in bright images, 'Sunlight on a broken column', 'a tree swinging'; but then, alas, 'Between the emotion / And the response / Falls the Shadow'. What Eliot meant by the Shadow is clear enough and it is not a Shadow that we encounter in his poetry without sorrow.

Ash Wednesday should be read with a poem of the same year, *Marina*, where the new resolution is made clear in these lines:

> This form, this face, this life
> Living to live in a world of time beyond me; let me
> Resign my life for this life, my speech for that unspoken,
> The awakened, lips parted, the hope, the new ships.

The problem of poetry and belief was endlessly discussed in these years

1925–30, in conversation and in print. But though it was always posed as a problem of poetry and belief, what Eliot and Richards and the rest of us were discussing was poetry and beliefs – there is a difference between a belief which is a belief in God, or in the Incarnation, and the beliefs which are formulated as the Thirty-Nine Articles of the Church of England or the Constitutions of the Society of Jesus. It is perhaps the same kind of distinction that Eliot himself made between poetic assent and philosophical belief, and I am only suggesting (following Kierkegaard) that we must distinguish between Christianity and Christendom. Eliot wrote (in his essay on Dante) that the advantage of a coherent traditional system of dogma and morals was that 'it stands apart, for understanding and assent *even without belief*, from the single individual who propounds it'. This distinction between dogma and belief would allow us to assume that belief is a process of psychic integration, precariously maintained. As such it need not conflict with poetic intuition, which is also a delicate process of psychic integration. In this both belief and poetry differ from those inflexible moral commands to which a man must, if he resigns his life and would have peace, assent. This was made clear by Pascal, and by Unamuno in *The Agony of Christianity*. The Jesuits, we are told, do not ask for faith but for obedience; and Unamuno suggests that it was such a demand that led Pascal, in a moment of fear, to cry: *It will stultify you. (Cela vous abêtira.)* The fragmented conclusion of 'The Hollow Men' is the same cry of despair, the same broken utterance:

> For Thine is
> Life is
> For Thine is the

Perhaps the key to Eliot's agony lies in this essay on Pascal; his was the same agony as Pascal's, but I think that in the end Eliot resigned his life for that life, *stultified his speech* for that unspoken law. Pascal, he said, was to be commended 'to those who doubt, but who have the mind to conceive, and the sensibility to feel, the disorder, the futility, the meaninglessness, the mystery of life and suffering, and who can only find peace through a satisfaction of the whole being'. Eliot himself, I believe, was not of those who doubt, but rather one of those great mystics who, in his own words, 'like St John of the Cross, are primarily for readers with a special determination of purpose'.

I am not trying to suggest that there is any incompatibility between the religious *belief* of a man like Eliot and his poetic *practice* – how could I with the examples of George Herbert and the later Donne to prove the contrary, not to mention Dante? But a problem does exist for the poet who has 'a special determination of purpose'; such a phrase implies a process of rationalization, by which we mean a conscious justification of dogma and morals as distinct from beliefs that are essentially irrational or instinctive. The habit of rationalization sustains the mystic, but it is a deadly habit in the poet.

I do not presume to judge Eliot; I even tremble as I attempt to reveal some of the dimensions of his agony. But if in this context I am to give my first allegiance to poetry (and I do not for a moment question the allegiance that a Christian poet must give to one whom Kierkegaard called 'the unique person'), it is not honest to pretend that the poet can have any other life or kingdom but poetry. The Shadow that falls between the emotion and the response is the shadow of the moral judgement, the Tables of the Law, the Commandments. For a year or two the old images will haunt the mind –

> Distraction, music of the flute, stops and steps of the mind over the
>   third stair,
> Fading, fading. . . .

But eventually

> We must be still and still moving
> Into another intensity
> For further union, a deeper communion. . . .

'In my end is my beginning' – yes, but it is the end of the earthly poet and the beginning of the redeemed sinner, 'The awakened, lips parted, the hope, the new ships'. The old ships are left burning on the waters

> Burning burning burning burning

SOURCE: extract from 'T. S. E.: A Memoir', in *T. S. Eliot: The Man and His Work*, ed. Tate, pp. 38–41.

David Ward The Ariel Poems (1973)

The first of the Ariel poems, *The Journey of the Magi*, was written in 1927, the year of Eliot's conversion and of the second section of *Ash Wednesday*. It exploits the theme of the journey which is also central to *The Waste Land*, but perhaps it is more immediately to the point to compare the transit it describes with the phrase from *Ash Wednesday*, 'this brief transit where the dreams cross'. Eliot takes as a mythical vehicle for his dramatisation of the journey of the soul the journey of the Magi as described by Lancelot Andrewes: 'A cold coming they had of it at this time of the year, just the worst time of the year to take a journey in. The ways deep, the weather sharp, the days short, the sun farthest off, *in solstitio brumali*, the very dead of winter.'

Their journey is towards the Christ child; towards the evidence of Incarnation, or the entry of the divine spirit into the world and into the flesh. It is also a journey towards the New Testament, the new Covenant between man and God, which destroys the old dispensation. The mythical complex of which the journey is part can be taken as describing, not just a historical event (perhaps not *even* a historical event), but an event in the life of the soul; a death and rebirth in a spiritual sense. The poem was written in the year of Eliot's conversion: it is a kind of mythical record or re-enactment of that event.

The images seem to have evolved in a most interesting way. In *The Use of Poetry and the Use of Criticism*, Eliot remarks (p. 148): 'only a part of an author's imagery comes from his reading. It comes from the whole of his sensitive life since early childhood.' [Ward quotes further from this passage; see above, Part One, section 3. III – Ed.] Eliot's personal memories enter into the poem as they must; the water-mill, for instance, invested with an evocative power for him which is as little, or as much, 'understood' by ourselves as it is by Eliot. But the six ruffians change more radically: Grover Smith has pointed out the complex of echoing allusions to the soldiers casting lots for the garments of Christ (Matthew 27 : 35) and to the blood money of Judas in 'Six hands at an open door dicing for pieces of silver'; the image which emerges from the process composes personal memory and the public memory of myth, convention and religious iconography into a peculiar compound. The prolepsis of the Crucifixion in 'three trees on the low sky' has somewhat the same effect: the extraordinary and boundlessly significant symbol sheathed in the most ordinary and unimpressive accidental image. Both the six hands and the three trees change aspect as one looks at them in different ways; with one eye open they *seem* to be unremarkable and insignificant memories; with the other, they *seem* to be conventional mythical icons; with both eyes opened they are a fusion of both, so that the marvellous and the ordinary are attuned in one vibrating chord.

The speaker returns to 'these Kingdoms' of the old dispensation, but as aliens: the ambiguous birth or death, of Christ, of an old world, of themselves, is a revelation which does not immediately end the journey. On the contrary, it initiates the journey, since it convinces him of the transitory nature of his existence, which awaits a final consummation: 'I should be glad of another death.' 'The dream crossed twilight between birth and dying' of *Ash Wednesday* VI lies between the dream of memory and the dream of anticipation, and is itself a dream: in the Magus's world of exile in his own kingdom Christ (a death and a birth for a world and a self) persists both as memory and anticipation. Alienation can only end with the fusion of the dreams in a new death.

A Song for Simeon, written in 1928, is based upon the 'Nunc dimittis', or 'Song of Simeon' which follows the second lesson in the order of evening prayer. The prayer is taken from chapter 2 of Luke, where it was revealed to Simeon 'that he should not see death, before he had seen the Lord's Christ' (Luke 2: 26). Simeon comes to see the Christ child and says 'Lord, now lettest thou thy servant depart in peace, according to thy word: for mine eyes have seen thy salvation, Which thou hast prepared before the face of all people' (Luke 2: 29–31). Joseph and Mary marvel at this, and Simeon prophesies to Mary, 'this child is set for the fall and rising again of many in Israel; and for a sign which shall be spoken against; (Yea, a sword shall pierce through thy own soul also,) that the thoughts of many hearts may be revealed' (Luke 2: 34–5).

This poem is not, however, a simple revision and augmentation of Simeon's prophecy: it is in only a limited sense another Song *of* Simeon, though the voice which speaks is in some sense Simeon. 'Simeon' speaks of his own age; of his own realization that he must accept a spiritual destiny which is less dramatic and joyful than that of the saint: 'Not for me the ultimate vision'. The prophetic mood of Simeon in the Bible story enables him to prophesy the ministry and suffering of Christ and the grief of Mary – this foreknowledge makes him the first to attain

salvation by that ministry, the first Christian. Being the first Christian
he is able to foretell the troubles and sufferings of the Christian
community because he is at one with that community. But he is a very
special case. He is the only Christian whose participation in the
Community does not involve participation, while in life, in the suffering
and death of Christ and the glory of His resurrection. He may prophesy
the Crucifixion, but only in anticipation. Whilst every other Christian
enacts the martyrdom within his own life – as the prime condition of his
life as a Christian – Simeon only *sees* (in the sense that Tiresias, or any
other prophet *sees*) the passion and the ecstasy. Thus, his position is a
paradox piled on a paradox: he misses the ecstasy but wins the peace of
salvation; he misses the pain and the glory of the Christian's life, but
suffers the weariness:

I am tired with my own life and the lives of those after me,
I am dying in my own death and the deaths of those after me.

He is, in the same senses as Tiresias and Gerontion, 'old man', and in his
life exists within the old covenant, but by a very extraordinary grace, by
prophecy of the new life, *knows* the new world 'Before the time of cards
and scourges and lamentation . . . Before the stations of the mountain
of desolation / Before the certain hour of maternal sorrow', that is to say
before the act of redemption in the passion. He therefore is and is not an
image of the Christian; the ways in which he is say something about the
Christian condition; his prophecy of those ways in which he is not, but
others will be Christian, says everything else that it is necessary to say.

The complex perception which gives rise to the figure of Simeon
ensures a moving and accomplished poem, an intentness and a dignity
of utterance which is quite remarkable. The quiet gravity of the first
movement, with its irregular slant rhymes imposing a ghostly echo of a
formal structure (perhaps, too, an echo of the windless calm in which
the aged Saturn waits described by Keats in the opening of the first
Hyperion) seems to repeat the description of the waiting-period at the
end of an old life in 'Gerontion', but transforms it with a tranquillity
which is not within reach of that tense and puzzled poem. The Roman
world, the world of the old dispensation, continues to move in its
accustomed ways, the hyacinths blooming in the return to the repeated
natural rebirth, but slowly, coldly, with entranced hesitance – 'The
winter sun creeps by the snow hills' – reflecting the old experience and

the new knowledge of the speaker. Simeon, too, is in transit between two worlds; the world itself is in transit between two states: not only does 'memory in corners' survive, awaiting the change, but 'dust in sunlight', the debris of change flecking the weak light of the winter sun, waits for the wind.

The quiet strength of the poem enables the allusions to be used in such a way that the mind is held back, forced to pause and consider; take for instance, '(And a sword shall pierce thy heart, / Thine also)'. This is an allusion in Luke also: Simeon, addressing Mary, foretells her grief and Christ's – Christ will be pierced through the side by the soldier's sword; she also will suffer as if by the sword '(Yea, a sword shall pierce through thy own soul also)'. But in the new context the words extend in their meaning to cover the sufferings of all Christians, who praise and suffer, who bear the derision as well as sharing the glory of the passion.

Animula appeared in 1929. Again, it is a poem about the condition of transit; of immediacy and innocence of experience which we, as adults, seem to remember in our childhoods. There are three stages in the poem. The first is introduced by an adaptation of Dante, 'Issues from the hand of God, the simple soul', and traces the distorting process by which the immediacy of childhood experience is disrupted into distinction and relation. The second stage, introduced by a parody of the first line, 'Issues from the hand of time the simple soul', laments the inadequacies of the human condition, the fearfulness and lack of purpose and direction which mark the human dream. The third stage is a prayer in which stock figures of the displacement of human energy are made to stand for the whole of humanity in its failure to achieve reality.

The quotation from Dante is spoken by Marco Lombardo, one of the spirits who is being purged of wrathfulness on the third terrace of Purgatory. He laments the degeneracy of the times, and asks Dante to pray for him. Dante asks what the cause of earthly vice is, whether it is decreed by heaven or proceeds from the inherent vice of man. Marco sighs and reproaches him for blindness, for thinking in terms of necessity rather than in terms of free will. He then says:

Issues from the hand of him who cherishes her before she exists, in the manner of a little child that plays, now weeping, now laughing, the simple soul, who knows nothing, save that moved by a joyful maker, she turns willingly to whatever delights her. First she tastes the savour of a trifling good; there she is deceived, and runs after it, if no guide or rein turns her love aside. So it was necessary to

put law as a curb, necessary to have a ruler, who could at least discern the tower
of the true city. Laws there are, but who puts his hand to them?
None. (*Purgatorio*, XVI, 85–98.)

Dante follows the psychological pattern of Aquinas, and adopts a late
mediaeval concept of the nature of kingship and law. Eliot's psychology
is somewhat more modern, entails a closer and more attentive
observation, and is not concerned with political or legal commentary.
But, like Dante, he is concerned to explore the relationship between free
will and environmental circumstance.

Experimental observations of a kind which were already beginning
when Eliot wrote *Animula* tend to support his account of the growth of
perception in a child, but the spirit of Eliot's account is more
Augustinian than clinical, and the development he describes is very
much in keeping with his own speculations in *Knowledge and Experience*.
The child begins by being conscious only of the disorganized sense
perception; as it begins to move and to respond to the world around it,
response is immediate and unreflective – 'Advancing boldly, sudden to
take alarm, / Retreating to the corner of arm or knee' – the verse
renders with delicacy the lack of the 'space between the impulse and the
reaction' of which Jane Harrison speaks. 'Between the emotion / And
the response /Falls the Shadow' for the Hollow Men, but it takes time
for the child to reach that stage. In the interim sense and action, thought
and feeling, reality and the imagination interpenetrate each
other – sense is confounded with sense ('the fragrant brilliance of the
Christmas tree'); emotion is immediate and unselfconscious; the story
and the common reality merge into each other ('What the fairies do and
what the servants say'). But as the child enters into the responsibilities of
the adult state distinctions are forced upon him – ' "is and seems" /
And may and may not, desire and control', distinctions which warp the
immediate impulse by subjecting it to reflection. The mental life of the
child warps in the process, makes living into pain, and causes the retreat
into dream – and we have already discussed the idea of the dream in
Eliot's poetry enough to make further discussion of it unnecessary.
These processes 'Curl up the small soul in the window seat / Behind the
Encyclopaedia Britannica' – cause it to withdraw into second-hand
experience, analytical and reflective rather than direct and truthfully
immediate.

'Issues from the hand of time the simple soul' – time distorts what
God creates, but does not make the soul any the less simple. The

harmony of impulse and action which allows the infant to grasp at kisses and toys, accepting without question the offered good, which allows him to seek comfort and reassurance so innocently and unselfconsciously, which allows him to accept pleasure as his right and without question, is destroyed. For once in his poetry Eliot approaches some part of the way towards a Blakean or Lawrentian sympathy towards the natural impulse as against the distortion of 'civilised' convention.

Perhaps the poem does not have the energetic suggestiveness of Eliot at his best, and perhaps the impulse towards religious and philosophical investigation dominates a little too much, somewhat enervating the verse. But nevertheless it shows a most sensitive awareness of childish perception and the problems of growth and life: within its limits it works well enough.

Each of the Ariel poems so far has been centred around a dramatis persona – the Magus, Simeon, Marco, old men, dying or dead, whose actions or words have been taken as a mythical vehicle for the expression of some incident or stage in the development of the soul, or in the case of *Animula*, the whole life of a disordered soul from creation to death (or birth) and after. Each of them is a new and different discovery of the ambiguity of death and birth. The little soul of *Animula* lives first 'in the silence after the viaticum'. The 'viaticum' is the Eucharist administered to one who is dying; the Latin word means provisions for a journey. And the final line, with its substitution of birth for death, again stresses the ambiguity, the idea that death is the beginning of a journey out of a dream state into a reality.

The dramatis persona whose history is the mythical vehicle in *Marina* is another old man, Pericles. In Shakespeare's *Pericles* both Thaisa and Marina have suffered a kind of death and rebirth, Pericles a kind of death by separation. His reunion with Marina his daughter, and later Thaisa his wife, effects a resolution of human pain and suffering into new life. The Pericles myth is combined with the Senecan myth of Hercules by an epigraph from *Hercules Furens* in in which Hercules awakes from a mad fit which the jealous Juno has thrown him into, and wonders where he is. In the course of his insanity he has shot his own children with poisoned arrows. The composite Pericles / Hercules who is the persona, then, is awaking from a dream. As Hercules he is half aware of the most terrible, unforgiveable sinfulness in the madness of his dream world. As Pericles he is aware of the resolution of suffering and loneliness, a return to sweetness and peace through an extraordinary grace.

The whole poem echoes and develops the questioning mood of the Senecan epigraph, from the breathless, unpunctuated incantation of 'What seas what shores what grey rocks and what islands' (mimicking the repeated lap of water on the hull) to the end; and it is this wondering uncertainty, this tentative, entranced movement, which gives the poem much of its evocative power.

Consider the ambiguities of this:

> What is this face, less clear and clearer
> The pulse in the arm, less strong and stronger –
> Given or lent? more distant than the stars and nearer than the
>   eye
>
> Whispers and small laughter between leaves and hurrying feet
> Under sleep, where all the waters meet.

Our attention is caught first by the hesitant step of the words (continuing the wave-lapping movement of the opening lines), so that we, too, seem to be suspended between near and far, between new understanding and greater mystery. There are, as one would expect, a whole host of metaphysical, theological and literary memories suspended here: Marina is, one might say, another Beatrice figure, a 'blessèd face' like that of *Ash Wednesday*, an image which bears in some sense or other the grace of God. And the ambiguities of this gracious image, one might say, are precisely the ambiguities which Christian doctrine would discover in the divine presence, immanent yet transcendent, 'more distant than the stars and nearer than the eye'. But if these things matter at all to us as we read the poem, they are subdued, merged into something more fundamentally interesting than any doctrine or metaphysical idea; a lightly suggested tone or mood, a phase of thought or feeling which, perhaps, lies behind most religious nostalgia. It's an image which Eliot frequently returns to, this elusive whispering and laughter of children in a garden; not because it means, or is intended to mean, anything firm or definite, in the sense that any doctrine or philosophical idea is intended to have meaning. By its elusiveness the image prompts the reader to recall images of his own, memories, or something less catchable than image or memory – moods, shapes of feeling – which nevertheless may be as distinct as can be as episodes in the reader's experience. The poem exploits our own memories of a dream world, and our sense of the unresolved, the wonderful, which so often envelopes our memories of dreams, and so often dominates the period between sleep and waking.

But there is another accent in the poem too, a far more distinct accent: 'Those who sharpen the tooth of the dog, meaning / Death', and what follows, with its repeated heavy emphasis on 'Death', tolling out at intervals on its own separate line. In a poem so full of delicate uncertainty this kind of emphasis destroys the finely attuned poise so rudely that its dramatic and emotional rightness of purpose must be absolutely secure.

But dramatically it is wrong. It is far too deliberate and heavy a rhetoric for the imagined situation; too plainly it is an elaborate embroidery of the words 'sensuality', 'pride', 'sloth' and 'lust' because by themselves those words would sit too baldly. And it is emotionally wrong: the assertive negative morality doesn't fit with the air of tentative discovery. And, most important of all, the failure of tone here may seed some doubts about the validity of the rest of the poem. Delicate uncertainty of tone may collapse into cultivated vagueness of expression if we are not prepared to co-operate, and this poem, depending as it does upon our own memories imaginatively re-creating dream and waking, depends peculiarly upon the co-operation of the reader.

Source: extract from *Between Two Worlds: A Reading of T. S. Eliot's Poetry and Plays*, pp. 164–71.

SELECT BIBLIOGRAPHY

M. C. Bradbrook, *T. S. Eliot* (1965). A sound, short introduction, with an excellent bibliography.

Northrop Frye, *T. S. Eliot* (1963). Also introductory, but employing a more sophisticated mode of analysis.

Helen Gardner, *The Art of T. S. Eliot* (1949). A general account of Eliot's development, particularly good on the poetic technique.

Hugh Kenner, *The Invisible Poet: T. S. Eliot* (1960). A very original, witty and perceptive account.

F. R. Leavis, *New Bearings in English Poetry* (1932). An excellent period placing of Eliot and the general state of English poetry at the time.

F. O. Matthiessen and C. L. Barber, *The Achievement of T. S. Eliot* (1935; enlarged edition 1958). An informative all-round account of his work.

J. Grover Smith, *T. S. Eliot's Poetry and Plays: A Study in Sources and Meaning* (1956; revised 1960). The prime account of Eliot's sources; an invaluable reference-handbook.

B. C. Southam, *A Student's Guide to the Selected Poems of T. S. Eliot* (1968; revised 1977). Provides detailed information on the sources, references and factual content of the poems chosen by Eliot for the volume of *Selected Poems*.

David Ward, *Between Two Worlds: A Reading of T. S. Eliot's Poetry and Plays* (1973). An account of the poet's intellectual development and its relationship to the poetry. Particularly valuable for its relating of Eliot's philosophical work to his poetry.

NOTES ON CONTRIBUTORS

F. W. BATESON: Formerly Fellow of Corpus Christi College and Lecturer in English, University of Oxford. Founding editor of *Essays in Criticism*, editor of *Cambridge Bibliography of English Literature*.

WALLACE FOWLIE: American critic. Professor of French, Duke University, he has written extensively on French literature of the nineteenth and twentieth centuries.

NORTHROP FRYE: Professor of English, University of Toronto; probably best-known for *The Anatomy of Criticism*.

DAME HELEN GARDNER: Formerly Merton Professor of English, University of Oxford. Her books include *The Art of T. S. Eliot*.

ROBERT GRAVES: British poet, novelist, essayist and critic.

D. W. HARDING: Formerly Professor of Psychology, Bedford College, University of London; a notable contributor to *Scrutiny*.

HUGH KENNER: Professor of English at the University of California, Santa Barbara; has written extensively on the Pound–Eliot era.

F. R. LEAVIS: Formerly Fellow of Downing College, Cambridge, and University Reader in English and Visiting Professor, University of York; founding editor of *Scrutiny*.

F. O. MATTHIESSEN: Wrote extensively on Eliot and Henry James.

P. G. MUDFORD: Lecturer in English, Birkbeck College, University of London.

GEORGE ORWELL: English novelist, journalist reviewer and essayist, best-known for *Animal Farm* (1945) and *Nineteen Eighty-Four* (1949).

GERTRUDE PATTERSON: Author of *T. S. Eliot: Poems in the Making* (1971).

EZRA POUND: American poet and critic; with Eliot, the leading poet and critic of the modern movement.

B. RAJAN: Professor of English, University of Windsor, Ontario, he has written extensively on Milton and Eliot.

JOHN CROWE RANSOM: American poet and critic; editor of *The Kenyon Review*, 1939–59.

HERBERT READ: British poet, critic and essayist; a leading participant in the literary and cultural politics of the 1920s and 1930s.

I. A. RICHARDS: British critic and poet; a founding father of modern criticism in his two classic works, *The Principles of Literary Criticism* (1926) and *Practical Criticism* (1929).

EDGELL RICKWORD: British critic, essayist and journalist; editor of the *Left Review*.

LAURA RIDING: American poet, essayist and critic.

ERNEST SCHANZER: taught English Literature at the Universities of Toronto, Liverpool and Munich. His publications include *Shakespeare's Appian* (1956) and *The Problem Plays of Shakespeare* (1963). He died in 1976.

J. GROVER SMITH: Professor of English, Duke University; an authority on twentieth-century literature.

C. K. STEAD: Professor of English, University of Auckland. His books include *The New Poetic* (1964) and an edition of *New Zealand Short Stories* (1966).

DAVID WARD: Lecturer in English, University of Kent. His books include *Swift* (1973) and *Between Two Worlds: A Reading of T. S. Eliot's Poetry and Plays*.

W. B. YEATS: Irish poet, playwright and essayist, belonging originally to the generation before Eliot, yet his great, perhaps greater, contemporary until his death in 1939.

MORTON D. ZABEL: American critic, during his lifetime his publications included *Literary Opinion in America, Craft and Character in Modern Fiction* and editions of works by Conrad and Henry James.

INDEX

This index includes only significant references. Works and names merely mentioned in passing are not included. Major discussions are printed in bold.